MW00784933

Turkey

modern architectures in history

This international series examines the forms and consequences of modern architecture. Modernist visions and revisions are explored in their national context against a backdrop of aesthetic currents, economic developments, political trends and social movements. Written by experts in the architectures of the respective countries, the series provides a fresh, critical reassessment of Modernism's positive and negative effects, as well as the place of architectural design in twentieth-century history and culture.

Series editor: Vivian Constantinopoulos

Already published:

Brazil
Richard J. Williams

Britain
Alan Powers

Finland
Roger Connah

USA
Gwendolyn Wright

Turkey

modern architectures in history

Sibel Bozdoğan & Esra Akcan

REAKTION BOOKS

Published by Reaktion Books Ltd
33 Great Sutton Street
London EC1V 0DX, UK

www.reaktionbooks.co.uk

First published 2012
Copyright © Sibel Bozdoğan & Esra Akcan 2012

The publishers gratefully acknowledge support for the publication of this book by the
Graham Foundation for Advanced Studies in the Fine Arts

All rights reserved
No part of this publication may be reproduced, stored in a retrieval system,
or transmitted, in any form or by any means, electronic, mechanical, photocopying,
recording or otherwise, without the prior permission of the publishers.

Printed and bound in Great Britain by Bell & Bain, Glasgow

British Library Cataloguing in Publication Data
Bozdoğan, Sibel
    Turkey. – (Modern architectures in history)
    1. Architecture – Turkey – History 20th century
    I. Title II. Series III. Akcan, Esra.
    720.9'4961'0904-dc22

ISBN 978 1 86189 878 4

Contents

Introduction

> After attaining a new culture and a new civilization, the new Turkey wants a
> new container for its life – a new envelope for its ideals. The new Turk wants
> new cities, new roads, new houses, new schools and new work but does not yet
> know what the new is all about . . . The excitement of revolution and the pas-
> sion for democracy are edifying the souls; but we are not yet able to build the
> outer shell of an egalitarian and individualist country that will edify the bodies,
> families and people of Turkey.
>
> İsmail Hakkı Baltacıoğlu, *Demokrasi ve Sanat* (Istanbul, 1931) pp. 11–12

Written at the height of the Kemalist Revolution that led to the foundation of the modern Turkish Republic upon the ruins of the Ottoman
Empire, the above words of prominent early republican intellectual,
educator and art critic İsmail Hakkı Baltacıoğlu vividly capture the
historical context within which modern architecture and city planning
was charged with the urgent mission of nation-building in Turkey starting in the mid-1920s. Also reflected in these words is a strong belief in
the power of form (architectural, urban, institutional) to both mirror and
transform (social) content – a belief also shared by most Turkish architects at the time. What makes this quotation even more interesting is
that the desired future implied by it is as yet formless: 'modern' is still an
aspiration for form rather than a recognizable style; an as-yet unrealized
potential. This utopian investment in modernity is one of the defining
characteristics of modernism in Turkey, as in many countries, where it
was precisely this 'not-yet' condition that gave modernism its evocative
power and allowed modernizing actors (architects, planners, political
leaders, intellectuals) to employ modernist visions as a way of shaping
people's desires.

The early republican quest for modern form in Turkey coincided
historically with the rise of the Modern Movement in interwar Europe
and initially found an appealing answer in the progressive discourse and
abstract aesthetic of the latter. It would soon become evident, however,
that this was far from being a fully convincing answer, nor one that
would succeed in soliciting unambiguous commitment. Although many
early republican architects, critics and commentators would first embrace

The Tulip Room by
SOM and Sedad Eldem
at the Istanbul Hilton
Hotel; photo by Ezra
Stoller.

the Modern Movement as the most appropriate formal expression of the country's civilizational switch from a dynastic, Islamic and imperial past to the desired modern, secular and Western-orientated future, their enthusiasm would always be counterbalanced by their nationalist discomfort with the term 'international style' and their anxieties regarding the homogenizing effects of modern technologies and the implied loss of cultural distinctness. After the Second World War, this earlier preoccupation with form and mobilization of modern architecture for national identity construction would give way to entirely new challenges posed by industrialization, capitalist development, democratization and rapid urbanization, bringing formidable problems of housing and infrastructure to the forefront. These issues would engage a highly politicized Turkish architectural culture during the 1960s and '70s, and would, in turn, themselves be superseded after the 1980s by a renewed interest in architectural form reflecting the spatial practices of globalization and economic liberalization. It is possible to argue that, some 80 years and numerous experiments after the founding of the Republic, Turkey is still a country in search of new forms (architectural, as well as social and cultural) for its evolving project of modernity – one that has taken many twists and turns along the way and is still caught in between the country's international aspirations and foundational nationalism.

In this book, we tell the story of these ideas, experiments and interventions to give architectural and urban form to Turkey's engagement with modernity. Even though the beginnings of modernization can be dated back to much earlier developments during the period of the Ottoman Empire, this book picks up the story from when Turkey became a secular nation state and sovereignty was handed to the people rather than the Sultan. In nine thematic and loosely chronological chapters, we offer an overview of modern architecture in Turkey, placing it in the larger social, economic and political context of the country's development as a modern nation in the twentieth century – from the end of the First World War when the new Turkish Republic was born out of the disintegration of the Ottoman Empire, to the country's democratization after the 1950s in the midst of the Cold War's competing ideological forces, and finally to the present when Turkey continues to be dramatically transformed through globalization, economic integration with the world market and transnational cultural influences, as well as its renewed preoccupations with identity, Islam and Ottoman heritage.

While presenting a critical and comprehensive account of modern architecture in Turkey over the last century, the premise of the book, and the series to which it belongs, is a commitment to emerging global perspectives in writing the history of modern architecture. It has been some time since the inherited Eurocentric biases of the mainstream historiography of modern architecture have been dismantled in favour of recognizing the plurality, heterogeneity and difference of modern architectures across the globe. More significantly, recent critical theories have articulated the need to abandon the very idea of a central, singular and canonic modernism or 'a European master narrative' claiming distinction from its allegedly lesser, derivative extensions in peripheral geographies ('non-Western', 'Third World' or 'other' modernisms to cite some of the terms in circulation). What is proposed instead is a 'cosmopolitan modernism' – one that is decentred, worldwide and heterogeneous, a global history that admits the circulation and translation of architectural ideas and forms.[1] Debunking the notorious east-west polarities in art/architectural historiography, these theories draw attention to the plethora of cross-cultural exchanges and complex power relations, not just between the industrialized west and the countries typically grouped under the term 'Third World', but among different 'Third World' countries themselves. Instead of looking at architects working in these peripheral geographies as passive recipients or imitators of an imported (read Western) modernism, they urge us to see them as active participants engaged in 'dense local practices of . . . domesticating, translating, selecting, mixing and reinventing'.[2]

Having participated in these critical debates in different ways with our own earlier work, we have sought to write this book, first and foremost, from such a cosmopolitan perspective.[3] While obviously inscribed within the country-by-country framework of the series, our account of modern architecture in Turkey underscores the inadequacy of bounded national categories, highlighting instead numerous trans-national exchanges, encounters and 'translations' between modernist Turkish architects and their European and North American interlocutors, as well as their counterparts in other 'non-Western' contexts. The forms of these trans-national encounters vary from architects' personal stories of travel, emigration or exile, to governmental recruitment of foreign architects and planners for major commissions, and above all to the global dissemination of ideas through modern mass media. Whatever the modes of transmission, however, the results are invariably hybrid and irreducible to either the canonic examples of an allegedly universal modernism or to essentialist discourses of 'national architecture' resistant to globalization.

In this book we conceptualize modernism, not as a recognizable style or a doctrinaire functionalism, but rather as the expression of contemporary experiences and shared aspirations of modern societies roughly from the First World War to the present. This, by definition, is something far more inclusive and pluralist than the accepted canonic forms (such as reinforced concrete frame construction, glass, absence of decoration, prismatic volumes and flat roofs) or the canonic chronological frameworks (interwar and immediate post-war) in terms of which 'modern architecture' has typically been discussed and understood. Accordingly, we have expanded the thematic boundaries of modern architecture to include not only the canonic works of modernism in Turkey (major public buildings by prominent designers) but also the expressions of 'ordinary' or 'everyday' modernisms resulting from informal, even illegal practices (anonymous residential fabric, squatter housing and speculative apartments in particular). Thus, against the top-to-bottom and State-sponsored projects of Turkish modernization, we sought to juxtapose the more spontaneous, anonymous and internalized everyday modernity of non-state actors, private developers and the building industry.[4] Likewise, we delineated the course of modern Turkish architecture in a broader temporal framework from the 1920s into the 2000s, including its 'heroic', 'revisionist', 'post-modern' and 'global' periods as parts of the same broader project of modernity, one that is defined by continuously self-modifying belief in the new.[5]

Turkey, as many other modern nations, exhibits an intense historical and cultural complexity, and has additional tangled and difficult dilemmas of identity resulting from the multi-ethnic and multi-cultural legacy of the Ottoman Empire – 'caught between two worlds', as many observers, scholars and journalists never fail to point out.[6] Historically, for more than five centuries Turkey and the preceding Ottoman Empire have been portrayed as the quintessential 'other' of Europe, a portrayal frequently at odds with the country's own official self-perception as an aspiring player on the European scene. For most of the twentieth century, the foundational doctrines and cultural politics of the 'republican revolution' were largely uncontested, constructing a modern Turkish identity that was orientated unequivocally towards the West. Meanwhile, modern architecture in Turkey was, by and large, a topic doubly neglected not only by historians of modern architecture (whose Eurocentric focus was mentioned above), but also by area studies (in this case Turkish/Middle Eastern studies, which was largely dominated by Ottomanists with an exclusive focus on earlier periods). The few descriptive and documentary scholarly studies and published histories of modern architecture in Turkey were mostly available only in Turkish.[7]

Since the 1980s, however, earlier republican certainties have given way to new pluralities with competing claims on the definition of modern Turkish identity. Today, perceived as Europe's oriental 'other' or 'the Europe' of the Middle East, depending on how you wish to see it, Turkey's identity remains profoundly ambiguous, hybrid and irreducible to worn out east-west polarities. Interdisciplinary interest in modern Turkey has mounted in recent years and Turkey's 'modernity project' has been the subject of numerous studies in the humanities, social sciences and, especially, the emerging discipline of cultural studies. Meanwhile, architecture and urbanism, while still maintaining their autonomous disciplinary concerns (with matters of design, form and technique), have become part of this interdisciplinary studies in mutually beneficial ways. A younger generation of architectural historians has given a new visibility to modern architecture in Turkey on the international scene, adopting approaches that are more critical, cross-cultural and interdisciplinary than those of the earlier generation.[8] Studies of representation, urban space, built form and visual culture are no longer marginal embellishments to the 'real content' of more traditional historiography (typically the work of political, social and economic historians) but rather the very substance of a new, critically and culturally conceived understanding of history itself, one that crosses traditional disciplinary boundaries in all directions. Looking at some recent publications that feature architecture as a constitutive ingredient in the making of modern Turkey (along with politics, society, culture, literature and gender studies among others), it is perhaps possible to talk about a 'spatial/visual turn' in modern Turkish studies.[9]

Hence, we have conceived this book as a contribution, not only to the historiography of modern architecture at large, but also to interdisciplinary modern Turkish studies. While 'autonomous' concerns internal to the design disciplines have given us our primary methodological tools and questions (analysis of form, construction, programme and meaning), we have also made it our objective to look at architecture in the larger political, social, economic and cultural contexts within which buildings, projects and ideas emerge. Above all, our history of modern architecture in Turkey seeks to illustrate how architecture and urbanism are as much the active means by which modern identities are produced and reproduced, as they are formally/stylistically determined by a confluence of diverse factors and historical experiences.

Within our broad chronology from the First World War to the present, our nine thematic chapters are implicitly clustered in three parts, corresponding to the three turning points in Turkey's history when major political, economic and cultural shifts transformed the practice of architecture in the country in visible and paradigmatic ways. Each initiated by a powerful political leader (Mustafa Kemal Atatürk in 1923, Adnan Menderes in 1950, whose rule was soon disrupted with three consequent *coups d'état*, and Turgut Özal in 1983), the transformations after these turning points also loosely correspond to the three distinct phases of modernity that most post-colonial and/or post-imperial nations have gone through, displaying more or less comparable experiences during the course of the twentieth century.

The initial period of independence and nation-building under the leadership of nationalist elites corresponds to what may be seen as 'modern architecture as national expression'. From Kemalist Turkey in the 1930s to Nehru's India in the 1950s, this is when modern forms were charged with a utopian power to evoke a thoroughly modernized, secularized and industrialized new nationhood, visibly dissociated from the country's own colonial or imperial past as represented by neoclassical and eclectic buildings in academic styles. In chapter One we discuss this phenomenon for the case of the Kemalist Revolution in Turkey, following it in chapter Two with the extensive modernist building programme of the republican nation state, primarily through the work of German and Austrian architects and planners invited by the new regime. In chapter Three we focus more specifically on residential architecture, especially on the pervasive 'modern house and city' discourse. We also look at nationalist reconstructions of the 'Turkish house', highlighting the fact that, in the search for the desired new *wohnkultur*, national expression was not an aberration of modernism, but an integral and constitutive dimension of it.[10]

As elsewhere, Turkey underwent major transformations after the Second World War, a period that ushered in urbanization, industrialization and democratization, the decolonization of the 'Third World' and, above all, the rise of modernization theories and discourses of development in the volatile bi-polar Cold War years. Underscoring our point about the profound ambiguity of modern Turkish identity is the fact that Turkey did not participate in the Bandung Conference convened in 1955 under the leadership of India to articulate a position of non-alignment and independence from both the capitalist and the communist blocs. Having been recently admitted to NATO, primarily due to her strategic importance on the border with the Soviet Union, Turkey then perceived herself as a bona fide member of the Western alliance, even though its problems of development were similar to those of the non-aligned nations. In this period, as modern architecture entered a revisionist, 'anxious' phase in the industrialized West, the aesthetic canons of International Style spread to the rest of the world along with the prevailing 'convergent theories of modernization', which stipulated that there was a universal path to modernity that all nations would follow and so end up resembling Western societies.[11] In chapter Four we discuss this 'modernism of development' in the context of Turkey's transition to multi-party democracy, capitalist development and the concomitant internationalization of modern Turkish architecture in the 1950s. In chapter Five we address the cracks in the optimism of modernization theory as reflected in architecture and urbanism, not just in Turkey but wherever institutionalized high modernism was unable to cope with the magnitude of problems posed by migration, urbanization and lack of housing. Through the Turkish example, we show how, under conditions of insufficient capital accumulation and absence of public housing and welfare programmes, a notorious informal sector emerged that, in the form of squatter housing and a speculative urban apartment boom, prepared the social and aesthetic plight of large Turkish cities. In chapter Six we demonstrate the intense upheavals in the context of bi-polar political

TOKI high-rise blocks in Istanbul; photo by Martinez Muniz, 2008/2010.

ambitions in the 1960s and '70s. We focus on the response of architects, both as designers engaged with revisionist/critical trends in modern architecture at large (from 'organic' architecture to discourses of 'regionalism' and 'new brutalism' challenging the aesthetic canons of International Style modernism) and as a highly politicized professional body, deeply engaged with and critical of the impact upon the urban landscape of capitalism and underdevelopment. These two decades came to an abrupt close with the *coup d'état* of 1980.

Starting in the mid-1980s, Turkey underwent unprecedented developments reflecting larger changes in the global order, representing a 'post-modern' world according to some theorists, or merely 'modernity at large' according to others.[12] In chapter Seven we offer an overview of the architectural/urban expressions of Turkey's shift to economic liberalization and integration with global markets (symbolized by the proliferation of shopping malls), at the same time that the foundational idea of a homogeneous modern Turkish identity was challenged in unprecedented ways (symbolized by the boom in mosque construction and the 'postmodern' turn in architectural experimentation). Thus we show how architecture is a powerful physical manifestation of what scholars have called 'divergent theories of modernity' – that societies are indeed becoming modern, but in their own very diverse and intertwined ways. In chapter Eight we again look at the dramatic contrasts and simultaneity of wealth and poverty, legality and illegality, aesthetic refinement and aesthetic plight that neoliberal urban politics have produced in the realm of residential architecture. These manifest themselves in the emerging new scales, new typologies and new sprawl of Turkish cities, which we see as local reflections of a global phenomenon from São Paolo to Shanghai in a world whose urban population has outnumbered its rural one, posing new challenges to the disciplines of architecture, planning and landscape. In the final chapter Nine we bring our history of modern architecture in Turkey as close to the present as possible, albeit in an inevitably tentative way. We zoom in on the work of a younger generation of architects, whose 'post-critical' focus on the disciplinary concerns of architecture (matters of form, quality and creativity) separates them from the political activism of the older generation. We also look at the highly visible 'trans-nationalization' of architectural practice in contemporary Turkey, not only through the success of these younger architects abroad but also through the arrival of international celebrity architects in Turkey. In this context, we conclude with a number of highly visible developments in Istanbul that demonstrate what is often characterized as the new 'post-national nationalism' – namely, governments' appeal to architectural spectacle, 'brandscapes' and urban renewal/gentrification schemes as a form of putting their countries on the global map.[13] At the end of these nine chapters, we hope to leave the reader not only with a comprehensive overview of modern architecture in Turkey in the twentieth century, but also with a palpable sense of the plurality, complexity and paradoxes of her still unfolding modernity project.

chapter one

Architecture of Revolution

Gentlemen, it was necessary to abolish the fez, which sat on the heads of our people as an emblem of ignorance, negligence, fanaticism and hatred of progress and civilization. It was necessary to accept in its place the hat, the headgear used by the whole civilized world . . .
Our thinking and our mentality will have to become civilized. We cannot afford to stop anymore. We have to move forward. Civilization is a fire that burns and destroys those who ignore it.
Kemal Atatürk, *Nutuk, 1927* (Ankara, 1952), pp. 720–21, and *Atatürk'un Söylev ve Demeçleri* (Ankara, 1959), pp. 207–10

Following Turkey's 'War of Independence' (1919–22) against the occupying allied forces after the First World War and the departure of the last Ottoman sultan into exile, the new Turkish Republic was established on 29 October 1923, bringing a six-century old dynastic Islamic Empire to an end. In the following years, under the personal directive of Mustafa Kemal Atatürk (1881–1938), the national hero and the founder of the Republic, a series of institutional reforms was launched, including the abolition of both the Caliphate (the supreme religious authority for all Muslims) and the Islamic *sharia* law (1924), the outlawing of the fez, the turban and other forms of traditional garb in favour of the Western-style hat (1925) and the replacement of Arabic script with the Latin alphabet (1927). Dissociating the new nation from its own Ottoman past, these reforms collectively amounted to a radical and comprehensive 'civilizational shift' from a traditional order grounded in Islam to a modern, secular, westernized society; or, in the words of its own protagonists, a 'revolution' (*inkılap*) that, under the rubric of Kemalism, became the foundational ideology of the Turkish state for decades to come.[1]

An exhibition hall (1933), a water filter station, and a casino/restaurant of a railway station (1937) in Ankara showing the pervasiveness of similar forms for different functions.

Although the proclamation of the Turkish Republic in 1923 is etched deeply in Turkish collective consciousness as the single most important event of modern Turkish history, it is important to point out that the main political and ideological objectives set earlier by the 'Young Turks' (the French-influenced group of late Ottoman reformers, bureaucrats and military leaders who sought to modernize the Ottoman state) continued to shape republican leaders and were consolidated into the single-party regime of the Republican Peoples' Party (RPP) after 1931.[2] This was an official programme of modernization to be implemented from above by the reformist elites of a paternalistic state, in the conspicuous absence of all the historical conditions within which Western modernity flourished: namely industrialization, urbanization, capitalism and an autonomous bourgeoisie. Inheriting a poor and war-weary country, Kemalist modernizers wished to 'skip stages' in a heroic leap. Like most other 'ideologies of delayed development' espoused by nationalist and/or post-colonial regimes in peripheral contexts, 'Kemalism was essentially revolutionary and "utopian" in Manheim's usage, its ideological position based on a zealous futurism to catch up with Western civilization'.[3] Given this sense of historical restlessness, it is not surprising that the exterior forms and recognizable symbols of modernity became the primary preoccupation in early republican Turkey. The words 'modern' (*modern*) and 'contemporary' (*asri*) were used synonymously in the 1930s to designate the new and desirable looks of anything (from women's fashion to architecture and urbanism) as opposed to their traditional counterparts under the Ottoman Empire. This assumption that form could transform content, coupled with the recognition of the power of representation, resulted in the systematic production and dissemination of a distinctly republican *visual* culture of modernity. Architecture, by its very nature, constituted a central component of this visual culture, further strengthened by the favourable historical coincidence between the Kemalist Revolution and the rise of the Modern Movement in interwar Europe. The formal and aesthetic canons of the Modern Movement – or the 'New Architecture' (*Yeni Mimari* in Turkish) – were enthusiastically embraced by the emerging professional community of young Turkish architects who saw modernism as the most appropriate expression of the rationalist and positivist ideals of the new republic.[4]

One of the well-known ironies in the history of modern architecture is that the label 'International Style' was coined precisely at the time of strong nation states and rampant nationalist sentiments everywhere between the two World Wars. While institutions like the League of Nations and the Congrès International d'Architecture Moderne (CIAM), both established in 1927, represented international ideals (in world governance and in architecture and urbanism, respectively), participation in them was primarily through national affiliations. It was, by definition, an inter-*national* order that implied the existence and primacy of the nation state and an understanding of nationalism as integral to rather than an aberration of modernity. Modernist Turkish architects, too, frequently expressed their distaste for the term 'International Style' and insisted on 'New Architecture', which they argued was neither 'international' nor 'a style': it was simply an anti-academic, anti-stylistic approach to architecture that was the most rational response to site, programme, climate and context, and was therefore by definition 'national'. The contradiction between this anti-stylistic understanding of modernism and its canonization as a recognizable aesthetic formula (of flat roofs, composition of cubic volumes, undecorated facades, band windows, *pilotis* and so on) would remain an unresolved tension in Turkish architectural culture throughout the early republican period.

CIAM's official account of modern architecture as a rational, scientific doctrine expressing the inevitable zeitgeist of the twentieth century conveniently became the basis of a symbiotic relationship between architects and the state. Embracing the rationalist / functionalist progressivism of modern architecture and urbanism legitimized revolutionary regimes as active agents of modernity, while identifying with these new nationalist regimes benefited the architectural profession in this great era of state patronage. While the specific form of the alignment between modern architecture and nationalist politics varied from country to country in interwar Europe, new nation states and/or revolutionary regimes like Kemalist Turkey and Fascist Italy were particularly receptive to modernism.[5] Turkish architects made no secret of their admiration for the latter.

Like Nehru after him, Kemal Atatürk was the paradigmatic nationalist modernizer who articulated the idea that the modern industrial civilization of the West constituted a universal and teleological trajectory of progress that every nation should follow by necessity. As he presented it, modern civilization was not the exclusive monopoly of Europe or the West just because it originated there. Rather, it was the stock of accumulated scientific knowledge, methods and tools, worldviews and lifestyles that constituted the very substance of the historical evolution of humanity and should therefore be seen as the property of all nations. The affinities between this teleological history of societal development and the official modernist polemic of the interwar years (authored by Sigfried Giedion and Le Corbusier in particular) are obvious: modern architecture too was constructed as a thoroughly rational and scientific fact of the modern industrial era (unlike earlier historical 'styles', which were the products of taste, convention and fashion) and was therefore a universal discourse that all nations should adopt if they wanted to catch up with modernity.

Throughout the early republican period it was this basic progressive model of history (shared by different forms of modern thought from Marxism to the Modern Movement in architecture) that gave republican leaders and Turkish intellectuals the necessary ideological grounds by which they could reconcile Turkey's revolutionary switch to Western civilization with their equally passionate commitment to promoting national culture. As fascinated by German philosophers' ideas of *Kultur* as they were by the rationalist and positivist ideas of French thinkers, they devoted substantial intellectual effort to demonstrating the compatibility of national (Turkish) culture with the basic precepts of modern Western civilization, including that of its new modern architecture. Architects and critics argued that modernism, far from being an alien import, was in fact an uncovering/recovering of what was already rational in Turkish architectural heritage, vernacular traditions and historical forms. The specific ways in which individual architects negotiated between the universal and the local varied, as we will articulate in more detail in the following chapters; but the search for the new Turkish architecture of the Kemalist Revolution (*inkılap mimarisi*), both 'modern' and 'national' at the same time, remained the dominant ideal.

The term *inkılap mimarisi* (architecture of revolution) conveniently collapsed two meanings into one: it signified both the aesthetic canons and rationalist/functionalist doctrines of the Modern Movement (that is, 'revolution in architecture', as the inaugural issue of the Turkish architects' professional journal *Mimar* characterized the newly completed Villa Savoie of Le Corbusier) and the specific building programme of the new Kemalist regime in Turkey ('architecture of the *Kemalist* revolution', especially government and railway buildings, schools, factories and the so-called 'Peoples' Houses' (*Halkevleri*) associated with the ruling RPP). What follows is a historical account of the ways in which modern architecture, under the rubric of *inkılap mimarisi*, was appropriated as a form of visual politics in Kemalist Turkey. First, we look at the radical break with the Ottoman revivalist 'National Style' of the late Empire, now construed as the academic and anachronistic 'other' of the new modern architecture. Secondly, we turn to the most symbolic showcase of modern architecture and urbanism in early republican Turkey: the construction of Ankara as a modern capital city and the building of the new infrastructure for taming the hostile nature of the central Anatolian plain in which it was located. Lastly we focus on factories, industrial complexes and model villages that were conceived as agents of social transformation disseminating modernity to the Anatolian hinterland. Together this serves as a bird's-eye view over early republican Turkey, mapping the ground on which modern architecture and urbanism was mobilized for Kemalist nation-building. Closer analysis of public buildings for the State and the private architecture of the modern house will follow in chapters Two and Three.

The Complex Legacy of Ottoman Revivalism

As we focus on the revolutionary self-representation of the Kemalist Republic, it is also important to mark the continuities with the final decades of the Ottoman Empire when major modern transformations in architectural theory, education and practice were initiated and art and architecture were institutionalized as self-defining and self-regulating disciplines with specific professional and political agendas.[6] Most visibly, between 1908 and 1918 a new architectural style emerged in Turkey representing all the cultural/ideological complexities of the patriotic 'dynastic nationalism' of the late Empire, the foundations of which were set in the latter part of the nineteenth century when the Ottoman intelligentsia sought to recast the Ottoman state as a modern nation and to construct a 'national self' based on a historicist interest in the cultural and artistic heritage of the Empire.[7] Retrospectively labelled by architectural historians as the 'First National Style', but known to its contemporaries as the 'National Architecture Renaissance', this Ottoman revivalist style combined elements derived from classical Ottoman architecture (especially semispherical Ottoman domes, wide roof overhangs with supporting brackets, pointed arches and ornate tile decoration) with Beaux-Arts design principles (symmetry, axiality and classic tripartite facade compositions) and new materials and construction techniques (reinforced concrete, iron and steel). Under the leadership of three prominent practising architects and educators – Vedat, Kemalettin and the Levantine Italian architect Giulio Mongeri – architects trained in the final decades of the Empire applied this hybrid style to the programmatic requirements of modern urban life, not unlike its revivalist counterparts in Europe, such as neoclassicism and Gothic Revival. Banks, offices, hotels, cinemas, ferry stations and other public structures were built in this style, first for the Young Turks before the First World War and later for the new Kemalist Republic in the 1920s.

The Ministry of Endowments offices (Vakıf Hanı, 1912–26), designed by Kemalettin and occupying an entire urban block in Sirkeci, Istanbul, is a most representative, technologically advanced, programmatically complex and aesthetically ornate example of a style that was pervasive in these years. Immediately after the proclamation of the Republic, the same style was employed for major public buildings in Ankara, mostly located in 'old Ankara' around Ulus Meydanı (Nation Square) below the Citadel. Among them is the canonic Ankara Palas (1924–6), the joint work of Vedat and Kemalettin, built as an ornate hotel with the latest technical infrastructure and modern conveniences to host the higher bureaucrats and foreign dignitaries of the new Republic. Also notable are the 'Ottoman',

'Agricultural' and 'Business' bank buildings (1926–9) of Giulio Mongeri, as well as a group of highly representative public buildings by the younger Arif Hikmet Koyunoğlu, lined along Ankara's main avenue: the Ministry of Foreign Affairs (1927), Ethnography Museum (1926) and Turkish Hearth Building (1927–30), which collectively display all the ornate stylistic elements that define the style, especially marble facades, tile decoration, Ottoman domes and 'crystalline' column capitals with *muqarnas* details. Similarly ornate 'First National Style' buildings proliferated in other cities of republican Anatolia such as İzmir, Konya, Kütahya and Sivas among others, mostly as government 'palaces' (*hükümet konağı*), schools, post offices, cinemas, hotels and other public buildings.

To this day, one of the most contentious topics in the historiography of modern Turkish architecture is the continued use of an Ottoman revivalist style by a secular and Western-orientated republic at a time when the new regime was seeking to dissociate itself from its Ottoman/Islamic past. Many architects and architectural historians, having internalized the modernist biases of republican historiography, tend to see this style as a 'temporary aberration' at best and dismiss its academicism and historicism as anathema to the revolutionary vision of the Kemalist project. What eludes this assessment is that, far from being an anachronistic architecture, the 'First National Style' was in fact a most appropriate expression of the volatile transition from Empire to Republic. Its Ottoman stylistic references applied to modern building types were effectively 'double-coded', capable of signifying both the glories of an Ottoman/Islamic past that continued to resonate with a traditional population and the new programmatic and technological needs of a society in transformation. As many revisionist scholars point out, in this period religion remained a powerful force for national mobilization, and the nation was conceptualized as a secular religion.[8] Understanding this shift from religious to national meanings is essential for historically contextualizing the 'First National Style' in the 1920s. Whereas during the final decades of the Ottoman Empire the relationship between the idea of Ottoman revivalism and Islam was analogous to that between Gothic revivalism and Christianity, increasingly after the turn of the century the nationalist republican intelligentsia succeeded in effectively recharging Ottoman forms with 'Turkishness' (not unlike the manner in which later Victorians looked upon Gothic revivalism as much as a symbol of 'Englishness' as that of the good Christian society that Pugin and Ruskin advocated). Such 'nationalization' of Ottoman heritage legitimized its continued use during the first decade of the Kemalist republic –not to mention the practicality of keeping an already established design and building practice at a time when resources were extremely limited.[9]

By 1930, however, as the single-party rule of the RPP was consolidated and the secular, Western-orientated cultural politics of the republic

Arif Hikmet Koyunoğlu, Ethnography Museum, Ankara, 1926, entrance view and column detail; photo by Sibel Bozdoğan.

A hotel in 'First
National Style' in
Bandırma, 1920s;
photo by İnci
Aslanoğlu.

became firmly established, 'First National Style' was rapidly abandoned
in favour of the 'New Architecture' (*Yeni Mimari*). This was the beginning
of an ideologically charged binary way of thinking in terms of contrasts
between the old and the new, the traditional and the contemporary (*asri*),
the reactionary and the progressive, which permeated the entire architectural discourse of the early republic. Prominent intellectuals like
Ahmet Haşim criticized Ottoman revivalist buildings as 'a reactionary
architecture (*mürteci mimari*)' antagonistic to the spirit of the Kemalist
Revolution.[10] Others proposed rationalist explanations for the necessity
of the New Architecture, portraying Ottoman revivalism as a romantic
and futile idea belonging to a bygone era. 'Each epoch produces its own
art,' wrote İsmail Hakkı Baltacıoğlu in 1929, 'today when it is possible to
build flat roofs, it makes no sense to modernize the dome. The dome is
not a national motif: it was merely a constructional necessity of the
past'.[11] In his seminal *Türk Sanatı* (1928), the influential art historian
Celal Esat Arseven wrote along similar lines: 'The Ottomans had no choice
but to make domes to span their roofs: after the advent of reinforced
concrete, this method was rendered obsolete. Fortunately it did not take
long to realize that it is a malaise to continue with the same method.'[12]
Three years later, in his *Yeni Mimari* (1931), adapted from André Lurçat's
book on modern architecture of 1929, Arseven would celebrate the arrival

24

of the 'New Architecture' in Ankara and praise the recent curricular transformations in architectural education as the emancipation of the architect from 'the stifling of talent by classicism'.[13]

The curricular reforms mentioned by Arseven were put in place from 1924 onwards by bringing in German-speaking architects and planners, including the Austrian-Swiss architect Ernst Egli, who was appointed head of the architectural section of the Academy of Fine Arts in Istanbul, the oldest school of architecture in Turkey (established in 1882). In a radical overhaul of the curriculum, the classical Beaux Arts model was replaced by the rationalist and functionalist precepts of European modernism and the 'First National Style' was cast aside as modernism's academic and anachronistic 'other' that had to be left behind in order to capture the zeitgeist of the modern age. By the early 1930s the triumph of the 'New Architecture' was complete: domes, arches and tile decoration were banished from republican practice as reactionary nostalgia. The fact that the only project with formal references to the Ottoman mosque among the 1937 competition entries for the new Grand National Assembly was promptly eliminated testifies to the radical nature of this break with the past.[14] In spite of the insistence of Arseven, Baltacıoğlu and other authors that the dome was 'a technical necessity, not a national, religious or symbolic motif', it was precisely this religious/dynastic symbolism that ultimately rendered it politically and ideologically impermissible in a modern, secular republic.

Contrary to the official doctrine that portrayed modern forms as a thoroughly rational consequence of function and technique, many early republican buildings defied the rationalist / functionalist explanations that were supposed to determine their forms. Three programmatically very different buildings in Ankara – the new Exhibition Hall (1933), the water filter station of Çubuk Dam (1936) and the casino-restaurant of the new Railway Station (1937) – illustrate how forms preceded function rather than followed it (see page 16). Despite their very different functions, these buildings shared a distinct, recognizable and recurring 'formal repertoire' of modernism: a long horizontal block (or group of horizontal blocks), rounded at one end or both (with allusions to a ship or ocean liner) and intersecting with a prominent vertical element (a clock tower or chimney). It was not their programmes or construction techniques that informed this distinct iconography, but rather their representative function as symbols of the 'new' (modernism) against the 'old' (Ottoman revivalism). Ultimately, in their programmatic zeal to equate modern architectural forms with the Kemalist Revolution, what eluded the republican intelligentsia was the 'transient' or 'fleeting' dimension of modernity: that what is cast as 'old' was once the 'new' and, more importantly, the 'new' is also historical and contextual (rather than objective, absolute and immutable).[15]

Ankara: Showcase of the New

On 13 October 1923 Ankara, an insignificant central Anatolian town from where the national War of Independence was directed, became the capital of the new Turkish republic. Nothing illustrates the 'old versus new' construct better than the contrast drawn in republican imagery between 'the nationalist symbolism, moral superiority and idealism' of the new capital and 'the imperial, dynastic, cosmopolitan and decadent' old Istanbul that had served as the seat of the Ottoman Empire since its conquest in 1453. 'Ankara is the city of future. Istanbul is a city of the past', declared the official publication *La Turquie Kemaliste* in 1943, 'In the latter the visitor thinks in terms of Ottoman rulers, mosques and history books, [. . . in Ankara] we drive along wide boulevards passing magnificent, modern, light-filled schools, parks and government buildings'.[16] Many issues of the same publication featured, under the heading 'Ankara Construit', a series of photographs (often employing European avant-garde techniques such as collage, montage and strategic framing) that conveyed the idealism, youthfulness and assertive enthusiasm with which the construction of Ankara was undertaken. The making of a modern capital city out of a small, poor, malaria-ridden and dusty town was celebrated as an epic accomplishment of the new regime and architecture became a powerful visual symbol of this accomplishment.

From the *Ankara Construit* series, in *La Turquie Kemaliste* (1935), showing a utopian image of new Ankara.

Today the physical fabric of Ankara bears the traces of the decisive stylistic shift around 1930 manifested in the architecture of its major public buildings. The 'First National Style' buildings of the 1920s are located in the older section of the city to the north, while the austere German and Central European modernism of the next decade dominates the newer southern extension of the city, appropriately called Yenişehir or 'the new city'. The main actors in the making of new Ankara were European (mostly German-speaking) émigré architects and

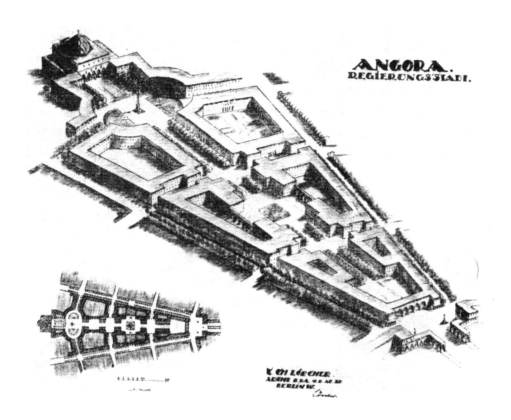

ANGORA.
REGIERUNGSSTADT.

Carl Lörcher, plan of the Governmental Complex, Ankara, 1924–5.

planners whose careers were threatened by political turmoil in Europe at a time that coincided favourably with the rise of a modernizing new regime in need of their expertise in Turkey. Between the two World Wars approximately two hundred German-speaking professionals served the Kemalist state, including some forty architects and planners who introduced modern architecture and urbanism into Turkish education and practice.[17] Starting in the mid-1920s, following the restructuring of the municipal administration in Ankara and the commissioning of the city's first survey map, the physical planning of the new capital was entrusted to German and Austrian architects and planners. The first Master Plan for Ankara, prepared in 1924–25 by the architect and planner Carl Christoph Lörcher from Berlin, would play a seminal (although long under-acknowledged) role in delineating the outlines of subsequent planning efforts in Ankara, especially in its governmental centre.

Lörcher's plan was conceived in two stages: the rehabilitation of the old city around the Citadel, which he highlighted for its historical significance and its dominant presence in the city's skyline, and the

construction of the new city to the south for a projected total population of 150,000 to 200,000 inhabitants. The baroque-inspired scheme
for the new city laid out the main north-south axis of Ankara (from
the Citadel in the north to the Çankaya hills in the south) as the backbone
of the plan, from which a diagonal grid of streets and large urban blocks
radiated at an angle. This main north-south axis, which Lörcher aptly
named 'Nation Avenue' (Millet Caddesi), was punctuated at regular inter-
vals by major public squares as formal focal points (with statues, fountains
and monuments), further accentuating the Beaux Arts principles that still
dominated urban design in the 1920s. The naming of these squares and
major streets after important events and prominent figures of the epic
War of Independence (such as Nation, Victory, Lausanne and Republic
Squares) constituted what architectural historian Ali Cengizkan calls a
series of 'urban metaphors' to nurture the nation's collective memory.[18]
The Government Complex (Regierungstadt) was laid out in an axial and
symmetrical arrangement with wide, straight promenades, squares and
monumental buildings with arcaded facades. The residential estates of the
Çankaya hills (Siedlung in Tschankaya) were conceived in the form of
loose-density, low-rise blocks and rows of houses around courtyards and
streets. Private gardens, public lawns and an overall proximity to nature
were presented as moral virtues in themselves, thus espousing the 'garden
city ideal' that would maintain its grip upon early republican thought
throughout the 1930s.[19]

Although the Lörcher plan was not implemented, aspects of it were
used in preparing the brief of the major international competition held
in 1927. Many of its features, such as the significance of the Citadel and
the old city, the imprint of the main axis and some cross streets, and its
plot and block sizes, have subtle imprints on the winning scheme by Hermann Jansen (1869–1947), another planner from Berlin.[20] Condemning
the dense, urban blocks of nineteenth-century European cities as
unhealthy, Jansen regarded the garden city concept as the ideal model
for planning the 'healthy and modern' city that Ankara aspired to be,
albeit one to be built by the political decision of a single-party state rather
than by the reformist impulses of private enterprise, as Ebenezer Howard's
original programme envisioned. Endowing the Citadel with a symbolic
significance as the Stadtkrone of Ankara (akin to Rome's Capitoline Hill
or Pergamon's Acropolis), he proposed isolating and preserving the old
city as some kind of museum piece while the new city developed around
and beyond it. Giving a literal, visual expression to the foundational
republican distinction between the old and the new, Jansen identified
'four essential concepts of modern city planning' that became the basis
of his new city – transportation, 'free areas' for recreational activities and

sports, 'community buildings' (the public, governmental and educational
buildings of the new capital) and residential areas – with belts of green
spaces separating these different functional zones. The location and
character of the residential areas were differentiated in relation to class
and income, with a workers' quarter (*Arbeiterviertel*) to the northwest
of the old city and an area for upper-class, single-family houses (*Land-
hausviertel*) to the south. While such ideas of functional zoning partly
connect Jansen to the emerging modernist urbanism of Le Corbusier and
the CIAM, the primary sources of the Jansen plan were the aesthetic and
preservationist approach of Camillo Sitte and the garden city model of
Ebenezer Howard.

In the 'community buildings' zone, Jansen proposed a Government
Buildings Quarter (*Regierungsviertel*) in the south and a Higher Education Quarter (*Hochschulviertel*) to the southeast of the old city. Along the
lines of Sitte's aesthetic urbanism, he studied their three-dimensional
architectural and urban qualities – their massing, heights and relationship to each other. He conceived his role as 'the author of the city',

single-handedly giving shape to a unified aesthetic to which he expected the architects of individual buildings to conform. Other German-speaking architects were brought in to design the components. While these 'community buildings' constituted the official face of modern Ankara under the new regime, the 'free areas' and green spaces were reserved primarily for recreational activities, sports and public leisure. These included the football stadium with adjoining hippodrome and parade grounds, as well as a large public park appropriately named the 'Youth Park' (Gençlik Parkı). Ankara in the 1930s was the ultimate embodiment of the strong cult of youth and health (central to the nationalist cultural politics of the interwar years, especially in Germany and Italy) and these spaces of public recreation and collective sports fulfilled an important ritualistic function above and beyond providing sports facilities or simply offering access to nature. The stadium (1934–6), designed by the Italian architect Paolo Vietti Violi, was not only a novel modern structure featuring a wide reinforced-concrete cantilevered canopy, but also the memorable stage set for extensively publicized national holiday celebrations, most symbolically the Youth and Sports Day of 19 May, when students (including female students in shorts) paraded in front of the public and performed in athletic and gymnastic exercises.

Paolo Vietti Violi,
Stadium, Ankara,
1934–6.

Three ambitious urban/infrastructural projects, the Çubuk Dam (1930–36), the 'Youth Park' (1935–7) and the Atatürk Model Farm and Forest (1933–8), stand out in creating the ethos of the new Ankara. They highlight Ankara's new relationship with Nature, one based on the idea of the scientific conquest of land, climate, terrain and vegetation for the habitation of a modern society. Deeply influenced by contemporary French theories of evolution and human geography – theories that correlated the racial characteristics of different peoples with their responses to their milieu or environment – many early republican intellectuals were interested in the significance of nature and climate in determining the character of a society and its settlement patterns. The German and Austrian architects of new Ankara articulated similar ideas: Ernst Egli, for example, wrote extensively on the significance of architectural 'context' or 'locality' (*mimari muhit*).[21] Atatürk was preoccupied with this correlation via the writings of Jean-Jacques Rousseau, who establishes in the *Social Contract*, a copy of which was in Atatürk's library, a direct link between more democratic forms of government and the fertility of the land.[22] Arid and poor, Ankara clearly did not qualify as a national capital, a sentiment shared by those nations that refused to transfer their embassies from Istanbul to this godforsaken city for many years. For

A national holiday 'Youth and Sports' parade on 19 May 1939.

republican leaders, to combat and reverse Ankara's 'fate' through irrigation and greening was therefore the first priority, a heroic national undertaking that commentators compared to the actual War of Independence.[23] The ambitious plan was to divert, regulate and utilize the waters of the three existing creeks (Çubuk Çayı, Hatip Çayı/Bentderesi and İncesu) to feed into three 'grand projects'.

The Çubuk Dam was designed and built by a team of Turkish and German experts as a concrete structure to regulate the waters of the Çubuk creek for Ankara's domestic, industrial and agricultural consumption as well as flood control. Contemporary documents, photographs and publications make it very clear that the dam carried a much larger representational and symbolic significance above and beyond its utilitarian purpose as a water reservoir. At a time when dams had a particular appeal to modernizing nation states and new revolutionary regimes everywhere (the Tennessee Valley Authority in the United States and the Dnieperostroi Dam in the USSR being the paradigmatic examples), Ankara's dam, modest though it was compared to these examples, was a proud showcase of the Kemalist determination to tame nature through technological means. After the construction of the dam was completed, a carefully landscaped public park was laid out at the foot of the concrete curve of the dam in 1935 and a restaurant-casino was built, projecting over the water's edge at the bottom of the valley. Thus a large engineering structure was effectively scaled-down, 'domesticated' for public use and adorned with a canonic modern building. The undulating facade of the restaurant-casino, counterbalancing the giant curve of the dam, not only displayed an elegant modernist aesthetic evocative of an ocean liner but, as contemporary photographs testify, was to become a popular place for dining, music and mixed-gender entertainment, a model setting for the republican project to transform society along Western lines.

The second 'grand project', the 'Youth Park' (Gençlik Parkı) was conceived as the primary 'free space' in Hermann Jansen's 1932 Master Plan: a large urban park in the middle of Ankara featuring an artificial lake to be constructed by diverting the waters of the Bentderesi creek to the site, by any measure a remarkable engineering feat for its time. Built on 26 hectares of marshy land stretching between the railway station and the old city at the foot of the Citadel, Jansen's vision for the park was one of terraces, cascading waterfalls and a dream world of waterside cafes and restaurants, with the new opera house and the exhibition hall in the background (see page 34). After successive budgetary revisions of the Jansen design, a modified version was constructed between 1935 and 1937 by Theo Leveau, a landscape architect and urban planner working for the Public Works Office (Nafia İşleri). An amusement park was added to the

Çubuk Dam outside
Ankara, 1930–36.

original scheme and the park was inaugurated on 19 May 1943, as part of celebrations for the national holiday for 'youth and sports'. In addition to its visual, aesthetic and recreational function, the lake was also used for swimming, rowing, sailing and ice skating. The Youth Park remains one of the most popular legacies of republican Ankara, not only symbolizing the redemption and greening of the city, but also providing the quintessential early republican public space, 'a school for socializing the people into modern citizens'.[24]

The third 'grand project', Atatürk Model Farm and Forest, was established on the vast reclaimed marshland to the west of the city. It was the largest and most significant of six similar state farms across the country, intended as laboratories for scientific agriculture (seed cultivation, vineyards, orchards, vegetable gardens, poultry and dairy farming) as well as light industry and commerce (brewing, dairy products, soda and ice-cream manufacture). After the draining of the marshes, the planting of trees and the setting up of the infrastructure, the architectural components of the project were entrusted to Ernst Egli who, between 1933 and 1937, designed the farm residence of Atatürk (Marmara Köşkü), the brewery building where state monopolized beer was produced (illustrated on page 46), the

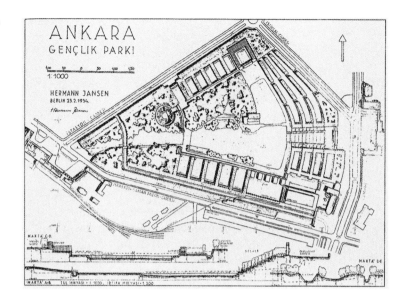

Hermann Jansen, plan and perspective sketch of the 'Youth Park', Ankara, drawn in 1934.

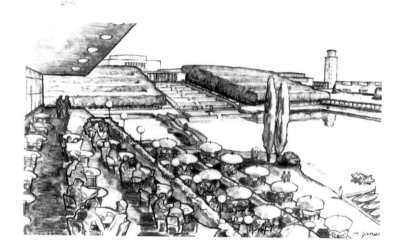

brewery workers' and farm technicians' housing and public baths. As with the Çubuk Dam, the model farm too was conceived as a place of popular entertainment and public recreation in addition to its promotion of scientific agriculture and forestry. It included tree-lined promenades, landscaped parks with meticulous flower beds, restaurants, cafes, two swimming pools (named after the two seas Marmara and Karadeniz) and a zoological garden popular with children and families.[25]

34

Collectively, these three projects (the dam, the park with the artificial lake and the model farm and forest) represent the republican 'high modernist project' of taming the wilderness, mastering the forces of nature and ultimately reclaiming the land as national property.[26] They also offer compelling case studies of how infrastructure (including dams, irrigation networks, canals and reservoirs) are not just utilitarian objects of engineering, but highly symbolic, aesthetic and political interventions for the creation of public space and the 'nationalization' of landscape.

Model Villages and Factory Towns

In early republican thought Istanbul was seen as the imperial city that owed its riches to the exploitation of the Anatolian hinterland by collecting agricultural produce, taxes and conscripted soldiers without giving anything back. By contrast, the new Ankara was idealized as the centre from which the Kemalist 'civilizing mission' would disseminate modernity to the remotest corners of the motherland, now defined by the new territorial consciousness of national borders. This would be done in two complementary ways: a comprehensive village programme (*köycülük*) to introduce agricultural reform, scientific farming and secular education to rural communities in villages and, at the same time, an ambitious programme of state-led industrialization (especially following the world economic crisis of 1929) through the establishment of new factory towns in Anatolia.

The village programmes were conceived in conjunction with the establishment of Peoples' Houses (*Halkevleri*) in 1932 as an organization directly connected to the ruling RPP, the self-declared 'agent of civilization' in early republican Turkey. Its primary aim was to provide popular education and indoctrination along the ideological precepts of the new regime, especially 'the foundational ideas of republic, nation and revolution' as *Ülkü* (Ideal), the official journal of the organization, put it in 1933.[27] Among other historical precedents for such revolutionary organizations, the Italian Dopo Lavoro organizations and fascist youth clubs were particularly inspirational for the *Halkevleri*. More significantly for our purposes, the programmes and the deliberately modernist aesthetic of *Halkevi* buildings in Turkey display remarkable similarities with the Casa del Fascio in Italy. Like their Italian counterparts committed to fascism, most famously Giuseppe Terragni, many Turkish architects saw the Kemalist state as the primary agent of modernization and so endowed the RPP's *Halkevi* buildings with a representational significance that would best be expressed through the progressive connotations of modern forms.[28] A canonic example is the Kadıköy Halkevi (1938) in Istanbul, designed by Rükneddin Güney with a 'pin-wheel' volumetric composition of interlocking blocks, flat roofs, circular windows and a rounded end to one of the blocks. The designs of the *Halkevi* buildings were variations on a basic theme: typically larger volumes containing the dual-purpose auditorium/gym would be located as a separate block connected to the main block containing offices, library, classrooms and spaces for different activity groups. It was common to arrange these blocks in L-shaped configurations to define an open courtyard for meetings, concerts, public festivals and weddings. By 1939 there were 163 *Halkevi* organizations in Anatolian cities and at its peak in 1946 (prior to its termination after the 1950 elections when the RPP lost power) the number of *Halkevleri* had reached 455.[29] It was in these *Halkevleri* that many provincial Turks, living in small towns, first encountered theater, classical music, books and art exhibitions.

The RPP's village programmes (*köycülük*) extended the same 'civilizing mission' to rural communities for both economic/utilitarian objectives (increasing and improving agricultural productivity) and ideological ones (turning illiterate, religious and conservative peasants into modern citizens committed to the republic). In the 1930s Turkey was an overwhelmingly agrarian country with more than 80 per cent of its population living in rural areas under extremely poor and primitive conditions. The modernization of these villages, as well as the resettlement of war refugees flowing in from the lost territories of the Ottoman Empire in the Balkans after the First World War, were formidable challenges that the early republic had to address. By 1933, when the RPP launched its ambitious programme, some 69 model villages based on garden city models, with standardized houses on a grid plan, had already been built for the refugees.[30] RPP ideologues made explicit analogies to and expressed their admiration for 'American missionaries' and the 'civilization bearing colonizers in Africa'.[31] Once again Fascist Italy was an inspiring model for republican projects of land reclamation and resettlement, crop irrigation, malaria eradication

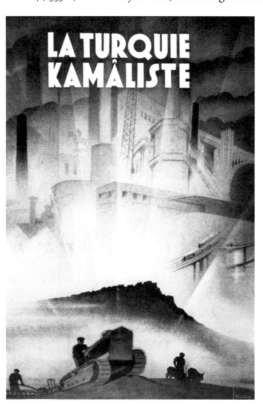

A cover of *La Turquie Kemaliste* idealizing agriculture and industry (1935–6).

Rükneddin Güney,
Kadıköy Halkevi,
Istanbul, 1938, model.

and combating disease in farm animals, and there were conspicuous similarities between the two regimes' commitment to the 'colonization of the countryside' – or, as the title of the Italian fascist magazine proclaimed, to the 'conquest of the land' (*La Conquista della Terra*).[32] It should be noted that in the 1930s, just like the word 'fascism', the word 'colonization' was devoid of its present-day negative connotations: it merely signified a progressive and enlightened state bringing modernity to the 'backward' countryside.

In the pages of *Arkitekt*, the journal of the emerging profession, the prominent modernist architect Zeki Sayar advocated the necessity of 'Interior Colonization' (*İç Kolonizasyon*), a common term in the German garden-city movement, proposing the professional architect/planner as the legitimate agent of civilization capable of transforming the architecture of the village along scientific lines:

> Although we must consider the habits and lifestyles of the peasants when we are constructing new villages, we should not hesitate to go against these traditions wherever they clash with contemporary social and hygienic standards. The new village plans should provide the users with the means for civilized living. A revolution in lifestyles is also necessary, to teach [the peasants] to sleep on individual beds rather than together on the floor, to teach them to use chairs and tables rather than eating on the floor.[33]

Model village in
Thrace for the
settlement of
Balkan refugees.

He also declared it a 'civilizational imperative' to eliminate the use of mud bricks (*kerpiç*), 'a primitive material utterly unfit for construction by the state', and advocated the use of concrete and cement for all village buildings, sanitary infrastructure, irrigation canals, stables and garden walls. He called for exploiting the economies of standardization and serial production of construction materials and building components (windows, doors and fixtures).

Along similar lines, 'villages are of paramount significance in nation building and must be designed by the professional architect', wrote Abidin Mortaş in 1935, illustrating his plea with a model village plan by Burhan Arif.[34] The latter featured a uniform grid of identical houses in both detached and row house typologies and a village centre consisting of a linear shopping street terminating at either end with a small square: one for government buildings and the other for the school, museum and village hall. The diagrammatic simplicity and exaggerated rationality of the proposal, like the rubber-stamp designs of most model villages built at the time, contrasted with the more organic morphologies of existing rural settlements. More conspicuously, the absence of the mosque, that unmistakable landmark of Turkish villages across Anatolia, was a strong architectural statement giving form to the RPP's radical, secularizing agenda. Proposing his own 'mosque-free' project for an ideal village, architect Aptullah Ziya wrote: 'the worst thing about a village mosque, which has been the only cultural and social centre for the village [under the Ottoman Empire], is that within its four walls it offers a bastion for the reactionaries who are the organizers of oppression and ignorance'.[35] His plan of 1933, reminiscent of Owenite utopian socialist communities in the nineteenth century, was laid out in the shape of a perfect square with

38

Burhan Arif, plan of a
model village, 1935.

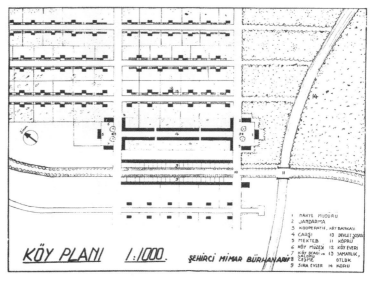

Aptullah Ziya,
Perspective sketch of
an 'ideal village', 1933.

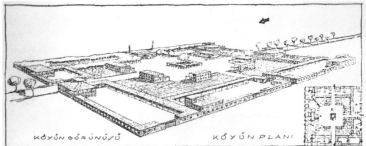

small farmhouses, stables and workshops arranged around a communal
central square flanked by the village school and the village coffee house,
which served as 'the library, the meeting place, the club and the cinema
of the peasant all at once: in other words a "modern temple" filled with
ample air and light'.[36] As Gülsüm Baydar has written, the 'silence' of the
peasants as the objects of such social engineering projects would come
to an end only after the Second World War, when the state's project of
transforming the countryside would give way to the peasants' large-scale
migration to cities, which would, in turn, transform the physical and
social fabric of Turkish cities in unprecedented ways.[37]

If modernizing the villages and making citizens out of peasants was
an urgent item on the republican agenda for the Anatolian hinterland, a
much bigger and more ambitious programme was its rapid industrialization. At the end of the War of Independence, Turkey was a war-torn,

capital-deficient country dependent on massive imports of foreign industrial products to meet domestic demand, while her meagre exports were limited to some raw materials and minerals. As early as 1921 Ferit Bey, the finance minister of the new Ankara Government, was lamenting Turkey's unfavourable balance of trade and declaring that what Turkey needed desperately was 'factories, factories and more factories'.[38] An Industrial Incentives Law (*Teşvik-i Sanayi Kanunu*) was passed in 1927 with the hope of creating a national entrepreneurial class in areas hitherto dominated by foreigners, Levantines and non-Muslim Ottoman *millets* who controlled 80.4 per cent of all industrial establishments in the final years of the Ottoman Empire.[39] Major incentives were extended to potential entrepreneurs, such as rent-free land for the building of factories and tax exemptions, as well as the duty-free importation of machinery and building materials, but the response was limited given the insufficiency of capital accumulation and the absence of an entrepreneurial culture.

The economic crisis of 1929, which marked the end of liberal economic policies everywhere, was the catalyst for Turkey's transition to a planned economy and massive state-sponsored industrialization programmes inspired by German, Italian and Soviet models. Many prominent Turkish intellectuals welcomed this as the most urgent and necessary precondition for true national liberation and the birth of a true national culture.[40] The geographic distribution of Kemalist state industries was informed by the larger 'civilizing mission' espoused by the regime. As the national hero Atatürk himself put it, 'it was necessary to distribute industrial establishments across the entire surface of the motherland . . . in order to introduce modern, civilized, progressive life styles into the remotest

Railway station, Sivas, mid-1930s.

corners of the country.'[41] Thus, in contrast to the concentration of factories in Istanbul and a few other coastal areas and port cities during the late Ottoman period, early republican factories and industrial plants were located across Anatolia, in medium-sized towns made accessible by the country's expanding railway network, a major state industry itself. The new railway stations of these provincial cities, repetitious and recognizable across Anatolia, followed a standardized prototype design produced within the Ministry of Transportation: two-storey buildings that displayed a distinctly modernist aesthetic with flat roofs and plain, albeit symmetrical facades.

The primary financing agent of early republican state-led industrialization was the national Sümerbank, established in 1933 with the objective of starting up new industries, most urgently for basic goods like textiles, leather, sugar, cement, iron/steel, chemicals and paper, the raw materials for which were all available in the country. Among the most significant of these were the iron and steel works of Karabük (constructed by the British company H. A. Brassert & Co. and completed in 1939), located near the coalmines of Zonguldak near the Black Sea coast in northern Anatolia, as well as five major textile plants: Kayseri and Nazilli, both designed by Soviet architects and technicians (1932–6), and Bursa, Malatya and Konya Ereğlisi, built by the Germans (1937–9). The idealized image of an industrialized Anatolian landscape is especially evident in a photograph (see overleaf) of the Zonguldak coke processing factory for the Karabük iron and steel works published in an official photograph album in 1938: the factory is depicted as a technological object harmoniously situated in an idyllic mountainside setting of northern Anatolia and as some sort of a 'machine in the garden', to use Leo Marx's famous phrase.[42]

The same vision of an industrial landscape stretching across the central Anatolian plain can be seen in the Sümerbank cotton textile plant in Kayseri (1934–6), designed by Soviet architects, built by the Turkish contractor Abdurrahman Naci Bey with long-term, low-cost Soviet loans, and operated by Turkish workers trained in the Soviet Union. The project also illustrates the overlapping of industrial, social and ideological objectives in the early republican period, when factories were conceived not as singular buildings or groups of buildings but as comprehensive 'factory towns' in the spirit of Soviet collectivist examples.[43] In addition to the immense production sheds, machine shops and electricity power plant designed by Ivan Nikolaev, the Kayseri complex included workers' housing by Alexander Pasternak and a cafeteria/social centre (daycare centre, cinema, infirmary and library) by Ignati Milinis, a former associate of Constructivist architect Moisei Ginzburg, along with a swimming pool and football stadium.[44] These mixed-gender workspaces and social /

recreational facilities significantly reinforced the secularization agenda of the republic, not unlike the ideological function of the 'workers' clubs' of Soviet Constructivism. In the same way that the latter were conceived as 'social condensers' to create the 'new man' of socialism, state-owned industrial complexes were conceived as instrumental in creating the new citizens of Kemalism.[45] Yet, unlike the Soviet communal housing experiments, workers' houses were typically based on family-orientated typologies that separated married workers and their families from unmarried workers and differentiated between different ranks and occupational hierarchies.[46] A more specific discussion of workers' housing in early republican Turkey will follow in chapter Three.

Coinciding with the rise of the Modern Movement in interwar Europe, early republican industrial buildings strongly informed the emerging discourse on New Architecture, which equated the functional/utilitarian with the aesthetic, an idea that was already pertinent in many countries before the First World War.[47] Moreover, this was a time when some of the Modern Movement's most iconic factories were built in Europe, most notably the Fiat Factory in Turin by Giacomo Matte' Trucco (1927), the Van Nelle tobacco factory in Rotterdam by J. A. Brinkman and Leendert Cornelis van der Vlugt in cooperation with Mart Stam (1926–30), and the Boots Wets Factory near Nottingham by Owen Williams (1933). While a newly emerging modernist architectural profession in Turkey followed European developments closely and talked about elevating the status of factories from that of utilitarian sheds to architect-designed modern objects, the practice rarely matched the discourse. Large-span structures of such immense scale or such levels of transparency were not possible in Turkey given the poor state of available building technology, as well as the tight budgets within which architects had to work with even in the major state factories. For example, some of the most visionary elements devised by Ivan Nikolaev for the Kayseri textiles plant were not built at all and what was completed looks more 'avant-garde' in perspective drawings than in the built versions, which relied heavily for the exterior finishing material on local stone that has aged badly.

The most recognizable formal element of modern factory design was the use of sawtooth roof forms or north-facing curved 'fins' for clerestory lighting to illuminate the main workspace, a formula that was well established with the Soviet-designed Kayseri and Nazilli textile plants, among others. Meanwhile, the sugar factories in Uşak (1926) and Turhal (1934) display a distinctly German brand of early modern factory design laid out as an industrial farm complex consisting of separate large-span steel frame structures with pitched roofs and classic proportions.[48] By contrast, the liquor factory/distillery in Mecidiyeköy, Istanbul (1931), by Robert

Coke-processing plant, Zonguldak, northern Turkey.

Sümerbank textiles factory, Kayseri, 1934–6.

Ivan Nikolaev, perspective drawing (top right) of an electricity power plant envisaged for the Sümerbank textiles factory at Kayseri, 1934–6, and the same building today.

Mallet-Stevens, the prominent French Modernist architect of the Corbusian school, and the brewery at Atatürk Model Farm, Ankara (1933–4) by Ernst Egli, both built for the Turkish state monopoly (Tekel), displayed the aesthetic canons of the Modern Movement with flat roofs, reinforced concrete frame construction and volumetric composition of the blocks.

Industrial imagery was central to the visual culture of the 1930s. Photographs of factories, bridges, railways, dams, power plants and grain silos featured prominently in official early republican publications. By celebrating industrial forms as aesthetic objects, these canonic photographs undoubtedly contributed to the emerging discourse of the 'New Architecture' (*Yeni Mimari*) in Turkey. In professional architectural journals, following the modernist polemic of Le Corbusier, airplanes, ocean liners and grain silos were portrayed as the real sources of the new architecture of the twentieth century.[49] There is, however, an important reason to distinguish between the early republican infatuation with the technological and industrial icons of modernism and the modernist avant-garde as it historically emerged in Europe. Modern technology and industry, which had been inspirational to Cubism, Futurism, Constructivism and other avant-garde currents in Europe, were idealized in early republican Turkey less as aesthetic and poetic inspiration, or as the sources of individual artistic experimentation, than as the goals, means and instruments

Sugar factories, at
Uşak, 1926, and at
Turhal, 1934.

Ernst Egli, Brewery at
Atatürk Model Farm,
Ankara, 1933–4,
photo by Markus
Hilbich.

Robert Mallet-
Stevens, Mecidiyeköy
Liquor Factory /
Distillery, gatehouse,
Istanbul, 1931.

of a larger national programme.[50] The original idea of the avant-garde as
a radical, even subversive challenge to official ideologies and established
artistic norms was anathema to the republican belief in art and architecture as subservient to a benevolent and modernizing state. Coupled with
the fact that, by the early 1930s, the avant-garde had already been eclipsed
in Europe by what scholars have labelled 'fascist', 'reactionary' and
'productivist' modernisms (in Italy, Germany and the Soviet Union,
respectively), it was not surprising that both Turkish architects and their
German and Austrian colleagues rejected the individualism or abstract

Collage from the
Ankara Construit
series, in *La Turquie
Kemaliste* (1937)
showing industrial
imagery.

Gasworks complex,
Ankara, 1928,
demolished 2006.

formal experimentation of the avant-garde, in favour of full commitment to the agenda (and patronage) of the Turkish state. The following
chapter looks more closely at this official state architecture, through
which modernism became both an expression and an active agent of
republican nation-building between the two World Wars.

chapter two

Building for the Modern Nation State

Hansen said: 'All good architecture is national' – but then after a brief pause he added: 'All national architecture is bad' . . . Whether the architects are forced to create national architecture through modern expressions . . . as in Fascist Italy . . . [or] they are forced to use historical styles . . . Both results are a disaster.

Bruno Taut, *Mimari Bilgisi* (Istanbul, 1938), pp. 333, 334

The Kemalist Revolution in Turkey created a dilemma over memory. While the aspiration for modernization and Westernization prompted representing the Revolution with European signifiers, the republican project of nation-building also motivated the revival of 'cultural roots'. Paradoxically this revival was also predicated on condemnation of the overthrown Ottoman legacy, necessitating new ways of constructing 'cultural roots' and finding alternative sources of national expression. 'If nation states are widely conceded to be "new" and "historical"', writes Benedict Anderson in his now classic study of nationalism, 'the nations to which they give political expression always loom out of an immemorial past and, still more important, glide into a limitless future'.[1] In Turkey too, the desired new Turkish architecture that would represent the new nation state needed to evoke both a futuristic and an archaic dimension. It had to connect simultaneously to both Western and national sources and, above all, to mediate the potential conflict between these aspirations. It was a formidable task with no obvious stylistic answer. This chapter examines the range of proposed answers, particularly with state-sponsored institutional buildings. It examines how the Kemalist revolutionary programme was substantiated with what its proponents liked to call 'modern and national architecture' (*modern ve milli mimarlık*).

Sedad Eldem and Emin Onat, Faculty of Sciences and Letters of Istanbul University, Istanbul, 1942–3; photo by Cemal Emden.

In the context of such a nation state-sponsored modernism, two themes rise to the fore that will appear throughout this chapter. The first is the concept of modern monumentality. As the physical bearers of collective memory, the erected monuments of the new Turkish state were charged with the symbolism of both modernization and nationalization.

Modern monumentality, however, was an oxymoron according to many European and North American modernists. Despite notable exceptions, including Peter Behrens and Alois Riegl, before the 1940s the majority of modern architects and theorists considered modern monumentality a contradiction in terms.[2] The historical antagonism between modern architecture and monumentality was summarized in Lewis Mumford's well-known motto, 'if it is a monument it is not modern, if it is modern it is not a monument'.[3] Monumentality was perceived as contentious to modernism, either because it symbolized permanence and the past whereas modernism embodied novelty and transition, or because monumentality had been historically tied to Classicism and traditional icons of stability that the modernist architects desired to abolish. Yet the construction of capital cities for nation states founded in the twentieth century, such as Ankara, Chandigarh and Brasilia, overthrew modernism's perceived antagonism to monumentality.[4]

The second theme is the invitation of European, particularly Austrian and German, architects to build the institutional symbols of Turkey as a new country. As contradictory as this may seem in the context of strident nationalism, the early Republican Turkish state relied exclusively on foreign architects and planners to shape its own representative buildings. Many of the experienced architect-builders (*kalfa*) of the Ottoman Empire in the eighteenth and nineteenth centuries had been from the Armenian and Greek minorities and the fortunes of their successors had dramatically declined after the advent of Turkish nationalism at the turn of the twentieth century.[5] At the same time, with the notable exception of some older architects associated with the now-discredited Ottoman revivalism, the newly educated modernist Turkish architects must have been perceived as too young and inexperienced for the task, prompting the Republican elite to look beyond home-grown talent. In any event, the solicitation of European architects in the 1930s not only constituted a historical precursor to the trans-nationalization of practice that would become increasingly pertinent in world architecture with globalization (see chapter Nine), but also raised the issue of modernism's 'translation' in Turkey.

German-speaking Architects of the Regime

The relationship between Germany, Austria and Turkey had taken numerous turns throughout history. The Ottoman and Prussian empires drew closer during the eighteenth century as part of the former's modernization policies and the pursuit of military alliances favourable to both.[6] During the period of industrialization Germany, competing against

France and Britain, sought to find new resources and markets on Ottoman lands, and German banks and schools were established in the Ottoman Empire. The Ottoman Army increasingly relied on German military experts throughout the nineteenth century, and the two countries remained allies during the First World War. In particular the excavations conducted by German archaeologists in Turkey (most famously at Troy and Pergamon) fed into the prevailing nationalist discourses on cultural origins in both countries. The cultural presence of the French, British and Italians had been relatively stronger under the Ottoman Empire, but the newly established Turkish state, antagonistic to both its own Ottoman precedents and to these three countries against which the War of Independence was fought, chose to cultivate Germany as the primary resource for its modernization and Westernization. The German-speaking experts invited by the Kemalist state were instrumental in the formation of Turkey's modern institutions and infrastructure.[7] During the late 1920s, in addition to the German planner Hermann Jansen, who prepared the master plan for Ankara (see chapter One), Austrian architects including Robert Oerley, Clemens Holzmeister and Ernst Egli were brought in to design all the major state buildings (ministries, schools and hospitals in particular) symbolizing the achievements of the Revolution.[8]

The year 1933 opened up a new phase in German-Turkish relations. Following the National Socialist takeover in Germany, many Jewish and socialist architects and city planners fled to Turkey, including Bruno Taut, Martin Wagner, Ernst Reuter, Margarete Schütte-Lihotzky, Wilhelm Schütte, Franz Hillinger and Gustav Oelsner. The same year also saw the introduction of university reform that put an end to the Ottoman *medrese* system and brought in about 180 German-speaking experts for the foundation of Turkey's new University Departments to offer higher education in fields equivalent to the modern European disciplines.[9] Istanbul University came to be known as *Emigré Universität* due to the numbers of German professors taking posts in many disciplines, while the Architecture department at the Academy of Fine Arts was restructured by Ernst Egli (1930–35) and later by Bruno Taut (1936–38), who both dismantled the Beaux-Arts tradition and replaced the traditional emphasis on classical facades and historical references with a new-found appreciation of rational and functional design. Egli introduced a competitive qualification examination for entry, and a two-stage education with two years of technical and two years of studio training.[10] Taut shifted the emphasis to social issues, including affordable housing projects.[11] Clemens Holzmeister and Paul Bonatz became influential professors at the newly founded Istanbul Technical University from 1940 to 1947 and from 1946 to 1954, respectively.

Atatürk Boulevard, Ankara, looking south: Holzmeister's Government Centre is visible at the top right; in the foreground is the Güven Monument (1935) by sculptors Anton Hanak and Joseph Thorak.

The political and cultural relation between Turkey and National Socialist Germany was ambivalent. Within months of the Nazi takeover, the German school and the official German organizations in Turkey started carrying its emblem, organizing National Socialist festivals and broadcasting its mission. The German-language newspaper *Turkische Post* closely followed the change of power on the European mainland, working almost as a propaganda medium for Hitler.[12] Nevertheless, Germans and Austrians in Turkey occupied an array of intellectual and political positions. For the most part professors working at Turkish universities who had themselves fled from the regime fought against National Socialist propaganda in Turkey, while others were representatives and promoters of Nazism. Among the architects the Schüttes and Ernst Reuter participated directly in anti-fascist activities, while Hermann Jansen and Paul Bonatz maintained ties with the National Socialist state.[13]

Hermann Jansen's master plan for Ankara mentioned in the previous chapter set the framework within which other German-speaking architects operated, especially in the Government and Higher Education Quarters, for both of which Jansen had provided preliminary site plans, as well as the Sıhhiye district where hospitals and other health-related buildings were being constructed.

The Austrian architect Clemens Holzmeister single-handedly designed all the buildings in the Government Quarter (*Regierungsviertel*), specified in both Lörcher's and Jansen's master plans. Holzmeister had studied at the Technical University in Vienna and been a professor at the Academy of Fine Arts in both Düsseldorf (until 1933) and Vienna (until 1938). He

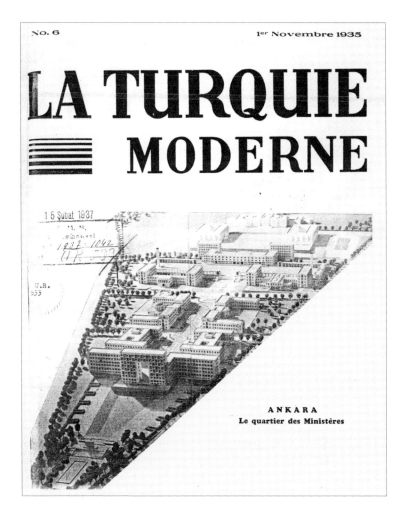

Clemens Holzmeister, Government Quarter, Ankara, 1929–35, model.

LA TURQUIE
≡ MODERNE

1 5 Şubat 1937

U.R.
533

ANKARA
Le quartier des Ministères

had already established a successful practice in his home country.[14] Approached by the Turkish Ambassador regarding the Ministry of Defence buildings in 1927, Holzmeister began working in Ankara for both the military and the government. In the course of his work for the new Government Quarter between 1929 and 1935, he retained the triangular site plan indicated in Jansen's drawings. He proposed eight U-shaped and H-shaped buildings placed symmetrically on two sides of the monumental axis, crowned by the Grand National Assembly that he would design in 1937–8 following an architectural competition. The unrealized Ministry of Customs and Monopolies building, conceived as the gateway to the complex, was probably over-ambitious for the

Clemens Holzmeister,
Drawing of the 'gate
building' (Ministry of
Customs and
Monopolies) for the
Government Quarter,
Ankara, 1934.

resources of the state, but it testifies to the vigorous desire for technolog-ical progress and a modern yet monumental symbolism. The Ministry buildings in the Government Quarter and Holzmeister's other institu-tional buildings, such as the Military Officers' Club (Ordu Evi, 1930–31), were harmonized with each other through the use of flat roofs, the avoid-ance of arches, domes and ornaments, and, most uniquely, the repetition of projected masses that formed different compositions with cubes. A new term, 'Viennese cubic architecture', was promptly coined by contempo-rary architects and critics to designate this style.

Although qualified as the 'First International Style' by some Turkish architectural historians, Holzmeister's buildings in Ankara hardly embod-ied an avant-garde Futurism, nor any antagonism or activism – values that historians of the European avant-garde deemed necessary. Despite their flat roofs and unornamented facades, these buildings employed quite conventional architectural tools for representing order, stability and authority, such as symmetry, massive blocks, elevated and centrally located entrances, colonnades and hierarchy of spaces. Their facades were punctured by vertical windows with traditional proportions rather than transparent surfaces; they featured conventional closed rooms with massive interior walls, rather than an open or free plan concept. This con-servative aesthetic has led some architectural historians to argue against the perceived modernism of Ankara's early Republican architecture and to claim that, while setting the stage for the progressive reforms of Kemalism, these buildings were not modernist or progressive themselves.[15] Nonetheless, contemporary accounts by architects and critics perceived these buildings as marking the 'beginning of a new era', especially when compared to the Ottoman revivalism of Mongeri, Vedat and Kemalettin.[16] They were modernist in another sense, bringing together representations of technological progress and novelty with monumental expressions of state power and authority. As such, these 'Viennese cubic' buildings testify to the non-monolithic nature of modern architecture, contrary to its portrayal by its own ideologues as a unified style. Their representation in propaganda media, newspapers, journals, posters and postcards has had the biggest impact on establishing them in the collective memory as carriers of Turkish modernism and the promise of the new.

In addition to the ministry buildings designed by Holzmeister, institutions for health and hygiene ranked high in the state's priorities. As part of the health reform, an immediate fight against tuberculosis, syphilis, malaria and other contagious diseases was initiated across the country: marshlands were reclaimed and people were vaccinated. Lörcher and Jansen had both emphasized the ideal of hygiene in their master plans, defining the modern city as a hygienic city.[17] The Ministry of Health building and the new hospitals in the Sıhhiye District (a word derived from 'health') just below the Ankara Citadel were designed by the Austrian architects Robert Oerley and Theodor Jost from as early as 1926.[18]

A collage of Clemens Holzmeister's buildings as published in *La Turquie Kemaliste* (1935).

Clemens Holzmeister,
Ministry of Defence
Building, Ankara,
1928–31.

The relation between hygiene, disciplined bodies and modernism has been emphasized by several thinkers; so has the maximization of human bodily performance as one of the main goals of modern organizational systems, not only Taylorism, but also scientific discourses (eugenics), as well as literal and visual representations of modernity.[19] In the modern world, human bodies were to be as healthy, clean, efficient and reliable as machines. Like other authoritarian states in the interwar period, Kemalism utilized sports spectacles on such occasions as the Youth and Sports Day to emphasize the importance of healthy, sportive and disci-

Theodor Jost,
Bacteriology Institute
(Hıfzıssıhha
Enstitüsü), Ankara,
1927–9.

plined bodies, and especially unveiled female bodies, for the making of
the modern nation.

In this context, one of the earliest buildings in Ankara's Sıhhiye
District, Theodor Jost's Bacteriology Institute (Hıfzıssıhha Enstitüsü,
1927–9) became an important landmark carrying multiple signifiers of
architectural modernism.[20] The flat-roofed building unmistakably promoted horizontality with its fenestration and the continuous sun-shading
lintel on its facade. Placed above its entrance was the nude sculpture of
Hygiene by the Austrian sculptor Wilhelm Frass, who depicted the Greek
goddess Hygieia, the daughter of Asclepius, the god of healing, and
granddaughter of Apollo. The relief of a nude woman on one of the new
regime's earliest public buildings in a country where no figurative public
sculpture previously existed, was definitely a revolutionary gesture, hinting at the changes to come not only in the sphere of health but also in
the making of the new Turkish woman.[21]

The major financial institutions of the Ankara government were
concentrated to the north of the Sıhhiye Health Zone (and past the
Higher Education Quarter, about which more will follow). After the
demise of Ottoman revivalism (represented by Giulio Mongeri's bank
buildings of the 1920s), New Architecture made its impressive appearance in this area, especially with Holzmeister's Real Estate Bank (Emlak
Bankası, 1931–3) and Central Bank (Merkez Bankası, 1933–4), and the
Turkish architect Seyfi Arkan's Municipalities Bank (İller Bankası, 1937).
Especially visible was the national headquarters of Sümerbank (1934–5,
the state's primary financial institution with a mandate to jump-start

Martin Elsaesser,
competition drawing
for Sümerbank,
Ankara, 1934–5.

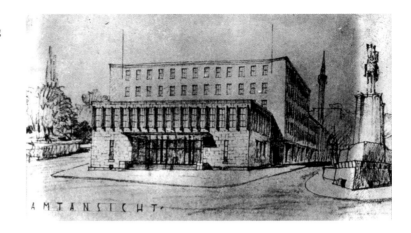

A construction photo
of Sümerbank,
Ankara, in September
1937.

national industrialization (see chapter One). This was designed by Martin Elsaesser, another German architect and one of the two directors of Das Neue Frankfurt. An international competition was held in 1934, and entries were received from Turkish and European architects, including such prominent names as Albert Laprade from France and Fritz August Breuhaus from Germany. Although first prize was awarded to the Turkish architect Seyfi Arkan, the commission eventually went to Elsaesser. Presenting an explicit contrast to the scale and fabric of the old city just below the Citadel, as well as to the adjacent Ottoman revivalist buildings of the 1920s, Elsaesser's building became one of the earliest examples of Turkish monumental modernism that shaped the new urban image of the old Ulus Square (Nation Square), in the midst of which the colossal new building arose in 1937. Apart from its symbolic significance, the building was also a technological milestone in Turkish construction industry, owing to its structurally challenging reinforced concrete mushroom columns, circular skylights and large spans designed by the German structural engineer Kurt Bernhard.

Higher Education Buildings

Whereas Ankara's Government Quarter is identified solely with Holzmeister's architecture, its Higher Education Quarter, the proud showcase of Kemalism's heavy investment in education, bears the stamp of the two most prolific German-speaking architects and educators of early republican Turkey: Ernst Egli and Bruno Taut. Egli had been Holzmeister's assistant at the Viennese Academy of Fine Arts and received his architectural diploma from the Viennese Technical University in 1918 and a doctorate in 1925.[22] He had an architectural office in Vienna from 1919 until 1927, when he moved to Turkey and started working at the Architecture Office of the Ministry of Education in Ankara. Three years later, he was also appointed head of the Architecture department at the Academy of Fine Arts in Istanbul. Between 1927 and 1940 Egli designed more than thirty buildings and worked on many more projects, as well as ten master plans, while also working closely with his students in Istanbul, many of whom received practical training in his office.[23] Egli handed over his posts to Taut in 1936 and left Turkey for Switzerland in 1940, where he worked as a professor in the Eidgenössische Technische Hochschule (ETH) in Zürich, taught courses on Turkish architecture and the history and theory of urban design, and continued to publish in both fields.[24]

His first designs in Ankara were for the State Music Conservatory (1927–8) and High School of Commerce (1928–9), but it was the İsmet İnönü Girls' Institute in Ankara (1930–31) that made an undeniable mark on modern architecture in Turkey. Girls' Institutes were introduced from 1928 at the suggestion of professionals such as the American progressive educator John Dewey, who was invited to Turkey for consultation. By 1940 there were 35 Girls' Institutes in major cities around the country and numerous centres for evening classes in small towns and villages, with some 16,500 women students enrolled.[25] The educational programme of these Institutes sought to transform traditional Ottoman housewives into thoroughly Westernized modern Turkish women. Egli's

Ernst Egli,
İsmet İnönü Girls'
Institute, Ankara,
1930–31.

building immediately had symbolic significance and photographs appeared in professional publications, propaganda journals and postcards, setting the stage for the making of the new Turkish woman.

Although Egli's and Holzmeister's buildings were often mentioned together by their contemporaries, many historians have noticed formal differences between the two architects, finding Egli closer to the aesthetic ideals of high Modernism. As Bernd Nicolai notes, this was commensurable with the fact that Holzmeister's governmental buildings were designed to communicate the power of the state and nationhood, whereas Egli's educational buildings sought to represent the emancipation of citizens, especially of women, through the spread of literacy and higher education.[26] Nicolai also highlights Egli's study trip to Central Europe with Turkish officials in 1929–30, where he must have been inspired by Erich Mendelsohn.[27] Whether a conscious choice of the regime or the result of the two architects' different aesthetic choices, Egli's buildings, especially the Girls' Institute, were notable for their use of continuous window sills, carved-in terraces and rounded corner balconies, which all accentuated horizontality, in addition to unambiguously flat roofs and unornamented facades. Along the same lines, Margarete Schütte-Lihotzky, the architect of the prefabricated Frankfurt Kitchen, arrived as an émigré in 1938 and designed an extension to another of Egli's projects, the Ankara Girls' Lycée. The unbuilt project featured a passageway connecting the new building to the existing one, and a classroom block placed at a lower level to take advantage of the site's slope. What stood out in Schütte-Lihotzky's design was how the cylindrical building served as a hinge joining the classroom block and the passageway to the existing building. Equally important were the outdoor spaces, especially the public walkways and the garden that occupied part of the roof of the classroom block. The coloured perspective drawings indicate that she particularly emphasized the outdoor spaces of the building, where women could be visible in the public space, rather than being confined inside.

As a consultant to the Turkish Ministry of Education, Egli designed numerous university buildings in both Ankara and Istanbul. By the time university reform was put in place in 1933, he had already designed three additional buildings for the campus of the Higher Agricultural Institute (1930–33). Soon after, Egli oversaw the School of Political Sciences (Mülkiye) in Ankara (1935–6), the Botanic Institute and buildings for the newly founded Cerrahpaşa Hospital in Istanbul (1933–5). With the exception of the Zoological School within the Agricultural Institute,

Margarete Schütte-Lihotzky, Extension to Girls' Lycée, Ankara, 1938.

Ernst Egli, Higher
Agricultural Institute,
Ankara, 1930–33.

many of these university buildings were quite eclectic, bringing together horizontal lines and unadorned modernist aesthetic with monumental colonnades, columns carrying slabs for balconies and classically proportioned L-, T- or H-shaped buildings that were frequently featured in contemporary photographs with their double-height spaces. One of his last but most characteristic buildings, the Civil Aviation School (1936), featured in the 'Ankara Construit' series in *La Turquie Kemaliste,* was particularly paradigmatic in earning him the reputation (and the praise) of being 'the architect who introduced New Architecture to Turkey'.[28] The canonic photograph (opposite) of the building, showing it freshly completed with construction rubble still on the ground, testifies to the impatient propaganda drive to publicize the newness and constructional zeal of the young republic.

Although Egli became the quintessential name associated with 'cubic' or 'New' architecture, his writings and the ambiguity of his buildings contradict such a designation. In some of his own publications and education practices, Egli explicitly promoted regionalist tendencies, defending a synthesis between universal principles and regional particularities. In his important essay *'Mimari Muhit'* ('Region and Architecture', 1930), Egli made a distinction between those who are attached to their regions and 'metropolitan people', who are shaped by international values.

The latter's intellect, Egli claimed, 'is not under the influence of the region. This intellect creates civilization. But at the same time it destroys itself'. This is seen in the 'so-called modern' houses in Ankara that 'copy European villas' but 'have nothing to do with modern architecture' or 'their region.'[29] 'The old Anatolian house (*eski Anadolu evi*) could guide a new movement of modern architecture in Turkey', Egli concluded: '[a] house like this, but one designed with modern means for a modern life, can be a model for contemporary and modern houses in Anatolian cities.'[30] Accordingly Egli initiated the National Architecture Seminar with Sedad Eldem, a multi-year research project to document examples of anonymous 'old Turkish houses' around the country (see chapter Three).

Bruno Taut replaced Egli at both the Ministry of Education and the Academy of Fine Arts. The leading architect of German Expressionism during the 1910s and of Berlin's social housing programme between 1924 and 1933, Taut fled from Germany as early as 1933 and arrived in Turkey in 1936 after spending three years in Japan. Taut built schools in Ankara, İzmir and Trabzon, and designed more than twenty buildings, including the Technical Universities of Ankara and Istanbul, although most remained unbuilt following his untimely death.[31] Among his realized university buildings, the significance of the Faculty of Language, History and Geography in Ankara (1937), adjacent to Egli's Girls' Institute, was soon recognized. In this building Taut's emphasis on tactile sensitivity and constructive ornament is manifest. Unlike the 'cubic buildings' of the period with surfaces devoid of texture or ornament, Taut used

Ernst Egli, Civil Aviation School, Ankara, 1936.

stones and tiles with different colours, textures and tactile qualities. On the exterior he treated the front facade as a hard skin of stones and bricks woven with the use of the *Almaşık* system – a traditional way of stone binding associated especially with Seljuk and early Ottoman communal buildings. The sensitive transformation from the stone of the front facade to the stucco of the side facade, refined joint details between the stones and the window frames, specially designed gutters and lamps, curved surfaces and expressive handrail details stand as notable features of the building. Just as in many of his high schools, Taut used a specific window detail with sun-shading beams placed at mid-height. Avowedly inspired by 'old Turkish houses,' this detail made it possible to both protect the interior from excessive sun at eye-level and let light into the building from above.[32] Inside the building, the main hall was designed as a collection of spaces within spaces with framed perspectives. These frames were further expressed by differentiating the smooth ceilings from the textured wall surfaces. Taut could elaborate the space in this way because he freed the plan from conventional classical conceptions and made use of the structural potentials of the new material, reinforced concrete. Unlike the formalism of Holzmeister and Egli, Taut's plans were more dynamic, as manifested most clearly in the Atatürk High School in Ankara (1937–8), which responded to the complex conditions of the site and the programme, rather than prioritizing a pure geometric form over functionalist concerns.

Judging from the references to traditional construction techniques, some of his colleagues and later commentators have claimed Taut an advocate of nationalism in architecture; Taut's own intentions, however, as formulated in books and essays written both in Japan and Turkey – most notably his last book, *Mimari Bilgisi* (Lectures on Architecture), published in Turkish – might be better identified as a cosmopolitan call

Bruno Taut, Faculty of Language, History and Geography, Ankara, 1937, a postcard from the 1940s.

Bruno Taut, Atatürk High School, Ankara, 1937–8, plan.

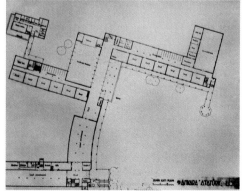

Interior details of the Faculty of Language, History and Geography, Ankara; photo by Esra Akcan.

to architects.[33] Most of his gestures were in the name of 'fighting against' the architectural approach 'labelled as *cubic*' in Turkey, as he explicitly stated in his letters.[34] Based on his experiences in Japan and Turkey, Taut observed with insight that modernism's basic dilemma outside Europe was the contrast between the 'slavish imitation of foreign styles' and 'uninspired' nativism.[35] His writing and buildings were meant as critical strategies to resist these two unproductive tendencies, without either closing a country to foreign sources or uncritically accepting them. Taut criticized those who rejected foreign influences in rejuvenating domestic norms. Yet he advocated a foreign influence that would be, he said, 'no false Internationalism, no uniformalization of the world (*Weltuniform-ierung*), no dullification (*Langweiligmachen*) of the whole earth', but a hybridization that would 'make both sides richer.'[36] This cosmopolitan ideal found its architectural manifesto in Taut's own house in Istanbul (1938), commonly known as the 'Japanese house', but combining sources from Germany, Japan and Turkey on both overt and hidden levels.[37] In a country wide open to influences from its west, but equally closed to those from its east, accentuating the visible influence of a 'Japanese house' in Istanbul was definitely a critical gesture.

Turkish Architects and State Commissions

The complex impact of foreign architects on the new Turkish Republic needs to be conceptualized as multiple forms of 'translation', acknowledging both their varied attempts to respond to the local conditions and the cross-cultural encounters that took place with their Turkish colleagues, students and clients.[38] On their part, the new generation of Turkish architects whose education overlapped with the curricular switch at the Academy of Fine Arts from the classical Beaux-Arts model to the New Architecture under Egli and Taut were particularly active in constructing a new professional identity committed to the search for a new 'national-modern' Turkish architecture. Many of them had received part of their professional education in Germany and France. For example, after graduating from the Academy of Fine Arts, Sedad Eldem and Burhan Arif Ongun received state fellowships in 1928 to continue their education in Europe. While Eldem pursued a three-year study tour in Europe, particularly in Paris and Berlin, that significantly influenced his development, Ongun worked in Le Corbusier's office in Paris.[39] Seyfi Arkan studied architecture in Berlin and worked in Hans Poelzig's office (1930–33), Arif Hikmet Holtay studied in Stuttgart and Berlin (1926–30), Emin Onat in Zürich (c. 1933–4),[40] Emin Necip Uzman worked in the office of the Berlin-based architect Fritz August Breuhaus (1937–9), and Rüknettin Güney studied architecture in Paris and worked in Auguste Perret's office after graduating in 1932.[41]

After establishing the professional organization Güzel Sanatlar Birliği (Fine Arts Association) in Istanbul in 1928 and launching their professional journal *Mimar* in 1931, the struggle of modern Turkish architects for professional legitimacy intensified. They were faced with the profound paradox of both respecting their prominent foreign teachers and colleagues who introduced New Architecture to the country, and at the same time feeling blocked by them from access to important state commissions. The tendency of Turkish political leaders to prefer foreign architects and planners was a primary grievance voiced in the pages of *Mimar*. Most of the time they evoked the rationalist/functionalist doctrines and the scientific/technocratic claims of the Modern Movement at large as the basis of their eligibility for public commissions. At other times they fell back on an overtly nationalist discourse to claim that, as Turks, they were better equipped to give expression to the Turkish Revolution than foreigners. The early republican dictum 'Western in technique, national in spirit' became an appealing formula for architects as well:

We need to learn from the techniques of European experts. However, the spirit and outlook of the Turk is higher than what they can attain. We must turn to the young generation of Turkish architects who, bearing the blood and the talent of the Great Sinan, are now walking along a contemporary and logical path. The leaders who wrote nationalism and populism into the principles of the republic must commission the architects of the revolution from which a modern and national architecture will be born.[42]

One of the first major international competitions that resulted in a Turkish architect receiving the commission was the Ankara Exhibition Hall (1933–4). The competition brief explicitly called for a building 'in the style of modern architecture' and two projects from the 26 entries were selected as finalists, designed respectively by the Italian architect Paolo Vietti Violi (who also designed the stadium in Ankara) and the Turkish architect Şevki Balmumcu. When the estimated cost of the former proved to be too high, Balmumcu's project was constructed.[43] The building became the pride of the entire Turkish professional community, since it stood as proof that a Turkish architect was as capable of designing and seeing through the construction of a large institutional building as his European counterparts.[44] With its dynamic horizontal mass rounded at both ends and balanced with a vertical tower, its horizontal ribbon windows, white unornamented facades and tube-like continuous interior space, the building quickly acquired canonic status. Embodying the idea of exhibition in multiple senses, not only did it offer the public a visible

Şevki Balmumcu,
Exhibition Hall,
Ankara, 1933–4.

Othmar Pflerschy, first photography exhibit in Balmumcu's Exhibition Hall, 1936.

manifestation of Ankara's new 'cubic architecture', but also functioned as the space where the accomplishments of the Kemalist Revolution were displayed.[45] Many important exhibitions took place here, including those devoted to painting, hygiene, Soviet art, arts and crafts, as well as the first photography exhibit of 1936, suitably introduced by Othmar Pflerschy who was the main photographer of *La Turquie Kemaliste*.[46] This was followed in 1937 by the Industrial Exposition that filled the longitudinal space with machinery, mining and metallurgical displays from major state industries.

The Ankara Exhibition Hall stands out as the only major public building designed by a Turkish architect before 1937. In the absence of large public commissions from the state, which relied almost exclusively on foreigners, modernist Turkish architects were largely limited to designing individual houses and apartment buildings (see chapter Three). There were indeed a handful of exceptions, but none with the political and aesthetic significance of the Exhibition Hall. Istanbul University Observatory (1934–6) by Arif Hikmet Holtay was a relatively small, albeit a remarkably modern building, and the State Monopolies Offices in Antalya and Konya (1934–5), designed by Tahir Tuğ, were provincial variations on the 'Viennese cubic' style of Holzmeister. It was only around 1937 that Turkish architects were able to break through this predicament, especially with the completion of the Municipalities Bank in Ankara

Arif Hikmet Holtay,
Istanbul University
Observatory,
Istanbul, 1934–6.

Seyfi Arkan,
Municipalities Bank,
Ankara, 1935–6.

(1935–6) by Seyfi Arkan, the railway station at Ankara (1935–7) by Şekip Akalın and the State Monopolies General Directorate building in Ankara (1937–8) by Sedad Eldem. By that time, however, the aesthetic preferences of the state were already shifting in the direction of a more monumental and classicized modern architecture reflecting the rampant nationalist politics of the time, one that would also bring about the tragic conversion of Balmumcu's Exhibition Hall into a nationalist state monument.

Classicized Modern-National Architecture

With the death of Atatürk in 1938, and under the shadow of approaching war in Europe, the nationalist component of Kemalism hardened into a statist ideology that allowed no liberalization or democratization until after the Second World War. Architectural culture became particularly nationalistic in this period and the representation of state power took precedence over all other architectural matters. Monumental public buildings of overpowering scale, stone-clad facades and an official, stripped-down classicism dominated the building scene. In spite of Turkey's success in remaining neutral and uninvolved in the Second World War (at least until its very end when joining the winning side made strategic sense), its arts, architecture and cultural politics increasingly resembled those of Nazi Germany and Fascist Italy, both of which were admired as paradigms of strong nation states.[47] Along these lines, Aptullah Ziya praised the Fifth Architectural Exhibition for Mussolini, as well as the entire fascist programme in Italy:

> The greatest virtue of modern art is its national character . . .
> Fascist Italian art is growing with giant steps in the hands of
> young Italian artists who are supported by their state. Italians
> have created a Fascist Architecture. The Turkish nation has
> achieved a much greater revolution than what the Fascists of
> Rome call their change in regime. But our Revolution lacks
> an important feature. It has not been monumentalized.[48]

Some compared the commissioning of German-speaking architects in republican Ankara to the employment of Armenian and Greek minority architects by the Ottoman Court in the nineteenth century.[49] Sedat Çetintaş, Bedri Uçar and others employed chauvinist and exclusive overtones in their writings. According to Çetintaş, Turkish architecture, which allegedly influenced the 'wonders' of the world from China to Anatolia, went into eclipse during the last centuries of the Ottoman Empire because of 'Western influences, Armenian masons and sly women of the Ottoman palace'; copying Western forms in the twentieth century hence meant 'forgetting one's horse and going into the race with someone else's mangy donkey.'[50] The pages of the three professional journals *Arkitekt* (*Mimar* until 1935), *Yapı* (1942–3) and *Mimarlık* (1944–53) abound with such sentiments, which became increasingly paradigmatic in the 1940s, while the demands for state support to Turkish architects rather than foreigners became more vocal.[51] Several architects made repeated pleas to the state to organize open competitions for major public

Şekip Akalın, Ankara Railway Station, Ankara, 1935–7, front facade.

Bedri Uçar, State Railways general Directorate/Ministry of Transportation, Ankara, 1938–41.

buildings and others referred to Fascist Germany and Italy to justify their idea that a national and unified architecture could only be achieved by the support of strong states.

One of the first manifestations of this shift can be seen in the Ankara Railway Station (1935–7), a building of great symbolic significance as the primary point of entry to the capital. Designed by Şekip Akalın, an architect within the Ministry of Public Works, it displays an imposing symmetrical facade with a tall colonnaded entry flanked by round projections on either side. Its spacious main passenger hall, meticulously

71   Building for the Modern Nation State

The rear facade of
Ankara Railway
Station, facing the
tracks.

detailed in marble, brass and wood, is lit by a diffused light filtering through the roof trusses and a large glazed facade gives access to the platforms at the back. A few years later the State Railways General Directorate/Ministry of Transportation building (1938–41) was completed on a site adjacent to the station. Designed by Bedri Uçar, another architect within the Ministry of Public Works, a four-storey colonnaded entrance gives access to the stone-clad building topped with the winged emblem of the State Railways. It was, not surprisingly, 'the most beautiful building in Ankara', according to the German architect Paul Bonatz, whose stamp on this later phase of early republican classicized modernism will be discussed below.[52]

The 1937 international competition for the Turkish Grand National Assembly epitomizes the mood and aesthetics of this classicized modernism. Out of fourteen entries, those by Clemenz Holzmeister, Albert Laprade and the Hungarian architect Alois Mezara were awarded the first prize by an international jury. These projects all had monumental, classicized facades with tall colonnades and wall reliefs, overlooking vast

Albert Laprade, competition project for Grand National Assembly, Ankara, 1937.

plazas with statues and flag posts. Holzmeister's project was the one eventually built, its completion extending well into the 1950s. The ultimate nationalist state monument of the republic, however, is Atatürk's Mausoleum, the Anıt-Kabir, literally the 'monument-tomb'. Located at the summit of Ankara's Rasattepe Hill, it remains one of the holiest sites of modern Turkey. As many scholars have pointed out, the Anıt-Kabir gives profound spatial expression to the conceptualization of nation as secular religion: it is the nationalist substitute for a space of religious ritual, prayer and spirituality.[53]

The near deification of Atatürk had already started in his lifetime with the ubiquitous presence of his statues, busts and portraits. After his death, an international competition for his mausoleum was held in 1942, seeking a design that would commemorate Atatürk 'as soldier, president, statesman, scientist, intellectual and great creative genius' and would evoke feelings of 'respect, dignity and immortality'.[54] The entries for the competition collectively demonstrate a fascinating mix of historical precedents and nationalist references – from pure solids in the spirit of

Clemenz Holzmeister,
Grand National
Assembly, Ankara,
postcard from 1961.

Boullée and Ledoux, such as a monumental pyramid by Giovanni Muzio, to a Roman pantheon by Arnoldo Foscini with frescoes and gold mosaics. Among the projects by Turkish architects there were references to Seljuk tombs (Kemali Söylemezoğlu, Kemal Ahmet Aru and Recai Akçay), to Turkic-Islamic tombs with cylindrical forms (Sedad Eldem) and to Egyptian temples with Hittite symbols (Necmi Ateş). The winning scheme by the Turkish architects Emin Onat and Orhan Arda is an abstract, monumentalized version of the classical temple form, incorporating prehistoric Anatolian references in its decorative programme. As the architects stated in their explanatory text, it was a built manifesto of nationalist Turkish history theses, extending the history of the Turks back to pre-Islamic Anatolia (to the Hittites in particular) and connecting it to the classical roots of Western civilization.[55] Whereas motifs like the paired Hittite lions lining the sides of the 'processional alley' or the prehistoric style of the wall reliefs on either side of the monumental stairs leading to the mausoleum (depicting the saga of the War of Independence) unmistakably evoke an 'archaic' dimension, the monumental colonnaded portico of the mausoleum has conspicuous affinities with Albert Speer's architecture in Germany.

Poster for the New
German Architecture
Exhibition, Ankara,
1943.

Emin Onat and Orhan
Arda, Atatürk's
Mausoleum (Anıt
Kabir), Ankara, 1942.

In 1943 Paul Bonatz, the leading jury member in Atatürk's Mausoleum competition, brought the National Socialist propaganda exhibition 'New German Architecture' (*Neue Deutsche Baukunst*) to Turkey. Bonatz was one of the foremost architects in Stuttgart, especially known for its main railway station and as an influential professor at the Stuttgart Technical University.[56] After joining the conservative architects Paul Schultze-Naumburg and Paul Schmitthenner in Der Block, as well as the campaign against the Weissenhofsiedlung,[57] he had built autobahns, petrol stations and bridges for the Third Reich.[58] Albert Speer's 'Introduction' for the New German Architecture exhibition catalogue, published both in German and Turkish, started with Hitler's statement 'No Nation lives longer than the documents of its Culture'. The exhibition displayed the absolute monumentality and the Greco-Roman classical references in the buildings of the National Socialist programme.[59] Bonatz's introductory speech for the opening ceremony in Ankara, as well as his talk at the Academy of Fine Arts in Istanbul, maintained similar arguments. After glorifying Greco-Roman Classicism, Bonatz complained about the loss and oblivion of this glorious tradition due to 'industrialization', 'liberalism' and 'individualism'. Accusing modern architecture, Expressionism and Romanticism, in particular, of 'murdering' classical architecture and of creating 'ugly buildings of technique' and fashionable individual styles for the sake of originality, he repeated the plea for the revival of cultural roots and the search for nationalist architecture.[60]

Bonatz also drew parallels between Hitler's Germany and Atatürk's Turkey, both moving towards a powerful architecture under the guidance of strong statesmen.[61] Turkish circles seemed quite receptive to Bonatz's and Speer's statements. No author criticized the ideology of the National Socialist exhibition in professional journals (though some criticized it on a stylistic basis),[62] and critics including Behçet Ünsal marked it as the sharp turn to another era in world architecture.[63] As paradoxical as Bonatz's rhetoric of rootedness was in Turkey, and as inappropriate as Greco-Roman classical vocabulary was as a convincing symbol of Turkish nationalism, both Turkish and foreign architects increasingly incorporated monumental colonnades, stone cladding and historical motifs during the 1940s.[64] For Bonatz, Classicism was not a 'period style' but a timeless archaic principle that had to be integrated with techno-scientific modernization. 'For us, classical means the will to attain the final and the absolute. In other words, it means a distance from the fashions of the day and the whims of the individual.'[65] This idea of classicism as perfectly compatible with the search for modern and national architecture was particularly appealing for Turkish architects.

When one compares student projects at the Academy of Fine Arts in 1931 and in 1943–5, one cannot fail but notice the stark difference in the ruling architectural taste: the white undecorated surfaces, horizontal windows, flat-roofed masses of the 1930s gave way in the 1940s to monumental stone buildings, small vertical openings and colonnades.[66]

The same classic and monumental tendencies permeated the official buildings executed throughout the 1940s, many of which Bonatz dictated as the leading architectural authority.[67] In addition to the competition for Atatürk's Mausoleum that brought him to Turkey, he served as a jury member in the most important architectural competitions of the time, including those for the Radio Hall and Court House of Istanbul and the Çanakkale Monument in Gallipoli. He also collaborated with Sedad Eldem in the design of Ankara University and acted as a consultant with Emin Onat and Sedad Eldem regarding the Faculty of Sciences and Letters of Istanbul University (1942–3). The latter, at the heart of Istanbul's historic peninsula, is a blown-up version of Eldem's traditional 'Turkish House' paradigm (see chapter Three) with its modular windows and wide overhanging eaves perched on top of a monumental colonnaded lower level bearing conspicuous echoes of Bonatz's Stuttgart railway station. Other traditional elements are incorporated into this classicized modern building, such as Ottoman composite walling techniques and open loggias on upper levels supported by tall, slender columns – a motif

Sedad Eldem and Emin Onat, Faculty of Sciences and Letters of Istanbul University, Istanbul, 1942–3; photo by Cemal Emden.

Paul Bonatz, State
Opera, Ankara,
1946–8, converted
from the Exhibition
Hall by Balmumcu
illustrated on
page 67.

that can be traced to a wide range of sources from Iran and Central Asia to Ottoman imperial kiosks and pavilions.

Perhaps no other example illustrates the shift of state architecture to classicized modernism and nationalist historicism in this period as vividly as Bonatz's conversion of Balmumcu's Exhibition Hall in Ankara into the State Opera (1946–8), a task that he would later describe as 'being forced to get married to an ugly woman'.[68] In order to add 'cultural roots' to the building and make it more monumental, Bonatz irreversibly destroyed the modernist aesthetic and constructivist composition of the original building. He demolished the tower, added pitched roofs and ornament, converted the horizontal windows into small vertical openings, changed the colour and reclad parts of the facade with travertine, designed a new entrance and wrapped the front facade with a monumental colonnade of classical Ottoman column capitals. If Balmumcu's original project represented the republic's collective amnesia towards its own past, Bonatz's conversion introduced a new amnesia, this time towards the New Architecture of the 1930s, as if the memory of what was erased by the latter could be rewritten simply by destroying it – as if one could rewind the process of modernization. It is a monument to how modern Turkish architecture erased (and continues to erase) its own collective memory and the traces of its own recent history along the way.

Both foreign and Turkish architects who designed the state-sponsored institutional buildings of early republican Turkey constantly struggled, in their different ways, to reconcile the representations of modernization and a refurbished memory of the Turkish nation, to connect simultaneously

78

to both Western and national sources. Despite the varying degrees of futurist and archaic impulses, opposing political positions, and the obvious differences in style between the horizontal-lined buildings of the 1930s and the classicist and historicist references of the 1940s, the aspiration to find a synthesis in architecture that would be both modern and national persisted. After these public buildings, we will now turn our attention to the residential visions of the Kemalist elite and the private houses built during this time.

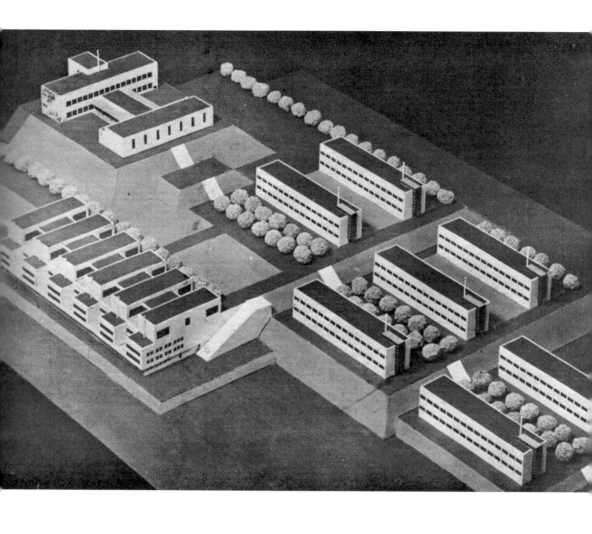

chapter three

The Modern House

House with a garden or apartment? All the well-known urbanists of the
world have agreed on the answer of this question: house with a garden
. . . An apartment is a symbol of rootlessness, temporariness, and a sort of
modern nomadism; a house with a garden on the other hand implies one's
attachment to life and a country, to cultivating roots and continuity.
Vedat Nedim Tör, *Karınca* (March 1936), p. 83

'One goal of modern city planning is the single family house', Hermann
Jansen stated explicitly in his report for the master plan of Ankara
(1929–39), while explaining his suggestions for the design of Turkey's
new residential areas.[1] Following pre-war garden city ideals, he advocated close relation to nature, correct orientation in relation to the sun
and planned neighbourhoods with ample light, air and green space as
the quintessential principles of modern hygienic living. Jansen repeated
the same land settlement decisions in six other master plans commissioned from him, believing that low-rise, low-density houses, and consequently sprawling urban development, were suitable for modern Turkey.
Apart from lower income families who could share small housing
blocks, the whole population in these cities would reside in private houses
with private gardens, and no new building would exceed three floors
in total.[2]

By inviting a German architect to determine the new residential types
for the Turkish population, the Kemalist state extended its modernization and westernization programme to the private lives of its citizens.
The main urban housing stock in Turkey up until then comprised either
anonymous, or vernacular, wooden houses or, in a few parts of Istanbul,
apartment blocks that emerged during the Ottoman modernization in
the nineteenth century. Seyfi Arkan, Adil Denktaş, Emin Necip Uzman
and others continued to build important examples of the latter type in
the 1930s, but Jansen himself referred to apartment buildings with the
pejorative German term *Mietskasernen* (rental barracks), and criticized
them as 'bad Western models' that needed to be replaced by correct
models of city planning.[3] There had already been a couple of collective

Seyfi Arkan, Türkiş
Workers' Housing,
Zonguldak, 1935,
model.

Typical residential
fabric at Ankara
Citadel, c. 1930.

housing projects in Istanbul (including in the area of Akaretler), and
Ankara's Sakarya neighbourhood had been built outside the Citadel walls
with wide streets on a grid plan. Nevertheless, it was by Jansen's master
plan that the Turkish state intended to interfere through institutionalized means in order to change the living habits of the population and
replace them with European models. Jansen followed the prewar garden
city ideals in determining the new land settlement patterns and residential types of Turkey, repeating similar principles in each city regardless
of their regional differences. Not surprisingly, this approach coincided
favourably with the nationalization programme of the Kemalist state,
which sought to regulate the living patterns of different ethnic, religious
or regional groups under one unifying ideal.

Jansen elaborated on four class-based residential areas and their
corresponding building types, which, he hoped, would thereafter regulate a new standard of living for the entire Turkish population.[4] The first
was the traditional anonymous, vernacular, wooden house, such as those
in the Ankara Citadel, commonly known as the 'old Turkish house'.

Even though Jansen treated the Citadel as the symbolic and geometric centre of the city, acknowledging its attraction in the skyline, he refrained from suggesting any rehabilitation plan for these houses. The Citadel had to be envisioned as if it were covered with a 'glass dome',[5] so that the new residential neighbourhoods could grow in visible contrast to the old. This official decision to leave the 'old Turkish houses' as picturesque ruins had serious consequences, establishing a sharp distinction between the old and the new. The Ankara Citadel remained as an isolated fringe, where the city's lower income residents continued to live, while the new inhabitants' life began in the new city, which was constructed with public parks, private gardens and wide streets. It would take an Istanbul-based architect, Sedad Eldem, to draw attention to these 'old Turkish houses' not as museum pieces, but as the sources of a desired national-modern Turkish architecture.

Dividing Ankara in relation to its economic classes, Jansen reserved the southern hills of the city for his second type, the villas of the new bureaucratic elite of the regime (for which he used the German word *Landhaus*), including Atatürk's presidential residence. As a third type, he envisioned that the upper middle income families would live in free-standing and row houses built collectively as cooperative housing with garden city principles. Finally, far away from the elite private residences, Jansen proposed a workers' residential quarter in the northwestern

Seyfi Arkan,
Apartment block in
Ayazpaşa, İstanbul,
1935, exterior view;
photo by Iskender.

section of the city, establishing single-storey row houses with affordable building materials suitable for the lower income citizens. Each of these residential types will be examined more closely below.

The Cubic House/Villa

Atatürk's presidential residence (1930–32), designed by the Austrian architect Clemens Holzmeister, rose on the southern hills of Ankara as a symbol of the new aesthetic vision, stripped of Orientalist connotations though retaining a sense of tradition meant to allude to a proud national heritage. It stood in strong contrast to the original vernacular house where Mustafa Kemal (Atatürk) resided in the first years of the Republic. The choice of Holzmeister, who had already been designing 'Viennese cubic' buildings for the Government Quarter (*Regierungsviertel*) and the Military Officers' Club, indicated that Kemalist stylistic preferences would also be extended to domestic spaces. In both the institutional buildings and the presidential residence, Holzmeister repeated similar window proportions, accentuated lintels around the windows and projected masses, making the president's house look like a displaced extension of the governmental complex, blurring the boundaries between the public and the private. As the public face of the president for both the international and national audience, this new house had to erase memories of war against Western countries on the one hand and symbols of Ottoman grandeur associated with the old regime's rulers on the other.[6] Seeking such a double-erasure, Holzmeister's design used modern monumentality in representing state authority with hidden layers of classicism. As an easily recognizable modernizing gesture on the exterior, the architect eliminated the pitched roof, which quickly differentiated the house from the surrounding ones. Moreover, he refrained from extensive decoration or historicist symbols, using stucco instead as the finishing material to attain smooth surfaces. Nonetheless the project's plan and arrangement of interior space followed more conventional norms, establishing sharp divisions between rooms, rather than using open plan or permeable boundaries. The symmetric U-shaped building encircled a closed courtyard, which was completed on both levels with an arcade and a covered gallery. The interior furniture, mechanical fixtures and finishing materials were imported from Vienna, giving the house a technologically advanced and aesthetically austere look.

Other examples of modernist design stood on the southern hills of Ankara, among which Seyfi Arkan's two houses for the Kemalist state deserve special mention. As a Turkish architect building for the state at a time when almost all the commissions for institutional buildings went to German and Austrian professionals, Arkan had an exceptional relationship with Atatürk. The foreign minister's residence (1933–4) comprised a private house and a reception area (with a ballroom), distributed over separate floors with separate entrances. The building's long cantilevered flat roof provided wide extending eaves for the balcony on the upper floor and the winter garden (instead of traditional semi-open spaces such as courtyards or *sofas*) introduced a gleaming new image to the city,

Clemens Holzmeister, Presidential Residence, Ankara, 1930–32, model and study room next to the library; photo by J. Scherb.

despite its unsuitability for Ankara's rough climate. Unlike Holzmeister, Arkan carried over modernist conceptions into the interior, using an open plan that was made possible by modern construction materials. The house for Atatürk's sister Makbule Atadan (1935–6), also designed by Arkan and known as the 'glass villa', was immediately charged with the task of representing 'how far Turkey has progressed in providing a setting for femininity'.[7] Arkan's design with large span horizontal windows, fully glazed surfaces and winter gardens (a glass pavilion was intended but remained unbuilt) followed the ideals of European architectural circles that advocated transparency as a distinguishing sign of modernist progress. The private and public realms of the house were not only separated but also gendered: the daily living and sleeping spaces of Makbule Atadan, as well as a 'women's common room', were reserved as private areas, while the large reception halls, a music room and winter garden were designated as public areas. The two were placed on the same level with translucent boundaries in between, underlining the separate existence of the feminine realm while veiling it from the space of public appearance, and thereby paradoxically maintaining a traditional patriarchic way of controlling women's place in society with modern materials.[8]

The emphasis on media appearance and public receptions in these domestic spaces was not coincidental. These houses for the Kemalist elite were also meant to disseminate new standards of taste to the nation and exemplify how to lead a modern life. Soon 'cubic houses', as they were commonly called, became recognizable signifiers of the new vision

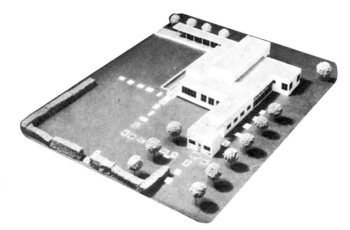

Seyfi Arkan,
Residence for
Makbule Atadan,
Ankara, 1935–6,
model and living room
with semi-transparent
walls separating the
women's realm; photo
by Veli Demir.

Ernst Egli, Ragıp
Devreş House,
Istanbul, 1934; photo
by Esra Akcan.

Seyfi Arkan, Atatürk's
House at Florya,
Istanbul, 1935; photo
by Esra Akcan.

Beş Odalı Fakat Çok Kullanışlı Bir Villâ ..

Villânın cephesinden görünüşü ile muktar ve muhtelif görünüşleri.

Bazı kimselerin köylük fakat çok göserişli evlere karşı meclûbiyetleri vardır; Bu hafta derzettiğimiz proje bu kimseleri memnun edecek şekildedir.

Bu villânın hususiyeti bol taraçalı ve son derece kullanışlı olmasındadır. İlk katta geniş bir salon, iki oda, bir mutfak ve bir helâ vardır. İkinci katta çok geniş bir taraşaya açılan iki yatak odası ve bir banyo salonu vardır.

Bu villâ büyük bir bahçe ortasında inşa edilecek olursa çok cazip bir manzara arzeder. Arsaiinin dür olması, bilhassa dış yanasında bulunması bu villânın dahilî tertibatı noktal nazarından elzemdir. Gözden kaşmıyacak bir noktada villânın damonan tamamen taraşa halinde olmasıdır. Yaz günlerinde bu dam hasır İskemleierle güzel bir salon halini alır,

Birinci ve ikinci katların tafsilâtlı plânları.

ve mizaflir kabul etmiye, ve danslı şay lar tertip etmiye çok müsaii olur.

Arzalsi hariç olmak üzere bu villânın mssliyeti beş bin lira raddesindedir.

'A five-room, functional villa' in the popular magazine *Yedigün* (September 1938).

of living. Ernst Egli's Fuat Bulca house (1935, demolished), another house built on Ankara's hills for a statesman, and the Ragip Devreş house (1934) in Istanbul were memorable examples of the type. The project for the Fuat Bulca house, for instance, employed an open plan, used porous internal boundaries between rooms and had a fully glazed winter garden, three new additions to Turkish domestic environments. Similarly Seyfi Arkan's Florya residence, built as a holiday house for Atatürk and, with its white-washed walls, flat roof and horizontal windows, spectacularly appearing to float in the middle of the sea, became another icon of modernism. This was somewhere the president would have close contact with the masses as he holidayed just metres away from the public beach, waving at them from the deck of his ship-like house. In press releases in which Atatürk was portrayed as the 'the most democratic president in the world, who cruises in a rowing boat among the masses',[9] the Florya residence provided the background for state-sponsored modernism.

In the first two chapters we discussed the architects and cultural critics who promoted 'cubic/new architecture' as the quintessential metonym for the Kemalist revolution. In addition to the professional discourse, cubic architecture became a widespread topic in popular magazines covering fashions in domestic living.[10] The series 'House and Furniture', 'Beautiful Houses' and 'The House of your Dreams', published in the magazine *Yedigün* from the mid-1930s and through the 1940s, promoted such houses as symbols of becoming modern and Western. In almost every issue the editors published examples of an ideal house, with promotional captions that emphasized the difference between cubic houses and the 'gloomy darkness and dim heavy air' of congested apartments in Istanbul.[11] Typically, these pages reproduced designs from foreign magazines and included photographs of recent buildings either abroad or in Ankara and Istanbul. Unlike in Weimar Germany, for example, where the language of *Neues Wohnen* usually represented a hope of achieving a social utopia, emancipation from excessive housework, and better living conditions for middle- and low-income individuals, the cubic house was used as an expression of the modernized and Westernized elites in

Turkey. *Yedigün* often promoted houses beyond the reach of many Turkish families, even though they were constructed as the ideal vision of living in modern times.

Cooperative Housing

The second residential type in Jansen's master plans was cooperative collective housing suitable for middle-income families. It was envisioned that most of Ankara would be built as an accumulation of these planned and single-handedly designed collective housing neighbourhoods. Jansen himself prepared the projects for the Bahçelievler, Emlak Bank and Agricultural School cooperative housing in order to illustrate the character of the city space that would emanate with this residential type. Detached or row single-family houses of one or two storeys stood on private building plots with large backyards and smaller front gardens, all placed parallel along a tranquil street with rows of trees leading to a busier highway to the city. These houses shared some common spaces, such as sports fields, parks, playgrounds, schools, shops and garages.[12] This was the residential image Jansen anticipated for the future of Ankara, and by extension for the rest of Turkey's growing cities. These low-rise low-density neighbourhoods on prewar garden city planning principles were promoted as revolutionary visions of living, yet Jansen was actually following the conservative values of his time. Already by 1924 architects in Europe, especially in Jansen's home city of Berlin, were disillusioned with many of the prewar garden city layouts, largely because of the model's inability to support an appropriate metropolitan density. They were thus working on much denser collective housing projects within the boundaries of the existing metropolis, designing multi-family horizontal building blocks or taller apartments. Housing settlements designed by architects who would later emigrate to Turkey, such as Bruno Taut and Martin Wagner in Berlin or architects in Ernst May's circle in Frankfurt, became the canonic examples of this new tendency. By contrast, Jansen's plans for Turkey failed to foresee the vast urbanization process awaiting a country with aspirations to rapid industrialization.

Nowhere are the results of this miscalculation clearer than in the story of the Bahçelievler housing scheme (1935–9), which was designed by Jansen himself, drastically transformed by members of the cooperative and architects they employed, and gradually completely destroyed by the forces of urbanization and the real-estate market.[13] Bahçelievler was built on the west side of Ankara as a model settlement for government officials to generate future housing. In the mid-1930s cooperative

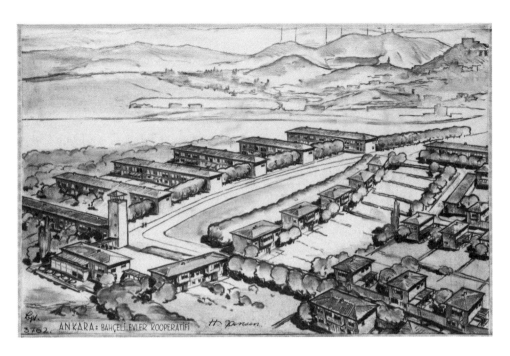

Hermann Jansen, aerial perspective of Bahçelievler (row houses to the left, double houses in the middle, single houses to the right).

housing was promoted intensely in Turkey. Opposing both 'old Turkish houses' for their perceived inability to integrate contemporary technological amenities on the one hand, and on the other hand the perceived failure of modern, isolated and unplanned apartments to create an ordered city with healthy qualities of light, air or green space, government officials increasingly advocated cooperative housing. A cooperative was an organization empowering its members by combining their financial resources and constructing affordable housing on cheaper land. The Emlak & Eytam Bank, founded in 1926, was established to give credit for the construction of housing and by 1935 some 900 cooperatives, mostly for agricultural activities, had been set up in Turkey. On 26 January 1935 Bahçelievler was officially launched as the country's first cooperative housing scheme with full support from the Turkish Society of Cooperatives, whose officials clearly promoted garden city models.[14] Jansen's plans for Bahçelievler involved detached, semi-detached and row houses (a second row house type was added in the second version), each with three to six rooms and all with large gardens. In his design Jansen followed functionalist principles, such as direct access from the house to the garden, correct orientation to the sun, efficient inner circulation patterns and mass production of window and door units. His attempts to integrate regionalist elements, such as projecting bays,

91   The Modern House

Typical cooperative housing promoted in the 'Villas of Ankara' series in *La Turquie Kemaliste* (1941).

loggias and courtyards reminiscent of 'old Turkish houses', were immediately rejected by members of the cooperative, who were upper middle-class government officials determined to eliminate all possible allusions to the traditional forms of living in the Citadel and so mark their social status with houses of European inspiration.

As anticipated, the Bahçelievler housing cooperative became a model for other settlements in Ankara and during the course of the 1940s and early '50s a number of cooperatives succeeded in constructing similar garden city housing settlements nearby. Much of Ankara was developed during this period as a series of garden city type housing schemes. By 1945 fifty building cooperatives had been founded across Turkey,[15] usually following site planning principles similar to those established in Bahçelievler, even though individual units were modified.[16] Bahçelievler and its adjacent housing cooperatives were promoted in the 'Villas of Ankara' series published in *La Turquie Kemaliste,* and they continued to be the neighbourhoods where bureaucrats and upper middle-income citizens lived until at least the 1960s.

Today, however, hardly any of the original garden city houses from this period remain. Many could not survive the growing pressures of urbanization and the real estate market, a process that will be considered in more detail in chapter Five. Prioritizing representational issues and, in this case, the residential identity of the new governmental elite must have prevented the Kemalist bureaucrats as well as future governments from confronting some of the serious economic and social problems with necessary sense of caution. One of the most visible consequences was the lack of adequate housing for the lower income groups and for the newly urbanized population migrating from the countryside after the Second World War. It was precisely this outcome that Zeki Sayar and Martin Wagner had predicted in their contemporary essays on housing, where they criticized the government for supporting a few cooperatives intended for upper middle-income government officials, but neglecting affordable housing that should have been a priority in the Turkish cities.[17]

Housing for Workers and Peasants

The third residential type in Jansen's original plans was working class collective housing, but neither his own project nor any other significant housing programme for the urban poor was implemented. Only a few notable exceptions can be recorded, such as the Türkiş and Kömüriş housing projects (1934–6) designed by Seyfi Arkan for the coalminers of Zonguldak on the Black Sea coast (see page 80). According to the Turkish nationalists of the early republican period, the fact that the rich Zonguldak mines were owned and administered by European companies was an indicator of the Ottoman Empire's semi-colonization. Therefore, improving the living conditions of the workers during the early years of the nation state was a matter of Turkish independence itself. Arkan combined free-standing single-family houses with multi-family housing blocks placed parallel according to the *Zeilenbau* model. He put special emphasis on the topography of the site and provided all houses with a view by using the land's slope efficiently. The dormitories and multi-family housing blocks were placed parallel to each other with a specific emphasis on a southwest-northeast orientation to make the most of sunlight. The units were standardized and minimally designed with only the most essential elements for modern living. In addition to dormitories for single workers and houses for families, the projects included spaces for community living, such as common dining halls, laundries and showers, as well as a primary school for the workers' children (only in the Türkiş settlement), anticipating that the workers would permanently settle in the town rather than return to their villages. Arkan's projects, however, were not free from the newly established class distinctions. The houses for the director and engineers were designed with different amenities than were available to the workers and were sited on top of a hill to reflect their social status. The Soviet-designed textile factories in Kayseri and Nazilli (1932–6, see chapter One) also provided workers' housing. The housing at Kayseri was

Lodgings for the Silk Factory personnel in Gemlik, c. 1937.

Abidin Mortaş, Type for village houses, 1940.

built as reinforced concrete apartment blocks, accompanied by a social club, cinema, swimming pool, daycare centre, infirmary and soccer stadium.[18] However, the lodgings for factories in Bursa, Gemlik and elsewhere often followed garden city models.

It was in immigrant settlements and model villages that the principles of collective housing were implemented with the highest rigour in early republican Turkey. The typology of village housing thus became a common theme in the late 1930s and early '40s. In the pages of the influential *Ülkü* magazine and the newly founded nationalist journal *Yapı*, designing villages was promoted as one of the highest ranks of 'building for the people'. Abdullah Ziya Kozanoğlu, Hatif Öğe, Burhan Arif Ongun, Abidin Mortaş and Behçet Ünsal planned the most notable models for typical Turkish villages.[19] The detached village houses were usually placed on a grid plan, with local elements that would slightly differentiate them from their urban and European counterparts, such as a big courtyard, stables for horses and other barn animals, or an outdoor toilet. These projects clearly indicate that modern mass-housing was perceived as a civilizing agent to be distributed to the remotest regions of Turkey. Industrialized building production was not a prospect for these village houses. Many of the architects insisted on local materials and low-tech structural systems. Nonetheless, the very idea of a planned and standardized village house emerged from a discourse that originated in response to the effects of industrialization. Despite the architects' aspirations to preserve local 'lifestyle and needs', the standardization of village houses in relation to a central building programme was a patronizing extension of the urban mind into the rural surroundings. While this 'missionary' attitude was yet another example of top-down modernization, it was also driven by a sincere goodwill and a matter-of-factness that was made necessary by the harshest facts: this became particularly evident in the context of deadly earthquakes in 1939 and 1940, especially the one around Elazığ that destroyed around 80,000 houses and took 40,000 lives. This prompted Turkish architects like Behçet Ünsal and German émigrés such as Wilhelm Schütte and Martin Wagner to think about earthquake damage prevention and post-disaster housing in terms of standardization, which they believed was connected to the village reforms.[20] Unfortunately these studies hardly made a lasting effect, and frequent earthquakes have since continued to take lives and destroy settlements in Turkey.

94

The most visible impact of industrial housing models on the Turkish scene was not so much in housing schemes for low income families, only a couple of which were realized before the 1950s, but rather in the principle of 'rationalization' itself. Ideas in favour of mass-produced and standardized housing, as well as projects designed to be functional, efficient and rational, abound even in the context of wealthier family homes. Already in the first issue of *Mimar* in 1931 (*Arkitekt* after 1935), the editor Zeki [Sayar] promoted standardization as an indispensable fact of modern times: 'The essential idea of this new spirit [industrialization] . . . is "serial" production and "standardization" . . . In "standardized" construction, the plans are idealized. They have a rational and generic form with minimized construction costs.'[21] What 'rational' meant for Sayar is particularly noteworthy. Unlike the term's use in much European discourse on mass housing, where the emphasis would be on economy, efficiency and functionality, Sayar redefined rational design as one that took into consideration both these and the 'climate, life style, conventions, economy, agriculture', and local building materials.[22]

According to the *Arkitekt* circle, the standardized modern house had to be prioritized for the establishment of a new architectural vision. The architecture critic and historian Behçet Ünsal promoted the 'abandonment of traditional architectural solutions' in favour of 'new' principles of rationalization, which were making the biggest impact in house design: 'The goal of our times is to combine rational and economic methods with an aesthetic expression in housing. In its most general sense, the new architecture is characterized as "People's architecture". The old architecture started from a monument, palace, fortress . . . The focus of new architecture is the "House".'[23] *Arkitekt* published hypothetical projects by Bekir Ihsan, Abidin Mortaş, Sedad Eldem and others in their search for the most efficient, minimal and industrial house that would also be appropriate for Turkey.[24] Many designers of wealthier villas and city apartments also cited functionalism and efficiency as their utmost architectural criteria.

These examples demonstrate the aspiration for minimal, standardized and industrial housing in Turkey, but also the lack of financial and administrative rigour as well as systematic research to determine the most efficient and functional residential types. In that, they bear witness to one of the paradoxes of the Kemalist programme: the makers of the new Turkey were intensely occupied with the representative qualities of the country's institutional buildings and houses, turning bare sites into modern cities, inviting foreign architects and carrying the tropes of Westernization to the remotest villages, publishing publicity journals filled with the images of brand new construction. However, this mass

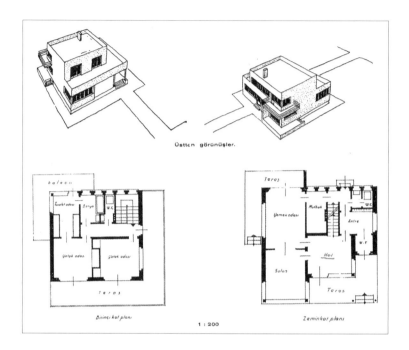

Üstten görünüşler.

1 : 200

Birinci kat planı

Zeminkat planı

housing programme paid less attention to the determination of structurally rational and financially sound solutions for the lower income
majority, a fact that took its toll on Turkish cities after the mid-1940s
with the spread of squatter settlements (see chapter Five).

The 'Turkish House'

The dissemination of European-inspired cubic houses to the major Turkish cities was not accepted without certain objections. One of the major
criticisms was their association with a misunderstood modernism. The
novelist Yakup Kadri Karaosmanoğlu ridiculed the new elite's cubic
fantasies in his novel *Ankara* in 1934.[25] In a letter to Walter Gropius,
Martin Wagner undermined Seyfi Arkan's Florya seaside residence of
1935 for Atatürk as a 'mishmash of Le Corbusier and Mies ... that copies
functional houses' from Europe while failing to understand the functional
logic behind their creation.[26] Behçet Ünsal cautioned against the mis-
use of the term 'cubic' in Turkey: the fact that the new building material
reinforced concrete favoured right angles and linear lines that resembled
a cube should not have legitimized every cube-like building as a modern
work.[27] The co-editor of *Arkitekt,* Abidin Mortaş, also warned against
the adoption of European modern architecture in purely aesthetic and

formal terms, without taking into account climate-specific and nationally orientated forms of modern architecture: 'new architecture appears with different forms and characters in different climates, customs, lifestyle and mind-frame of various countries . . . Therefore it is simply wrong and meaningless for us to desire putting a beautiful house published in a book in the middle of any site.'[28] Another major criticism against cubic houses was the inappropriateness of modern construction techniques for Turkey's conditions, and consequently the poorly executed buildings, which ended up creating distasteful replicas of Western masters' buildings.[29] The writer Peyami Safa, for one, denounced the malpractice of cubic buildings as the work of an 'uneducated builder, tasteless carpenter, catalogue lover, copycat architect and talentless painter', creating 'distorted, short and flat apartments built out of cheap cement with low ceilings and narrow rooms'.[30]

As a result, cubic architecture came to be associated with a decadent and pretentious cultural colonization jeopardizing the emergence of an architectural expression that could be both modern and Turkish at the same time. The rising controversy against it was coupled with a melancholic appreciation of the 'old Turkish houses'. Intellectuals and architects in Istanbul grieved over the loss of the urban tissue – old

Köprülü Amcazade Hüseyin Paşa waterfront house, Istanbul, 17th century; photo by Esra Akcan.

Sedad Eldem, Typical plans for 'Turkish houses' without a *sofa* (top left), with *outer sofa* (top right), *inner sofa* (bottom left), and *central sofa* (bottom right).

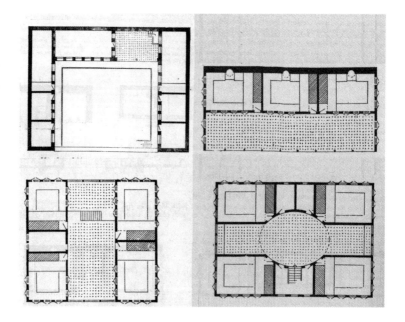

mansions and waterfront houses along the Bosphorus, which either burned in frequent fires or were left to decay because of the new cultural values. As such, these intellectuals initiated a timid yet persistent criticism against the early Kemalist architectural programme's exclusively European orientation.

In search of a culturally specific modernism, Sedad Eldem cultivated a recognizable style that he attributed to the influence of these 'old Turkish houses'.[31] As a recent graduate of the Istanbul Academy of Fine Arts in 1928, Eldem was already critical of the lack of a nationalist style in architecture and, for inspiration, was working on countless watercolours and sketches depicting anonymous houses around the country. In his diaries that record a three-year study tour in Europe, he often fluctuates between appreciating European modernism and hesitating over its worldwide dissemination. In a passage he later crossed out, he wrote: 'In the last ten years, European products colonized Turkey. This destroyed Turkish art. If this continues, we will be completely absorbed by Europe.'[32] To fight against this threat of oblivion, Eldem and Egli decided to launch the National Architecture Seminar at the Istanbul Academy in 1933. This was a research studio dedicated to the examination and documentation of the 'old Turkish houses' in various Turkish cities.[33] (Eldem extended the research into the Balkans in the following years.) Studies and competing theories that defined the 'Turkish houses' had been suggested before and continued to be produced well after the research at the Academy.[34] Eldem's unique contribution to this literature was his argument about the typological specificity and historical evolution of these houses.[35] He also led the way to a unique architectural style in new buildings that came to be known as the 'modern Turkish house'. Despite their geographical expansion and different layouts in urban or rural settings, these houses shared the 'same conception in plan'.[36] Eldem specified the multifunctional *oda* (room), *sofa* (common room) and transition areas (stairs, corridors) placed on the upper floor as their three main elements. Each 'old Turkish house' was a city in itself, according to Eldem: each *oda*, where the multiple functions of sleeping, eating and working could be accommodated with the help of flexible furniture, was a house in itself, and the *sofa* was the space of public appearance for the extended family. Eldem also worked out a typological matrix that differentiated four basic types of the 'old Turkish house', categorized in relation to the place and character of the *sofa*. He argued that the historical evolution was from the 'most primitive' type without a *sofa* in rural areas, to the one with an outer *sofa*, inner *sofa*, and culminating in the most advanced stage with a central *sofa*, examples of which were located in Istanbul.

In the eyes of its promoters, a new modern Turkish architecture based on the study of anonymous houses meant an implicit subversion of the existing cultural hierarchies perceived between Europe and Turkey.[37] It would empower what they perceived as the Turkish heritage against the threat of disappearance. However, the very categorization of the totality of these houses, ranging from the large mansions of wealthy Ottoman families to modest houses in Anatolian villages, under the single name 'Turkish house', and simultaneously the absorption of all the ethnic and religious groups including Armenians, Greeks, Kurds, Jews and Alevis under one overarching nationality of 'Turkish', indicated a vigorous appropriation of the Ottoman past into the nationalist ideals of the Turkish Republic. While this assimilation raised national consciousness as a guard against the loss of these houses, it erased the cosmopolitan texture of the former period.

Throughout his career Eldem remained committed to the creation of a modern 'Turkish house' style.[38] The institutional buildings that he had the rare opportunity to design during the early republican period were examples of a more monumental and classicist nationalism (see chapter Two), but he cultivated a clearly identifiable expression in the houses that became representative of the new 'Turkish house' style. In most of his residential designs during this period, Eldem used a central or outer *sofa* as the main organizing principle of the plan, such as the Ayaşlı house in Beylerbeyi (1938), arranged around an oversized central main

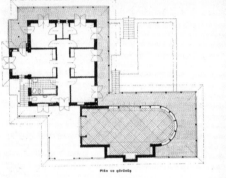

Plân ve görünüş

Sedad Eldem, Fethi Okyar House in Büyükada, Istanbul, 1936, view from the exterior and plan.

hall, and the Fethi Okyar house in Büyükada (1936), with a wooden outdoor gallery (outer *sofa*) encircling the building. The Ağaoğlu house (1936) also stands out with its oval *sofa* projecting onto the street. Even though this space is not programmed as the common hall of an extended family, or the public square of the house, it projects over the exterior wall as an evident allusion to the traditional 'old Turkish house'. The side facades have a projecting bay (*çıkma*), again reminiscent of a very noticeable element in Istanbul's wooden houses. Eldem's choice of white-washed stucco walls and horizontal windows, however, testifies to his aspiration for a dialogue with European modernism. The emphasis on horizontality was another major design strategy for Eldem in hybridizing the architectural character of 'old Turkish houses' with the designs of Western architects he closely followed, including Eric Mendelsohn, Frank Lloyd Wright and Le Corbusier. For instance, he usually designed flat roofs (or roofs with hidden slopes) with the wide extending eaves that would normally be present in a pitched roof. This detail highlighted horizontality and flat roofs, aligning Eldem with European modern architects, but it also alluded to the colourfully ornamented wooden eaves of traditional houses that provided shade from the sun.

The Taşlık Coffee House in Istanbul (1947–8) became Eldem's built manifesto, extending over a retaining wall with a large projecting bay (*çıkma*) and wide ornamented eaves. Its explicit reference to Köprülü Amcazade Hüseyin Paşa's waterfront house (see page 97), an icon left to decay in the early days of the republic, is a testimony to Eldem's unhesitating commitment to re-establishing continuity with Istanbul's past. The T-plan composed of three identical projecting bays was another recognizable element of traditional Istanbul houses, enabling maximum fenestration on a given span. Eldem made the most use of this possibility by encircling all the edges of the T-plan with continuous horizontal windows that let in the light and offer a panoramic view of the Bosphorus from inside the coffee house. The building also stands out for its extensive use

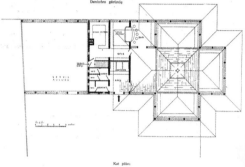

Sedad Eldem, Taşlık Coffee House, Istanbul, 1947–8, view from the exterior and plan.

of wood, including timber beams 'buttressing' the concrete cantilever, exterior woodwork and built-in wooden furniture in the interior. In Eldem's view this structural lightness not only alluded to the timber frames of traditional houses, but also made the new buildings compatible with European Modernism.

This compatibility was indeed one of Eldem's most typical arguments in explaining the intellectual agenda of his oeuvre. Toward the end of his career, he produced a summary of his research that reveals his long-standing conviction that the 'old Turkish houses' already embodied the principles of European Modernism: 'It became clear that the characteristics of Turkish houses had been embodied in a variety of traditions ranging from ancient Chinese domestic buildings to the residential works and architectural principles of the most modern masters like F. L. Wright and Le Corbusier.'[39] In his opinion the modular execution of exposed timberwork in traditional vernacular houses in Turkey followed the same constructional logic as Auguste Perret's exposed reinforced concrete structures; the horizontal low lines of these houses reminded him of Frank Lloyd Wright; the placement of living spaces on the upper level performed the same function as Le Corbusier's *pilotis*; close contact between the interior space and nature, secured through courtyards and outdoor *sofas*, pre-dated the garden city ideal; the sloping roofs of vernacular houses were more functional than functionalist architecture in preventing leaks. Although Eldem remained critical of the dissemination of Eurocentric modernization in Turkey throughout his career, he often declared himself a close follower of modernist principles that he perceived to be already implicit in 'old Turkish houses'. This helped Eldem resolve a very common dilemma of Turkish modernization – a dilemma derived from the simultaneous desire to be part of 'Western civilization' on the one hand, and of establishing an identity that would avoid the perceived threat of being 'absorbed by the West' on the other. This also became a common strategy in early republican historiography among influential historians such as Celal Esad Arseven and Behçet

Paul Bonatz,
Saraçoğlu housing
project, Ankara,
1944–5.

Ünsal, who rewrote the history of Ottoman architecture in ways that attributed to it an exclusively Turkish heritage, while interpreting modernism as a natural continuation of this heritage.[40]

Within a decade the 'old Turkish house' became a recognizable metonym of cultural heritage, employed as an architectural expression of nationalism even in projects officially sponsored by the state. Paul Bonatz's design for the Saraçoğlu housing project in Ankara (1944–5), intended for government officials, was a testimony to this shifting symbolism from the 'Viennese cubic' to the 'Turkish house'.[41] As an unwavering defender of nationalism in architecture during this period (see chapter Two), Bonatz added a few signifiers of 'Turkishness' to a collective housing project that was otherwise designed on site planning principles and using unit design patterns that had become commonplace in his home country. For each unit, Bonatz provided a balcony with wooden balustrades and projecting bays (çıkma) 'in accordance with the Turkish style', as he also underlined in his explanation,[42] even if this happened at the expense of efficiency and minimal space, which were regarded as higher values for collective housing during this period. Whereas the government officials of the Bahçelievler housing project firmly requested a design that would distinguish them from the residents living in

Ankara's 'old Turkish houses', a decade later these traditional houses were now marked as the official symbol of Turkish architecture through Bonatz's design.

The residential culture of early republican Turkey was caught between temptation for Western living models and a simultaneous aspiration for a unique Turkish identity. While European, particularly German and Austrian, modernism provided major models of translation, the traditional wooden buildings commonly referred to as 'old Turkish houses' equally shaped the outline of the modern house. The governmental elite and architects, both German and Austrian émigrés and their Turkish colleagues, together envisioned new models of living for the whole population. Large sections of the population, however, were to have their lives changed by these transformations, but they were not given the chance to participate in the decisions shaping their living spaces. The Kemalists' over-emphasis on nationalism and representational values not only ignored the hybrid histories that had produced the former living patterns, but it may also have diverted the focus away from the housing problems awaiting Turkish cities in the wake of rapid urbanization.

chapter four

Populist Democracy and Post-war Modernism

With the 14 May elections an important step [was] taken in a revolution
that is far more important than anything that had been accomplished
previously in our country . . . It used to be that only one person ruled and
only a few hundred participated in politics. With our democratic revolution,
with one leap, millions and millions of citizens acquired the vote and . . .
became real citizens.

Adnan Menderes, *Cumhuriyet*, 2 February 1960[1]

With the landslide election victory of the Democratic Party (DP) on 14
May 1950, Turkey's early republican period came to a decisive end.
Abandoning the secular authoritarianism, statist economic policies and
nationalist self-sufficiency of the Republican Peoples' Party during the
previous two decades, the DP regime promoted populist democracy,
private enterprise and a more ambitious regional role for Turkey in
the post-war international order. The initial Western-orientated cultural politics of the nation (as established by Atatürk in the 1930s) did
not change, but the meaning of 'Western' in the nation's collective
consciousness shifted considerably from 'European' to 'American'.
Owing to her strategic importance for the American policies of containing communism and Soviet expansion during the Cold War, Turkey
was included in the Marshall Plan of 1947 and admitted to NATO in
1952. American governmental and private agencies poured generous
packages of development aid and technical assistance into Turkey to
modernize her agriculture, industries and transportation network.
Images of John Deere tractors in rural Anatolia or Mack trucks on the
newly built roads across the country still offer vivid symbols of the
mechanization of agriculture and the switch from railways to highways
in the 1950s.

That the DP was able to deliver a brief 'economic miracle' in its first
few years in power offered ample grounds for optimism in the early
1950s. Turkey was heralded as one of the most successful models of a
universally defined process of modernization better known as 'modernization theory', as articulated by American social scientists and area

Hayati Tabanlıoğlu,
Atatürk Cultural
Centre in Taksim (AKM),
Istanbul 1956–69,
1977; front elevation
facing Taksim Square.

studies experts.[2] Central to modernization theory was a basic dichotomy between modernity and tradition, presenting the former as an unambiguous blessing and the latter as an obstacle to its realization. It was postulated that as societies became more 'modern' by increased literacy, increased mobility, spirit of enterprise, use of communication technologies, urbanization and other such indicators, their traditional traits and cultural practices (like fatalism, religion and lack of curiosity about the world) would give way to new patterns of thought and behaviour largely derived from the institutions and values of American society. Above all, the transition from a traditional to modern society was equated primarily with consumerism and entrepreneurship, thereby giving credence to Fredric Jameson's more recent characterization of modernization theory as 'a euphemism for the penetration of capitalism'.[3]

The capitalist expansion of Turkey's economy in the two decades after 1950 would usher in dramatic consequences in the form of social change, demographic movements, massive urbanization and environmental degradation. These decades witnessed, before everything else, the increasing homogenization of the population and especially the consolidation of a national (Muslim-Turkish) industrial bourgeoisie following the departure of the remaining non-Muslim entrepreneurs, merchants and businessmen inherited from the cosmopolitan Empire. The establishment of a strong private sector, buttressed by the 'import substitution' policies adopted by the state after 1958, led to rapid industrialization, the creation of a national market (especially for household goods, refrigerators, washing machines, domestically assembled cars and construction materials) and the cultivation of a new culture of consumption (in stark contrast to the early republican values of frugality and self-sufficiency). Images of Arçelik refrigerators or domestically assembled Anadol cars remain powerful representations of the everyday culture and middle-class aspirations of Turkish society after the Second World War. Industrialization, in turn, led to the emergence of new social groups (an urban working class and migrants in search of work) and new spatial transformations, especially in the urban periphery of major cities (factories and industrial zones, accompanied by 'informal settlements' and squatter housing for migrant workers). This was the beginning of a new experience of modernity as mass-culture, based not on a project dreamt up by nationalist elites, but on the everyday experience of millions of people coming into contact with the simultaneously liberating and alienating effects of urban life.[4]

In stark contrast to the early republican project of taking modernization to Anatolian towns and villages, Istanbul now became both the centre stage and the leading actor of this unfolding drama. After two decades of relative insignificance in the shadow of the new capital, Ankara, the old imperial capital enjoyed a spectacular revival under the new DP regime and became the showcase for massive urban modernization projects following a master plan by the French urban planner Henri Prost (1874–1959): the opening of new roads, public squares and parks and the construction of new, iconic modern buildings that will be introduced below. In İzmir too, Turkey's third major city on the Aegean coast, French urbanists René and Raymon Danger prepared a *plan d'aménagement* in collaboration with Henri Prost in 1924, only partially implemented during the 1930s. After the Second World War, Le Corbusier also produced a schematic *plan directeur* for İzmir in 1949, structured around the idea of a 'green city' with a population of 400,000 people. It followed the functional zoning principles of the 1933 CIAM Charter, separated vehicular and pedestrian traffic, proposed residential blocks raised on *pilotis* and enforced a *tabula rasa* approach for the historical districts. Ultimately, however, its destructive approach and its disregard for the existing land ownership in the proposed new areas were found to be unrealistic by the municipal authorities. A new international competition was held in 1951 and the winning master plan of Kemal Ahmet Aru, Emin Canpolat and Gündüz Özdeş structured İzmir's urban development throughout the 1950s and '60s.[5]

A younger generation of Turkish architects established themselves in private practice outside state patronage and produced works that reflect the aesthetic canons of 'International Style' in all its post-war variations: from the American corporate style of the 1950s to works of Le Corbusier and Latin American modernism. Whereas early republican modernism manifested itself primarily in austere-looking government complexes, educational buildings and cultural institutions, cutting-edge architectural production after 1950 was most visible in hotels, offices, shopping centres, commercial and recreational projects, with taller apartment blocks emerging as the dominant residential typology. What follows is a closer look at the urban and architectural developments of the 1950s, setting the stage for this second major phase of Turkish modernity (1950–80) following the early republican period.

Urban Interventions in Istanbul

After its multi-ethnic and multi-religious population had grown steadily throughout the nineteenth century to reach 1,200,000 people on the eve of the First World War, Istanbul's urban population declined almost by half in the early republican period (691,000 in 1927), mainly as a result of losses in recent wars, the departure of non-Muslims and the transfer of the state bureaucracy to Ankara. During the years that Ankara was rising as the new capital, Istanbul was reduced to a shadow of its former self: a city shrinking in population, area and national significance, with crumbling infrastructure, old buildings and empty plots that were not rebuilt after successive fires had taken their toll. As discussed in the previous chapters, during the radical Kemalist nation-building of the 1930s the limited resources of the young republic were mostly directed to Ankara and other Anatolian towns. Istanbul had to wait until the 1940s for the first planning efforts and until the 1950s before catching up with and rapidly surpassing its turn-of-the-century population of one million inhabitants.

The urban interventions of the 1950s largely followed the blueprints laid out earlier by Henri Prost, who led the planning office of the Istanbul Municipality between 1936 and 1951.[6] Prost's 1939 masterplan for Istanbul equated modernity with open spaces ('*espaces libres*' as he called them): wide boulevards, large squares and public parks modelled after European precedents. As such, it responded to the early republican quest for making modernity visible by showcasing the openness, spaciousness and cleanliness of modern public spaces, positioning them as the antithesis of the congestion and unhealthiness of traditional (especially 'oriental') cities. As Dr Lütfi Kırdar, the popular governor/mayor of Istanbul, put it in 1943, 'Istanbul [was] a diamond left among the garbage' and the task of urban planning was to clear away 'the garbage' to reveal the diamond.[7] Demolishing chunks of the old fabric (old wooden houses, small shops, warehouses and unseemly derelict structures), opening new roads or widening existing ones, and laying out urban squares and landscaped public parks (in contrast to the more private Ottoman garden or *bahçe* tradition) were the primary devices employed by the Prost plan.

Although the implementation of the Prost plan was hindered substantially by the difficult circumstances of wartime, urban historians agree that the transformation of Istanbul from an Ottoman city into a republican one started in those years and continued in the latter part of the 1950s under the personal direction of the DP's charismatic prime minister Adnan Menderes, for whom the re-making of Istanbul was a colossal PR campaign – a 'prestige struggle' both at home and internationally.[8] Guided by a modern Haussmanian vision sponsored by the national government, extensive demolitions were undertaken during his administration, not only to build new roads and thus make the city compatible with modern traffic, but also (and in line with the more conservative and populist values of the DP, in contrast with the radical secularism of the early republican period) to clear the areas around mosques, *medreses* and

Demolition during
Istanbul's urban
renewal in the late
1950s.

other historically significant structures of the Ottoman era, making them visible for Istanbulites and tourists alike. Criticizing the neglect of the Ottoman capital in the early years of the republic, which his administration was determined to reverse, Menderes declared in 1957: 'Istanbul's redevelopment is a story of a triumphal parade . . . We will conquer Istanbul one more time!'[9]

The impact of these new roads on the subsequent growth of the city and its eventual macro-form is a vast topic beyond our scope, but a selective focus on a few urban fragments can effectively illustrate the unprecedented nature of the new scale and urban aesthetic introduced by them.

Istanbul's historical peninsula, with its centuries-old macro-form of domed Ottoman mosques on hilltops surrounded by the tight fabric of wooden houses, became the site of some of the most radical urban interventions of the 1940s and '50s. Following Henri Prost's proposal, Atatürk Boulevard, a major new artery 50 metres wide, was cut transversely across the peninsula, connecting it to the Galata-Pera-Taksim section to the north of the Golden Horn. Perpendicular to this first major modern intervention of the 1940s, Menderes added in 1956 what would become one of his most enduring urban legacies: the convergence of Vatan Avenue and Millet Avenue, two roads of an unprecedented width, on Aksaray Square, the busy hub of the historical city. The new coastal road along the Marmara shore to the west of the city was opened in the late 1950s, connecting the city to the new residential suburbs of Ataköy and

New avenues cut through the urban fabric of Istanbul's historical peninsula.

Yeşilköy, the beaches of Florya and, above all, to the new modern gateway to the city, Yeşilköy Airport, which was completed in 1953.[10]

The impact of this coastal road upon Istanbul's growth has been substantial. While the residential suburbs of Ataköy and Yeşilköy still constitute the most representative example of post-war modernist architecture in Turkey, the development of industrial zones in the hinterland along this coastal road (especially in Zeytinburnu, where a cement factory was in operation from 1938, and Kazlıçeşme, where highly polluting leather factories operated until their removal in the 1980s), would attract the first squatter settlements from the 1950s (see chapter Five). Outside the historical peninsula, roads along both shores of the Bosphorus were widened and another major new artery, the Barbaros Boulevard, was opened to connect Beşiktaş on the Bosphorus shore to what was then the outer limit of the city beyond the ridge overlooking the Bosphorus. As on the western shores of the Sea of Marmara, industrial developments, squatter settlements and new residential suburbs rapidly emerged along this hinterland, defining the future direction of Istanbul's northward urban growth towards what is today's CBD (Central Business Districts) along the Levent-Maslak axis. Istanbul's transformation from a shore city to a hinterland city would accelerate and become an irreversible sprawl after construction of the first Bosphorus Bridge and the city's ring road in the 1970s (see chapter Seven).

On a more architectural scale, the primary focus of modernist interventions in republican Istanbul was the Taksim area on the northern side of the Golden Horn, the major urban hub from which new roads radiated towards the historical peninsula to the south, the Bosphorus to the east and the newer residential and commercial neighbourhoods of Harbiye and Nişantaşı to the north. Following Prost's schemes, the traffic around Taksim Square was reorganized and the old military barracks flanking the square were demolished to make room for a large European-style public park (İnönü Gezisi), complete with rows of trees, flower beds, paved pedestrian paths and terraces. To complete this overall geometrical order visualizing modernity, the Taksim Municipal Casino (Taksim Belediye Gazinosu, 1938–40, now demolished) was built at the northern end of the park, giving Istanbul its paradigmatic early republican public

The public promenade park (İnönü Gezisi) Taksim, Istanbul, by Henri Prost and built during the 1940s. Taksim Municipal Casino is visible at the far end of the park.

Rükneddin Güney,
Taksim Municipal
Casino, Istanbul,
1938–40, dining hall
and plan.

Paolo Vietti-Violi,
Şinasi Şahingiray and
Fazıl Aysu, Palace
of Sports and
Exhibition, Istanbul,
1949.

space (café, restaurant, ballroom and wedding hall) where modern (that is, Western), secular norms of recreation, entertainment and civility were displayed. Designed by Rükneddin Güney, it was an elegant reinforced concrete structure with a double-height dining hall flooded with light, a semicircular transparent wall or bay window projecting towards the park and an open café terrace with a spectacular view of the Bosphorus.

The tree-lined Cumhuriyet Avenue connecting Taksim Square to the modern neighbourhoods of Nişantaşı to the north was conceived in the Prost plan as the new face of Istanbul, lined with modern apartments

Skidmore, Owings &
Merrill with Sedad
Eldem, Istanbul Hilton
Hotel, 1952–5 (isolated
in the centre of the
photo), which over-
looks the Bosporus.
The Open Air Theatre
(1947–8) can be seen
to the left of the
Hilton and State
Radio Hall (1945) in
the foreground.

connected at street level by a covered portico, a likely remnant of Prost's colonial urbanism in North Africa. The Avenue also gave access to the new Civic Centre (the sports, culture and arts zone of the city) perched at the high point of the valley overlooking the Bosphorus. The Civic Centre included the State Radio Hall (Radyoevi, 1945; architects İsmail Utkular, Doğan Erginbaş and Ömer Güney), the 'Open Air Theatre', an auditorium following the natural slope towards the Bosphorus (Açıkhava Tiyatrosu, 1947–8; architects Nihat Yücel and Nahit Uysal), and the Palace of Sports and Exhibition (Spor ve Sergi Sarayı, 1948–9; architects Paolo Vietti-Violi, Şinasi Şahingiray and Fazıl Aysu), where major sporting events were held over the years, especially basketball, volleyball, wrestling and weight-lifting. Completing this spatial display of the early republican cult of sports, youth and health, the Dolmabahçe football stadium (1946) was built at the lower end of the valley. Going against Prost's vision of keeping this valley as a large public park, the DP administration would give over a spectacular site at the top of the valley for the construction of the Istanbul Hilton Hotel, a symbol of post-war shifts in Turkish architectural culture, politics and society.

The Internationalization of Turkish Modernism

In the sharply divided Cold War world of the 1950s, Turkey was admitted to the 'Western club' as a new NATO member primarily for geopolitical reasons. The climate of optimism central to modernization theory and discourses of development constitute an important backdrop to the favorable reception of international architectural currents in Turkey at this time.[11] Although the centrality of the nation state as the primary agent of modernization remained unchallenged, Turkish architects mostly abandoned the search for a 'Turkish national style' and dropped their earlier misgivings about the term 'International Style'. The latter came to be seen as a new supranational aesthetic of bureaucratic and technocratic efficiency best symbolized, for example, by the recently completed UN Building in New York. Equally important, however, was the domestic fact that the state had largely succeeded in homogenizing the society and creating a national bourgeoisie, thereby removing a major motivation to search for a distinctly 'Turkish' national style. With the expulsion and departure of Greek, Armenian, Jewish and other minorities and the suppression of any expression of ethnic diversity on the part of the Anatolian migrants who replaced them in major cities (Kurds and Alevis), the Turkishness of the nation seemed to be no longer contested.[12] Hence, expressing Turkishness through architecture was replaced by the desire to adopt the supranational language of modern technological progress as visual testimonies to the success of Turkish national modernization in an international context. Most Turkish architects were still committed nationalists, in spite of the aesthetic shifts in their work, but nationalism was no longer a matter of style to be derived from historical or vernacular precedents, but rather a matter of national pride in the internationalization and increased competence of the profession.[13]

More numerous and less famous than their early republican counterparts, the architects of the 1950s constituted an entirely new generation in whose careers the new commitment to International Style coincided with a significant organizational transformation of professional practice.[14] An important institutional marker was the establishment of the Chamber of Turkish Architects in 1954 as a licensing and regulating body that affirmed the profession's autonomy and independence from the state. Throughout the early republican period, almost all of the practising architects in Turkey were either teachers in the architectural and engineering schools or salaried government employees in the planning and technical units of the various ministries. Railway stations were designed within the Ministry of Transportation, schools in the Ministry of Education and so on, which also accounted for a certain degree of aesthetic uniformity. Although the practice of providing major public architectural and planning services within the state bureaucracy continued under the DP government from 1950, the emergence of private clients brought in a conspicuous programmatic shift in the kind of buildings that best embodied the 'modern' in Turkish architecture: from governmental and educational buildings of the early republican period to commercial, industrial and recreational buildings (hotels, beach facilities, offices, shopping complexes and factories). Coupled with the broader emphasis on the role of the private sector in Turkey's new development strategies, the rise of private clients facilitated the emergence of what architectural historians consider to be the first truly 'private' architectural firms and the first major 'partnership' models.[15]

Especially notable among these new practices are the partnerships of Haluk Baysal and Melih Birsel, who produced residential designs of very high quality reflecting the international trends of the 1950s (see chapter Five) and the 'Construction and Architecture Workshop' (IMA – İnşaat ve Mimarlık Atölyesi) of Turgut Cansever, Abdurrahman Hancı and Maruf Önal, whose members continued with accomplished individual careers after the group split up. Collectively, these architects not only defined the distinct aesthetic canons of the 1950s, as will be discussed below, but also explored new forms of critical and collective practice outside the state sector.[16] Above all, it was with their work that the international canons of post-war modernism trickled down to mainstream practices, becoming an 'ordinary', 'anonymous' or 'everyday' modernism that no longer carried the strong ideological charge of the early republican 'civilizing mission', but still maintained its social purpose.[17]

Two primary sources of inspiration were especially important for these architects in their new receptiveness to international influences. The first was American corporate modernism, especially the glass curtain wall epitomized by such projects as Lever House, New York (1952) by Skidmore, Owings & Merrill (SOM) or Mies van der Rohe's Seagram Building (1958), both of which were widely publicized by the architectural media at the time. In his semi-autobiographical *Architectural Anthology of the 1950s Generation*, Enis Kortan remembers his 'mesmerizing encounter with Mies van der Rohe's Fransworth House' through publications and, more generally, the fascination of his generation with the work of SOM, Marcel Breuer, Richard Neutra, Eero Saarinen and Minoru Yamasaki among others.[18] Works by American architects were extensively published in Turkey in *Arkitekt*, many of them with the information provided by the United States Information Services (USIS) in Istanbul, an organization that translated American foreign policy and strategic goals into cultural propaganda abroad.[19] News items and announcements in *Arkitekt* also reveal that in the 1950s summer training programmes and various exchanges were offered to Turkish architects and engineers by the u.s. government through Fulbright grants. In 1956, in a conspicuous departure from the earlier German influence in Turkish architectural education, a new American-inspired school of architecture, the Middle East Technical University, was established in Ankara with a University of Pennsylvania committee headed by G. Holmes Perkins playing a major role mediating between the Turkish and u.s. governments.[20]

The second, equally powerful influence was that of the post-war work of Le Corbusier, especially the paradigmatic Unité d'Habitation (1948), as well as the Corbusian work of Latin American and Caribbean architects that were featured in Turkish architectural media. The 'tropicalization of post-war modernism' (the growing consensus that Corbusian elements like the *pilotis*, the *brise soleil* and the roof garden are more 'at home' in the tropics than in Europe or North America), is a vast topic beyond our present scope.[21] However, the many little-studied connections between Turkish and Latin American/Caribbean modernisms during the 1950s promise to open up new ways of 'triangulating' cross-cultural exchanges in modern architecture and so break out of the worn-out East-West dualities. Uniquely among Turkish commentators, the late Şevki Vanlı, an important Turkish architect of the post-war generation, has acknowledged some of these connections and, for example, cited the Ministry of Health and Education Building in Rio de Janeiro (1945; architects Lucio Costa and his team, including Oscar Niemeyer with Le Corbusier as consultant) as a major influence on the distinct facade aesthetic of 1950s Turkey.[22]

Reflecting all of these aesthetic influences, the Istanbul Hilton Hotel (1952–5), designed by Skidmore, Owings & Merrill (with Gordon Bunshaft as lead designer and Sedad Eldem as the local collaborating architect) is, by general consensus, the indisputable icon of post-war modernism in Turkey. It is also a textbook case of modern architecture's role in u.s. Cold War politics, at a time when the designs of u.s. embassy buildings and Hilton hotels were seen as powerful visual instruments of projecting a positive image of America abroad.[23] As Annabel Wharton and others have observed, to enter the Hilton was to gain admission to 'a little America', the paradigm of benevolent and democratic capitalist society that the DP regime embraced as a model.[24] Looking at the construction of the Istanbul Hilton as a political investment in a strategic location bordering the Soviet Union, the u.s. government heavily invested in the project and the construction was publicly financed by the Turkish

The entrance facade of the Istanbul Hilton Hotel.

Pension Funds (Emekli Sandığı) with loans from the Bank of America and with additional funds from the Economic Cooperation Administration (ECA). The construction was undertaken by German firms in collaboration with on-site Turkish engineers, and the hotel was opened with spectacular ceremony and a media extravaganza in June 1955.

Following the architectural precedent set by the 'tropical Modernism' of the Caribe Hilton in San Juan, Puerto Rico (1949; architects Torro, Ferrer & Torregrosa), the design of the Istanbul Hilton illustrates the basic typology that would become a pervasive paradigm thereafter: a horizontally placed narrow, two-sided prismatic block lifted on *pilotis* above a transparent ground floor and finished with a rooftop terrace. Given the non-availability of structural steel in Turkey, Skidmore, Owings & Merrill steered away from its signature glass and steel curtain walls,

Section and ground-
floor plan of the
Istanbul Hilton Hotel.

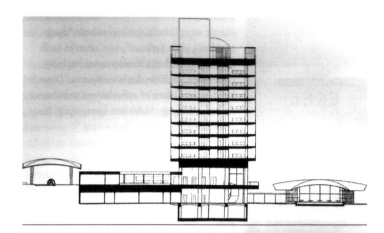

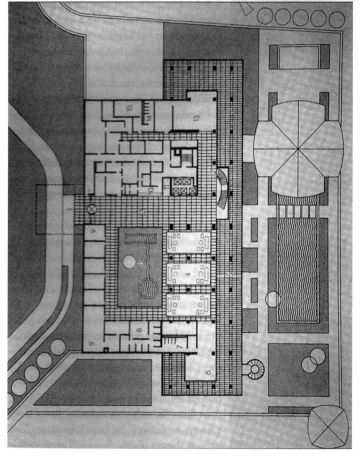

and employed instead a distinctly Corbusian idiom where the reinforced concrete structural frame is also the *brise soleil*, resulting in an appropriate solution to both the local climate and the limitations of the Turkish construction industry. Furthermore, the distinctly American ideal of democratizing comfort and luxury found its expression in the regular grid of the famous 'honeycomb' facade. On the one hand, the stacking of identical units (hotel rooms) was evocative of a democratic efficiency – everyone gets the same cell. At the same time, the interior of the hotel room signified American notions of modern comfort, consumption and the 'good life' through technological amenities, with air conditioning, a private bath, hot water, wall-to-wall carpeting and a radio cabinet in every room. With its novel form, structure and materials (including the imported white cement that gave it its clean look) the Hilton quickly became a symbol of technical perfection, precision and progress.

Yet, it was also evident to everyone involved that an imported building landing on a prime location in Istanbul like an alien spaceship was fraught with difficulties, not only for the pride of the host nation, but also for American 'soft politics', which understood the strategic need for some concessions to local culture, not to mention the latter's marketing value for commercial tourism. Posters and publicity material never failed to mark the exotic location of this ultra-modern new hotel (see overleaf). Ostensibly 'Turkish' (Ottoman) elements were incorporated into the design and contemporary commentators eagerly exoticized these elements using all the familiar orientalist clichés. For example, the wavy thin-shell concrete entrance canopy was promptly nicknamed 'the flying carpet' and the roofs of the restaurant and the small poolside pavilions were associated with the domed *şadırvans* of Ottoman architecture. Other local references included the ceramic wall tiles in the lobby, which were abstracted or stylized from Ottoman tile patterns, and the so-called Tulip Room with 'all the rich trappings of an Arabian Nights harem', as *Architectural Forum* put it in 1955.[25] In the end, the will for Americanization on the one hand, and the anxiety produced by this very process on the other (that is, the fear of a faceless, standardized International Style homogenizing the world and eliminating cultural difference), reproduced in built form some of the same notorious orientalist binary oppositions that modernization was supposed to eliminate. The rationality of the main hotel block was juxtaposed against the sensuality of the auxiliary structures and interior furnishings; the tectonics of the former against the decorative character of the latter, respectively; the functional against the merely entertaining; and ultimately the 'Western' against the 'Eastern'. The fruitful cross-cultural intentions of the project (the appropriation of the principles of International Style in relation to climate control and locally

Istanbul)K hilton

The Tulip Room at the Istanbul Hilton; photo by Ezra Stoller.

opposite:
Istanbul Hilton luggage tag.

Istanbul map from the hotel brochure, locating the Hilton in relationship to major monuments.

available materials) were thus suppressed by reintroducing the divide between 'us' and 'them'.[26]

The 'Hilton Style' Disseminated

The basic typology of the Hilton quickly became the paradigm of modern hotel architecture in Turkey throughout the 1950s, repeating with small variations the same horizontal block with a reinforced concrete grid/*brise soleil* of hotel rooms and balconies on the main facade, the same spacious

Rana Zıpçı, Ahmet
Akın and Emin Ertan,
Çınar Hotel in
Yeşilköy, Istanbul,
1959.

reception areas, bars and restaurants on the more or less transparent ground floors (or sometimes projecting from it as a separate block with more plastic roof forms) and the same rooftop bars, night clubs or discos on the flat roof. Among the most illustrative examples are the Çınar Hotel in Istanbul (1959; architects Rana Zıpçı, Ahmet Akın and Emin Ertan) situated on the Marmara shore along the newly opened coastal road connecting the city to the airport; the Porsuk Hotel in the inland city of Eskişehir (1957; architect Vedat Dalokay); and the Great Ephesus Hotel in the heart of İzmir (1957–64; architects Paul Bonatz and Fatin Uran). The Tarabya Hotel (1957; architect Kadri Erdoğan), on the water's edge of the Bosphorus north of Istanbul, is an important variation on the theme, bending the prismatic block into a slight curve along the shore and departing from the 'honeycomb formula' by differentiating the facade grid of the balconies.

Located in the historical context of Büyükada (the largest of the Princes' Isles off the Marmara shores of Istanbul), and the result of a national competition, the private Anadolu Club (1951–7; architects Abdurrahman Hancı and Turgut Cansever) is yet another horizontal prism, albeit a one-sided one, unlike the Hilton. While the sea-facing rooms, accessed from the single corridor at the back, have the familiar honeycomb balconies/*brise soleil* to the front, the back facade displays a different grid

Paul Bonatz and Fatin Uran, Great Ephesus Hotel, İzmir, 1957–64.

Kadri Erdoğan, Tarabya Hotel, Istanbul, 1957, aerial view.

composed of pivoted square panels of wooden lattice screens, filtering a soft light into the corridors and into the spacious hallways and stairwell space. The latter projects as a separate vertical shaft attached to the back of the horizontal block and topped on the roof terrace with a conspicuously Corbusian parasol. The joint work of a devoted follower of Le Corbusier, Abdurrahman Hancı (who worked in Paris for many years) and a culturally conservative architect, Turgut Cansever (who would later attribute the light filtered through the sun-screens of the back facade to the memories of traditional houses and Islamic *mashrabiyas*), the building subtly embodies multiple cultural references (Corbusian, tropical modernist, 'Hiltonist' and 'Islamic'), while remaining irreducible to any one of them. As such, it testifies to how, far from being passive recipients of an imported aesthetic in the 1950s, Turkish architects were active participants in the localization and naturalization of international modernism.

Nevzat Erol's winning design in the competition for the new Istanbul City Hall (1953) is another canonic building of 1950s modernism, marking the transfer of the basic Hilton paradigm from hotel buildings to offices and public buildings. As in the Hilton's main hotel block, the two-sided horizontal prism of the office block in Erol's design is raised on *pilotis* (with a facade articulation that differentiates between the reinforced concrete grid of office units and the tighter grid of the *brise soleil* corresponding to the vertical circulation shafts) and is finished on the roof terrace, with the more plastic form of a thin concrete shell covering the rooftop restaurant. The large auditorium, the singular element distinct from the repeating units of the programme, is separated from the main prismatic block and differentiated formally with a thin-shell concrete roof structure of intersecting parabolic vaults. The volumetric composition of the bigger horizontal prism and the lower auditorium attached to the front of it is completed by an open plaza contained within the L-shaped layout. It is, however, the urban impact of the building that brings the controversial legacy of Hiltonism into sharper focus. Unlike the Hilton or Çınar Hotels, located in the modern republican hub and the new coastal suburb respectively, the City Hall sits in the historical heart of Ottoman Istanbul. It is placed perpendicular to the newly opened Atatürk Boulevard, between the Ottoman aqueduct to the north and Aksaray Square to the south. Dwarfing the small Ottoman *hamam* behind it and introducing a new, foreign aesthetic unlike anything in the historical fabric, it stands as the quintessentially 'republican' monument inserted inside the old imperial city (see page 110).

Other office buildings of the time display the same prismatic block configuration, albeit with minor variations, as for example in the case of

Abdurrahman Hancı
and Turgut Cansever,
Anadolu Club,
Büyükada, Istanbul
1951–7.

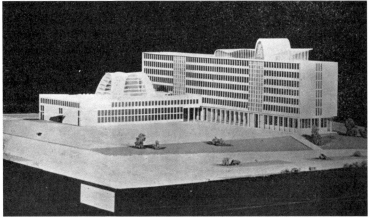

Nevzat Erol, Istanbul
City Hall, 1953, model.

the Etibank Offices in Ankara (1953–5; architects Tuğrul Devreş, Vedat
Özsan and Yılmaz Tuncer), in which the slightly concave curve of the
two long elevations introduce a subtle divergence from the geometry of
the regular prism. Similarly, the Ulus Business Centre in Ankara, a complex of offices and retail shopping (1954; architects Orhan Bozkurt,
Orhan Bolak and Gazanfer Berken) features a twelve-storey, two-sided
office block, this time with slightly convex facades. While some version of
the concrete *brise soleil* remained as the norm for the facades of office
buildings, the first important experiments with glass curtain walls
'draped' in front of the structural frame also emerged in this period, for
example the General Directorate of State Waterworks in Ankara (1958;
architects Behruz Çinici with Teoman Doruk and Enver Tokay). This

building is an interesting 'hybrid' combining the 'glass skin' of corporate American skyscrapers with the familiar Corbusian idiom: horizontal block raised on *pilotis*, approached by pedestrian ramps and completed at the top with a usable rooftop terrace. Given the limitations of the building industry, however, it is not surprising that high-rise towers clad in glass curtain walls remained a formidable technological challenge in Turkey during the 1950s, with the proud exception of Ankara's Emek Office Tower or simply 'the Skyscraper' (*Gökdelen*), as it came to be known in popular parlance (1959–64; architects Enver Tokay with Ilhan Tayman). A two-sided narrow prismatic office tower in the manner of the UN Building in New York, it rose above a three-storey 'plinth' of shops and

Orhan Bozkurt, Orhan Bolak and Gazanfer Berken, Ulus Business Centre, Ankara, 1954.

Enver Tokay and Ilhan Tayman, Emek Office Tower or 'the Skyscraper' (*Gökdelen*), Ankara, 1959–64; compared with the UN Building as it appeared in *Mimarlık*.

Birleşmiş Milletler, New York, A.B.D   *Emekli Sandığı Gökdeleni, Kızılay, Ankara*

Behruz Çinici, Teoman Doruk and Enver Tokay, General Directorate of State Waterworks, Ankara, 1958.

publicly accessed spaces. Not surprisingly, it earned a landmark status as a singular, free-standing object in the central hub of modern Ankara.

Perhaps the most iconic, not to mention controversial, example of the 'glass-and-concrete box' formula of 1950s modernism is the Atatürk Cultural Centre (Atatürk Kültür Merkezi, known as the AKM) in Taksim Square, Istanbul. The still unfinished saga of this building started in the early republican period, with the intention of building Istanbul's first opera house at the eastern end of Taksim Square as part of Henri Prost's urban modernization master plan. The preliminary project by August Perret reflected the architect's monumental stripped-off Classicism and was developed and detailed by Rükneddin Güney in the 1940s. Although foundations were laid in 1946 and the naked structure of the building was up by 1953, its completion was hindered by complex economic and

Hayati Tabanlıoğlu, entrance lobby to the Atatürk Cultural Centre, Istanbul, 1956–69, 1977.

political factors, including a change of government and a fiscal crisis leading to the transfer of the building from the Istanbul Municipality to the Ministry of Public Works. The latter, in turn, commissioned one of its own salaried architects, Hayati Tabanlıoğlu, who had completed a doctorate on theatre design in Germany, to redesign the project. Working with two German consultants (Willie Ehle for stage design and Johannes Dinnebier for lighting), and a competent group of Turkish architects, structural and electrical engineers and interior designers, Tabanlıoğlu's team produced an exquisitely crafted concrete and glass box.[27] Constructed between 1956 and 1969, it contained a 1,317-seat multi-purpose 'grand hall' with comprehensive backstage facilities and a spacious entrance foyer, and on the lower level a 530-seat concert hall, a 300-seat theatre and a small 'children's cinema'.

The damaged Atatürk Cultural Centre following the fire in 1970.

It was, however, the building's main Taksim Square elevation that gave the AKM not only its iconic status in Turkish post-war modernism, but also its famous public face for critics and admirers alike: a transparent glass skin thinly veiled by the geometric patterns of an aluminium lattice screen. Also enhancing the feeling of lightness and transparency were the spacious foyers with polished floors, the enchanting effects of the overhead lighting in the form of geometric chandeliers, 'halos' or 'stalactites', and, like a modern sculpture suspended in space, an elegant spiral stair of very light steel construction floating in the main entrance hall. The artwork and interior furnishing of the entrance hall and the main foyer were carefully selected and incorporated into the design, including an abstract sculpture by Cevdet Bilgin, paintings by two prominent Turkish artists, Oya Katoğlu and Mustafa Plevneli, and a 10m square Hereke carpet covering the floor of this temple to the republican, 'westernized' ideal of modern Turkish culture. By a tragic twist of fate, only a year after its grand opening in 1969, the AKM was burnt down in a fire and it would take the Tabanlıoğlu team another seven years to restore it for a second opening in 1977.[28]

Retrospective assessments of the Hilton Hotel's impact upon Turkish architecture have been mostly negative. The late Şevki Vanlı, who coined the term 'Hiltonism' (*Hiltonculuk*) writes that 'this easy rationalist template, [this] Cartesian honeycomb facade grid became a mainstream domestic typology to be repeated thousands of times . . . For almost every building type, repetitive cells and balconies were projected on the facade and monotonous horizontal prisms filled our cities.'[29] Even Sedad Eldem, who had collaborated on the design of the Hilton, would later write that after the Hilton 'buildings started to look like boxes, drawers or radios' and that 'Anatolian towns were now "invaded" by these glass and tin cans'.[30] While expressing a justified critique of the generic and often characterless reinforced concrete blocks that became a hallmark of mainstream commercial and residential architecture in Turkey after the 1950s, these views overlook some of the more interesting facade articulations that Turkish architects introduced during these years. In contrast to the early republican preoccupation with volumetric compositions, architects of the 1950s treated facades as a form of 'modern decoration' expressing the programmatic and structural properties of the building and using the reinforced concrete frame as a grid to be filled in with geometric compositions of glazed areas, brick or plastered infill walls, wooden or concrete screens and/or cantilevering balconies.[31] Climate and sunlight control was aestheticized through the use of variations on *brise soleil*: perforated bricks, pre-cast concrete screens and wooden lattices for facades, exterior corridors and vertical circulation shafts, connecting Turkish architecture of the 1950s to the prevailing 'tropicalized' or 'Mediterraneanized' modernism of architectural culture from the Caribbean to the Middle East and beyond, especially in the work of Edward Durrell Stone and Joseph Stein in India, Lucio Costa and Oscar Niemeyer in Brazil or Walter Gropius and Josep Lluis Sert in Baghdad.

Integrating the Plastic Arts

Another argument against the alleged monotony of 1950s Turkish modernism can be found in the 'integration of plastic arts', or the collaboration between architects, painters, muralists and sculptors. Advocating a synthesis of the plastic arts following similar experiments in the West, the Turkish branch of Group Espace was formed in 1955 by the sculptors Hadi Bara, Ilhan Koman and the architect Tarık Carım, 'marking an important milestone in Turkish modernism' as Turkish art historians see it.[32] During the 1950s and '60s many prominent Turkish architects, including Haluk Baysal, Melih Birsel, Utarit İzgi, Turgut Cansever and Abdurrahman Hancı, worked on the synthetic idea of combining modernist concepts of space and construction with abstract/non-figurative original artworks. Epitomized by the work of contemporary Latin American, Caribbean and Mexican architects, this was a welcome strategy, not only breathing life into the presumed sterility of International Style modernism everywhere, but also reintroducing stylized touches of cultural and national identity into otherwise anonymous buildings of post-war modernism.[33] It was therefore of particular interest for architects in peripheral geographies, perennially caught between the euphoria of internationalism and the anxieties of losing national identity. The stylized 'Turkish tiles' that Sedad Eldem designed for the Hilton's lobby, the abstract mosaic mural with folkloric themes that decorated the bar of the Çınar Hotel, or Katoğlu's 'naïve' paintings of Anatolian peasants decorating the foyer of the Atatürk Cultural Centre, all seek to negotiate a compromise between international aspirations and the desire to express local culture. It was a creative tension, albeit a precarious one that could easily end up further accentuating the very binary opposition that it sought to dissolve, as has been discussed above in relation to the design of the Hilton Hotel.[34]

Whereas hotels and cultural centres were, by their nature, more likely to include works of art as a way of expressing local or national distinctness, the integration of architecture with the plastic arts appears to have been widely embraced in the 1950s and '60s to add aesthetic quality and a certain degree of civic-mindedness to otherwise utilitarian or commercial modern buildings, from hospitals to shopping centres. While the large mosaic panels that Bedri Rahmi Eyüboğlu designed for the main hall of SSK Samatya Hospital in Istanbul (1959; opened 1960) or Eren Eyüboğlu designed for the Hacettepe Children's Hospital in Ankara (1955; opened 1958) are notable examples, it is the new shopping centres that gave particular prominence to this collaborative concept. This seemingly curious juxtaposition of high artistic ambitions with the crass materialism of commerce needs to be viewed in the specific social, economic and cultural circumstances of the 1950s. With the 'civilizing ideals' of the early republic still lingering on, this was a brief but favourable climate for capitalism and the arts 'to talk to each other' – a climate that largely accounts for the emergence of commercial structures and shopping centres as the unlikely testing grounds for international modernist trends and new aesthetic experiments. Most notably, at the Manifaturacılar retail centre in Istanbul (1959), a series of shopping galleries around courtyards featured original works by Turkish sculptors (Kuzgun Acar, İlhan Koman), painters, muralists (Adnan Turani, Nuri İyem, Arif Kaptan) and ceramic/mosaic artists (Bedri Rahmi Eyüboğlu, Eren Eyüboğlu, Füreya Koral).

Both the integration of the plastic arts and the defining aesthetic canons of the 1950s were embodied with particular elegance in one project that no longer exists: the Turkish Pavilion for the 1958 Brussels Expo, 'a lost icon of Turkish modernism' by Utarit İzgi (1920–2003) and his three colleagues Muhlis Türkmen, Hamdi Şensoy and İlhan Türegün (illustrated on page 134).[35] The result of a national competition held in 1956, the project consisted of two separate pavilions, an exhibition hall and a restaurant/café, connected by a 50m wall decorated with a mosaic mural by Bedri Rahmi Eyüboğlu (1913–1975). Supported by slender steel columns and clad in modular panels of plate glass and oxidized aluminium for the exhibition pavilion and of teak for the restaurant, the transparency and pristine modernist aesthetic of the pavilion distinguished it not only from the more overtly 'oriental' iconographies of other non-Western pavilions in the Expo, but also from similarly literal replications of 'national' forms that had represented Turkey in earlier international exhibitions, especially Sedad Eldem's project for the 1939 World's Fair in New York.[36] Yet the 'internationalism' of the 1950s (not to be confused with the more recent phenomenon of globalization) was still based on the primacy of the nation state. The national pavilions were expected to be showcases of these distinct national identities in the comparative (and competitive) context of an international fair. Nothing illustrates the complex negotiations between the emerging internationalism of the world and the deeply entrenched nationalism of the Turkish state than the contrast between the architecture of the pavilion and the exhibits within. Whereas the 'glass box' container visually celebrated post-war internationalism, its contents reproduced the official republican constructions of Turkish history and identity as laid out in the 1930s, displaying the art and archaeological treasures of pre-Ottoman Anatolia, as well as its Ottoman-Islamic heritage.

Above all the pavilion was a superb example of the 'integration of the plastic arts' paradigm. The long mosaic wall by Eyüboğlu, the central 'anchoring' element or backbone of the design, incorporated highly stylized motifs from Anatolian Turkish life, culture and landscape: a colourful modern mural depicting peasant women, fishermen, animals, rivers, mountains, trees, Anatolian *kilim* patterns and other folkloric themes arranged in a continuous visual narrative. Utarit İzgi, a firm believer in collaboration between artists and architects, and the chief architect of the project, regarded large ceramic or mosaic wall panels as simply the modern reincarnation of the tile decoration on the walls of Ottoman buildings. He would later write, citing the work of such artists as Miró, Rivera, Picasso, Noguchi and Calder integrated into twentieth-century buildings, that the relationship between art and architecture is fundamental to the discipline, 'compelling the architect to think of space as a potential setting for art and encouraging artists to innovate with their materials and techniques for a better fit with the architectural setting'.[37] One of the most notable examples of this integration was an industrial building, the Vakko Factory (for fine fabrics and textiles) in the Merter district of Istanbul (1969; architects Haluk Baysal and Melih Birsel). Original work by fourteen artists, including Eyüboğlu and the most prominent Turkish painters, ceramic artists, muralists and sculptors, such as

Kuzgun Acar, facade sculpture in the Manifaturacılar retail centre, Istanbul, 1959. The Centre's architects were Doğan Tekeli, Sami Sisa and Metin Hepgüler; photo by Didem Yavuz.

Sadi Çalık, Jale Yılmabasar and Mustafa Plevneli, were integrated for the first time into the design of an industrial building, not as a decorative afterthought but as constitutive elements of the original design concept. It was a rare early example of using the power of plastic and graphic arts to add an aesthetic value to the project, above and beyond sheer functionalism and capitalist rationality, and thereby enhancing the quality of workspaces at a time of Turkey's rapid industrialization.[38]

Sometimes brilliant, sometimes giving in to the 'orientalizing' impulses of 'anxious modernities', but always fruitful in its experimental rigour, this 'intimacy' between architecture and the arts was unfortunately brief. After the 1958 Brussels Expo closed, the components and mosaic wall panels of the Turkish Pavilion were dismantled and brought back to

Haluk Baysal and
Melih Birsel, Vakko
Factory in Merter,
Istanbul, 1969
(demolished 2006),
exterior view showing
wall reliefs by Bedri
Rahmi Eyüboğlu.

Istanbul, but the plan to reassemble them was never realized and the remains of the pavilion were tragically abandoned to neglect, oblivion and eventual loss, partly due to the dramatic events leading to the military coup of 1960, but largely due to what Ali Cengizkan aptly calls the 'culture of destruction' endemic to official Turkish modernization.[39] More recently the Vakko Factory was demolished in 2006, unable to withstand the lucrative urban development market resulting from Istanbul's phenomenal growth as a global city on the rise. Fortunately, the artworks have been incorporated into the new Vakko Head-quarters designed by REX (see page 295). Meanwhile, many of the ceramic wall panels that adorned the lobbies and bars in the hotels mentioned above have since been removed in subsequent renovations. Even the Manifaturacılar retail centre has recently been threatened with demolition to make room for new resi-dential development. As Turkish modernity continues to erase its own traces, the surviving fragments of the 1950s aesthetic in Turkish cities remain as sad reminders of a confident post-war modernism that is rapidly fading in the collective memory.

The post-war shifts in Turkish culture and politics outlined here were far from smooth or implemented without resistance. The traditional repub-lican elites (the military, bureaucracy and Kemalist intelligentsia) resented the new economic policies of the DP government, which depended on agricultural exports and foreign aid, replacing the earlier ideals of national self-sufficiency and industrialization through the agency of the state. Nor were the DP's ambitions entirely free of ambiguities. The slogan of turning Turkey into 'a little America' had been accompanied by an equally strong ambition to turn Turkey into an important regional power in the Eastern Mediterranean with strong ties to other Muslim countries of the Middle East. What was celebrated as Turkey's textbook case of internationalization and modernization during the 1950s went hand in hand with a renewal of nationalist and religious themes in the official discourse. The ethnic homogenization of Turkish society (and the harass-ment and departure of ethnic minorities) accelerated under the DP regime and many of the early republican restrictions on religious expression were lifted in what amounted to a populist reclamation of the Ottoman and Islamic heritage. Such relaxation of the radical secularism of the early republic, while gaining conservative, popular support for the DP, antagonized the republican elites who saw themselves as the guardians

Utarit İzgi, Muhlis
Türkmen, Hamdi
Şensoy and Ihan
Türegün, Turkish
Pavilion for the
Brussels 1958 Expo,
exterior view and
interior view of
the exhibition wall
showing the project's
'backbone' (the mosaic
wall by Bedri
Rahmi Eyüboğlu).

of Kemalist reforms against Islamic reactionaries – a conflict that remains endemic to Turkish society and politics.

As many critics have pointed out, modernization theory was the work of American social scientists and 'area studies' experts who offered an academic foundation to the expansion of American political, military and economic interests throughout the world in the aftermath of the Second World War.[40] The positive psychological effect of this theory on the emerging nations of the post-colonial world was considerable, giving them grounds to hope that, although historical and cultural differences separated them from the experiences of the industrialized West, they too could 'make it' one day along this linear, predictable and 'scientific' model of development. Where the older colonialist/orientalist constructs based on essentialist cultural categories suggested a built-in inferiority, modernization theory defined a universal process that applied to all societies. For architects it played a progressive role in replacing the nationalist obsession with identity in favour of international problems of modernization, such as development, urbanism, housing, construction and infrastructure. Before the end of the decade, however, modernization theory was proving incapable of delivering its promises, as even Daniel Lerner admitted.[41] Societies were indeed changing, but turning into something 'modern' in their own ways and not as theory predicted.

By the end of the 1950s the DP's massive demolitions and urban interventions in Istanbul had already run into financing difficulties. The lack of coordination and the damage wrought upon Istanbul's historical urban character drew increasingly harsher and more vocal criticism.[42] The country was not able to attract as much foreign investment as expected; corruption and mismanagement of funds were rampant; and, most ominously, the populist policies of the DP and relaxation of the militantly secular foundations of the republic were drawing increasing opposition from the military establishment and Kemalist intelligentsia. On 27 May 1960 the DP regime came to an abrupt end when tanks rolled in and the army took over in what was the first of a series of military coups. This was the first sign that Turkey's road to 'democracy' was going be difficult, just as had been the foundational project of modernity and its architectural/urban expressions. International Style modernism also fell from grace with the collapse of the DP regime, giving way to experiments with organic architecture, 'actual regionalism', new brutalism and other revisionist trends of the 1960s and '70s (see chapter Six). By then, the new strategies of capitalist development through incentives for private enterprise and the dynamics of rapid industrialization through import substitution policies had already made major cities strong magnets for rural migrants from Anatolia seeking jobs in the industrial sector. This resulted in an intensive housing shortage, and the consequent emergence and pervasive dissemination of generic and informal residential types, which will be examined in the next chapter.

chapter five

Housing in the Metropolis

One winter night, on a hill where the huge refuse bins came daily and dumped
the city's waste, eight shelters were set up by lantern-light near the garbage
heaps . . . Towards morning, unable to resist the wind any longer, one of the
huts collapsed. The baby who had flown off with the roof into the factory
garden was killed, trapped between fragments of stone and wood.

Latife Tekin, *Berji Kristin: Tales from the Garbage Hills* (London, 1993), pp. 15, 20

The grim life in a squatter settlement on Istanbul's urban fringe, as
described by Latife Tekin, is strangely evocative of that in the dense, middle-class apartment buildings of the city's congested neighbourhoods,
described by another prominent novelist Orhan Pamuk. 'Other things
could be found on the repulsive basement floor that was encrusted with
dirt a lot worse than manure', wrote Pamuk, speaking of the light-well
in the apartment building:

> shells of pigeon eggs stolen by mice who went up the spouts
> to the upper stories, unlucky forks and odd socks that had
> slipped from flower-print tablecloths and sleepy bed sheets
> shaken out the windows and fallen into the petroleum-colored
> void, knives, dust cloths, cigarette butts, shards of glass and
> light bulbs and mirrors, rusty bed springs, armless pink dolls
> that still batted their plastic eyelashes hopelessly yet stubbornly
> . . . It was a place [the apartment dwellers] . . . mentioned as
> if talking about some ugly, contagious disease: the void was
> a cesspool they themselves could, if they were not careful,
> accidentally fall into like the unfortunate objects swallowed
> up by it.[1]

They may be fictional, but these words portray vividly the two distinct
residential types that became prolific during this period and shaped
Turkish cities for years to come: small-contractor (*yap-satçı*) apartments
and squatter settlements (*gecekondu*). While the narrow and unkempt
light wells of the apartment blocks were like perpetual dustbins beyond

Danyal Çiper, Gemi Ev
(the ship house),
Ankara, 1968;
perspective drawing.

the residents' reach in Pamuk's depiction, the *gecekondu*s, self-built from flimsy materials salvaged from rubbish, were in Tekin's portrayal bound to be destroyed by factors beyond the residents' control.

The second half of the twentieth century in Turkey was marked by rapid urbanization that had its biggest toll on housing conditions. The population living in the 67 Turkish cities (largest of which were Ankara, Istanbul and İzmir) increased from 5.2 million in 1950 to 27 million by 1985 (and to 44 million in 2000). Whereas the percentage of the total

Cover of the professional journal *Mimarlık* illustrating *gecekondu* and anonymous apartments, 1967.

population living in urban surroundings had stayed almost steady at 25 per cent in the first half of the twentieth century, it reached 53 per cent by 1985 and 65 per cent in 2000. In the first five-year development plan of 1963 the housing need was officially specified as 265,500 units per year. Successive governments attempted to handle the housing shortage in different ways throughout the period covered by this chapter (1946–80), but none of these policies produced effective results to alleviate the emerging housing crisis. In 1951 city municipalities were assigned the task of regulating and producing housing to counteract the production of illegal settlements. In 1958 this task was also allocated to central government with the establishment of the Ministry of Reconstruction and Settlement (Imar ve Iskan Bakanlığı). After the 1960 *coup d'état*, the new constitution treated housing as part of the legal right to health services, and the consecutive five-year development plans recognized the housing shortage as one of the most serious problems in Turkey.[2] While liberal economies shaped the 1950s, as outlined earlier, the housing policies of the 1960s and '70s can be seen as steps in the direction of a welfare state, albeit one that would remain unrealized. Despite these efforts, it would be fair to conclude that these institutional measures produced similarly ineffective results from the viewpoint of the lower income groups and rural immigrants. By contrast, there were some creative leaps in architectural expression and residential typology for the upper- and middle-income families. Architects continued to design single family houses and cooperative collective housing, but their contributions to the overall development of the home remained minimal and ultimately insignificant in the presence of the massive housing shortage.

The House as Architectural Expression

The new generation of Turkish architects that came to prominence in the late 1950s and early 1960s did so through architectural competitions and by designing single-family houses for the new bourgeoisie – industrialists, businessmen and professionals from outside the state sector – that was emerging for the first time, especially as Istanbul regained the importance it had lost to Ankara during the early republican period. It is strikingly clear that the architects who served this new clientele were knowledgeable of the European and North American professional scene. Many were inspired by the established names of modern architecture, particularly by Le Corbusier, Frank Lloyd Wright and Richard Neutra, whose works were published in Turkish journals. Additionally, mature expressions of the 'modern Turkish house' style as it emerged in the 1930s and '40s also came onto the housing market during this time.

Architects took full advantage of reinforced concrete's formal possibilities in eliminating load-bearing walls and producing long horizontal lines, which translated into flat or inversely tilted roofs, long spanning beams, fully transparent facades or white painted non-decorated walls, cantilevered masses or houses raised on *pilotis*, large carved-out terraces, double-height living rooms, open staircases and open floor plans. These houses, unlike many of their early republican counterparts, were neither part of a governmental cultural programme of westernization, nor brought in directly by European architects. They therefore bear witness to the voluntary diffusion of the modern movement into the life of the Turkish elite and bourgeoisie.

In a series of houses built in Istanbul during the late 1950s and '60s, Utarit İzgi and his colleagues experimented with many of these features.[3] In the Haluk Şaman villa and Çiftehavuzlar villa (with Mahmut Bir), for example, the architect underlined the borders of the front facades with reinforced concrete frames that were elaborated differently in each case. While the covered terrace of the Çiftehavuzlar villa is elevated above ground to accentuate the borders of the frame, the building for Haluk Şaman incorporates two houses seperated by a narrow semi-closed garden but unified with the concrete frame. Quite a few architects in this period used accentuated reinforced concrete frames, which enabled them to design the facade with wall-to-wall and floor-to-ceiling glazing: these included the Barlas waterfront house (1966) by United Architects (Mahmut Bilen, Emin Necip Uzman, Ahsen Yapanar, Irfan Bayhan and Adnan Kuruyazıcı) and Haluk Baysal and Melih Birsel's villas in Istanbul (late 1960s).[4] As contemporary interior photographs of these houses testify (see overleaf), the architects and clients welcomed the total dissolution of the boundary between the outside and the inside. Some single-family houses built by Muhteşem Giray in the mid-1960s, including the Özgür and Uzunoğlu villas, found their architectural expression in cubic masses, white surfaces, large glazing on the front and horizontal windows on the side facades, as well as carved-out terraces.[5] The Uzunoğlu villa (1967) had an inversely sloped roof and lengthy cantilevers, features that came to be used frequently during this period, notably in the Arif Saltuk villa designed by Ercüment Bigat and İlhan Bilgesu (1958).[6] The unusual tilt of the roof expressed, in a way, the possibility of using reinforced concrete to subvert the older architectural norms of traditional building materials. The new trend reached one of its most eloquent manifestations in Abdurrahman Hancı's Ali Aksel house in Dragos, Istanbul (1972). The house not only benefited from cantilevered terraces and fully transparent surfaces, but also highlighted the white-painted balustrade beams and pergolas. The result is a white rectangular prism with carved-out exterior living spaces and a composition of white beams (see overleaf).[7] While these single-family houses interpreted Le Corbusier's five principles in unique ways, Danyal Çiper's Gemi Ev house in Ankara was an idiosyncratic example that took its inspiration from a mixture of Frank Lloyd Wright's Guggenheim Museum and Fallingwater House. Locally named 'the ship house', owing to its explicit references to marine windows, decks and long horizontal lines, its plan is conceptualized as a series of

Utarit Izgi, Haluk Şaman Villa, Istanbul, 1959; photo by Oruç Muradoğlu.

United Architects,
Interior of Barlas
waterfront house,
Istanbul, 1966.

free-standing rooms on a large circular podium, with differently sized circular balconies on the upper floor (see page 138).[8]

The international connection of this generation is perhaps best exemplified by Nezahat Arıkoğlu, whose career also exposes the difficulties of being a female architect. While many women graduated from architecture schools in Turkey, very few could continue their profession due to the lack of social and professional support. Educated at the Academy of Fine Arts in Istanbul, Arıkoğlu instead practised in Baltimore, Maryland, during the 1960s, while continuing to contribute to the Turkish scene by reporting from conferences and passing on publications from the United States.[9] In the Arıkoğlu house in Baltimore (1962–3) she used steel construction, unlike the reinforced concrete houses in Turkey, raising the major living spaces and bedrooms on steel columns and cantilevering beams. Despite an obvious allusion to Mies van der Rohe's Farnsworth house in Illinois, the Baltimore house does not intend to liberate the interior from columns or use totally transparent curtain walls: nor does the house seem to have generated the same type of controversy between residents and architect over privacy issues.

After the 1950s Sedad Eldem maintained a remarkably productive career until his death in 1988.[10] Commissioned by Istanbul's richest families to build waterfront houses along the Bosphorus and large villas on

its hills with uplifting views, he had numerous opportunities to develop the 'modern Turkish house' style, a lifetime exploration since the very early stages of his career. In the Uşaklıgil villa (1956–7), Kıraç waterfront house at Vaniköy (1965–6), Bayramoğlu waterfront houses at Kandilli (1969–74), Sertel villa at Yeniköy (1975–9), Koç villa at Tarabya (1975) and Komili villa at Kandilli (1978–80), to list some well-known examples, Eldem used a modular frame that regulated not only the structure and window frames, but also the intricate details of the roof and its over-hanging eaves. These modular structures alluded to the wooden frames of the 'old Turkish houses', which he believed combined their aesthetic refinement with the rationalism of the modern movement. In the Sirer waterfront house (1966–7), Eldem's explorations with the modular frame reached its unique interpretation. While the street facade of this house more typically alludes to the wooden *çıkma* (projecting bay) of 'old Turkish houses', the facade along the water repeats the same frame but empties it out. The dematerialization of the frame's infill results in an

Sedad Eldem, Sirer waterfront house, Istanbul, 1966–7; front and back facades.

Sedad Eldem, Rıza Derviş Villa in Büyükada, Istanbul, 1956.

abstract and slender facade, attuned with postwar modernist architectural taste in Turkey. In many of these houses, Eldem continued to organize the plan around a *sofa* in order to evoke another reference to 'old Turkish houses' (see chapter Three). Nevertheless, especially during the early part of this period, Eldem's practice also responded to some of the patterns of post-war modernism that became widespread among his colleagues. In the Safyurtlu house on the Yeniköy slopes, built in 1952, he raised the building on concrete columns and encircled the upper floor on three sides with a continuous terrace, the roof of which was

Sedad Eldem, House
in Yeniköy, Istanbul,
1952; interior 'sofa'.

Nezahat Arıkoğlu,
Arıkoğlu house,
Baltimore, Maryland,
1962–3.

supported by slender wooden stilts. This gave the house the expression of a totally transparent mass raised on slender columns. The interior *sofa* of this house takes full advantage of the open plan, large spans and low ceiling accentuated by the horizontal lines of the wooden texture. With its wide transparent surfaces, flat roofs, long-projecting cantilever slabs and accentuated gutters, the Rıza Derviş Villa (1956) in Büyükada, Istanbul, is another testimony to the influence of postwar modernist aesthetics on Eldem.

From Garden City to Free-standing Block

During the early republican period the German émigrés in Turkey, including Bruno Taut, Martin Wagner, Margarete Schütte-Lihotzky and Gustav Oelsner, took every opportunity to advocate mass-housing not only as one of the most creative modern architectural inventions, but also as an effective solution to the housing shortage caused by modernization itself. At the dawn of the 1950s, Gerhard Kessler calculated that there must have been 50,000 residents without legal or proper housing in Istanbul.[11] Meanwhile, the Americanization of Turkey during the 1950s shifted the source of 'Western' expertise in housing matters. Numerous foreign professionals from the UN agencies and the United States came to Turkey to research and advise on housing conditions, including Gordon Bunshaft, who arrived with a team from SOM in 1951, Donald Manson in 1953, Charles Abrams in 1954, Bernard Wagner in 1955–6, Fredrich Bath in 1958–60 and Richard Metcalf in 1963.[12] The SOM group, for one, warned about the 'illegal or 'mushroom' houses and the contemporary substandard quality of living, and suggested a national planning office to function in coordination with regional and city planning offices, as well as a separate housing office. They advocated a housing programme that would not only rely on government subsidies but also the stimulation of private capital, yet ensuring 'that the flow of capital is confined to essential low-cost housing, and does not benefit those who wish to speculate, or construct luxury or semi-luxury housing'.[13]

While governments relied on American expertise that promoted the stimulation of private capital, Turkish architects organized around professional institutions that addressed the housing shortage from a socialist perspective, especially after the mid-1960s. The Chamber of Turkish Architects published a manifesto in 1960 on the economic inequalities that translated into a lack of social housing: 'It is bluntly obvious, however, that there is a big social injustice in our country. The privileged population enjoys housing opportunities that would be characterized as luxurious even in rich countries, and thereby exploit our country's

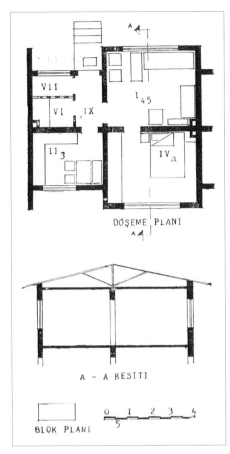

VII
VI . IX
I_{45}
II_3
IV_a

DÖŞEME PLANI

A — A KESİTİ

BLOK PLANI

0 1 2 3 4
5

Minimal dwelling (31.5 square metres usable area) established by the Ministry of Reconstruction and Settlement, 1963.

building resources at the expense of other classes.'[14] The fact that half of the population in big cities lived in informal housing and that collective housing catered to wealthier families confirmed these observations. The universities also organized several conferences and generated extensive publications on healthy, efficient and economic housing standards.[15]

New legal and financial regulations were implemented; a number of state institutions were established, including the Emlak Kredi Bank and Social Insurance Agency (Sosyal Sigortalar Kurumu); five-year development plans after 1963 reserved up to 20 per cent of the state's budget for housing (although this number decreased with each plan).[16] Mass-housing standards (*halk konutları standartları*) that determined who could benefit from state credit were legalized in 1964, defining a minimal dwelling as one that ranged between 30.5 and 63 m² for the lowest income group, and between 63 and 100m² for lower-middle income groups.[17] The Ministry of Reconstruction and Settlement generated nationwide standardized plans, and prepared housing projects for small cities such as Isparta, Denizli, Manisa, Kars, Adıyaman, and post-disaster housing in Erzurum, Çanakkale and Diyarbakır, albeit with little opportunities for realization.[18]

There was a big shift in the typology of collective housing from the early republican period to the second half of the twentieth century. Until the early 1960s cooperative housing settlements were built according to the pre-war garden city model, which had been introduced to Turkey by Hermann Jansen's master plan, and exemplified in his own design for the Bahçelievler housing (see chapter Three). Inspired by the English and German garden-city movements, this model generated sprawling neighbourhoods of one- or two-storey detached houses with pitched roofs and rectangular windows in large private gardens, organized together in a network of peripheral roads and larger boulevards. The state-sponsored sample projects in Ankara throughout the 1950s, such as Sümerbank houses (1947), the İller Yapı Cooperative (1950) and Yenimahalle (1961), usually followed this model.[19] Architects including Mithat Yenen and Abidin Mortaş continued to design garden cities, but explored alternatives

Advertisement of Lottery houses in the 1950s.

in individual housing units, such as houses organized around a central *sofa* (*karnıyarık*).[20] Also notable in this period are the new housing projects sponsored by banks (such as Emlak Kredi, Yapı Kredi and Iş Banks) with tens of units to be given away to their lucky customers in nationally publicized housing lotteries. Typically designed as single-family villas, or more seldomly as multi-unit small blocks, they testify to the fact that such practices by state-regulated banks catered primarily to middle and upper-middle income families who were the potential clients for savings and loans, and not to the poorest sectors of society.

The architectural shift from the 1950s to the 1960s can best be illustrated by the difference between the 1st Levent and 4th Levent housing schemes in Istanbul, both designed by Taut and Oelsner's student Kemal Ahmet Aru, and sponsored by the Emlak Kredi Bank. While the former (with Rebi Gorbon, 1947–52) followed pre-war garden city principles, the 4th Levent housing scheme (1956–60), in contrast, offered tall multi-family blocks that stood separately on large open spaces).[21] Even though streets with two-storey single-family houses (245–270 square metres) in private gardens also existed, another major contribution of the Fourth

Kemal Ahmet Aru,
Comparison of 1st
Levent (with Rebi
Gorbon) and 4th
Levent Housing,
Istanbul, 1952,
1956–60.

Levent housing scheme to the history of housing in Turkey was the
anticipation of a diverse neighbourhood with different family sizes and
multiple residential types. Planned for 1,800 people, the three-, five- and
ten-storey blocks contained dwelling units of diverse types ranging from
56 to 167m² with almost a dozen different options. The blocks with large
glazed surfaces, horizontal lines and carved-in or jutting-out repetitive
balconies contributed to the creation of a taste for the international style
in Turkey. The settlement was designed to contain shops, parking lots,
a cinema for 580 people, a petrol station, a sports club, a cultural centre,
a kindergarten and an administrative block, since it was not designed
simply to rectify the housing need, but also to offer city services in the
extended borders of Istanbul by taking into consideration the rising
influence of the car. Nevertheless, an environment composed of point
blocks rather than continuous streets and building fronts had its limits in generating a city life with social and cultural activities. Many of
the buildings incorporated retail and social services on their ground
floors, but as free-standing blocks on large lawns they did not create a

continuous street pattern. The Aksaray block apartments (1957) and Ataköy settlements (1958–69), both sponsored by the Emlak Kredi Bank, have also been considered milestones of collective housing in Turkey, employing the multi-family housing type, rather than the pre-war garden city model. Composed of 55 blocks ranging from three to 13 storeys, and 618 units with nine different dwelling types, the first Ataköy settlement, designed by Ertuğrul Menteşe (chief architect), Muhteşem Giray, Eyüp Kömürcüoğlu and Ümit Asutay-Yümnü Tayfun, was conceived as a satellite city with free-standing blocks on the outskirts of Istanbul.[22] Just like many other collective housing projects, it was controversial whether the unit plans and building materials were targeted at the population truly in need of social housing. The dwellings, which were as large as 140m^2, had spacious living rooms and four bedrooms. The Emlak Kredi Bank explained this choice as a response to the 'needs of large Turkish families that reside with children and even grandchildren'.[23] Nonetheless, many units contained two large living rooms and a 'maid's room', hinting at a way of life far beyond the reach of families with limited resources.

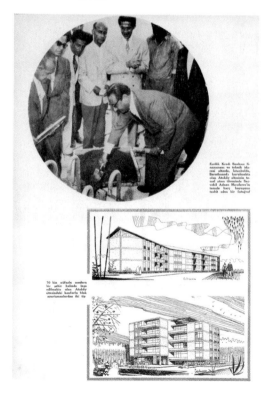

Ataköy Apartments, Istanbul, 1958–9, portrayal in *Istanbul'un Kitabı* (1957) with Adnan Menderes laying the foundations.

Haluk Baysal and Melih Birsel, Yeşilköy Housing, Istanbul, late 1970s; photo by Sibel Bozdoğan.

Unlike the experiments with perimeter block, terrace housing and other residential types elsewhere in post-war Europe, low-rise, high-density housing was conspicuously absent in Turkey. One other notable exception was the Yeşilköy housing project by Haluk Baysal and Melih Birsel (late 1970s) in a satellite of Istanbul, which stands out on account of its stacked duplex units along a two-level inner street. Smaller cooperatives, typically established by professionals pooling their resources, have produced some of the most architecturally interesting housing schemes during this period. The Hukukçular housing block (1960–61) in Şişli, Istanbul, designed again by Baysal and Birsel for a group of lawyers, stands out with its duplex and semi-duplex units that create a dynamic facade and a complex section. A formal allusion to Le Corbusier's Unité d'Habitation, which was introduced to the Turkish audience in 1957,[24] the 66 apartments in the Hukukçular block, in contrast, aspire to a bourgeois life style with three bedrooms, two bathrooms, an open kitchen and large terraces. The three dwelling types create an elaborate section, because they are placed in a block that brings together single-storey, duplex and semi-duplex units; but they do not encourage social diversity as they are composed of similar sizes and the same number of rooms.[25] Another significant scheme is the Cinnah 19 in Ankara, designed by Nejat Ersin for a small cooperative of architects and engineers, and realized with credit from the Emlak Kredi Bank. With its fifteen duplex units stacked in a horizontal prismatic block raised on *pilotis*, a roof terrace with a

Haluk Baysal and Melih Birsel, Hukukçular Sitesi. Istanbul, 1957–61, facades and plans.

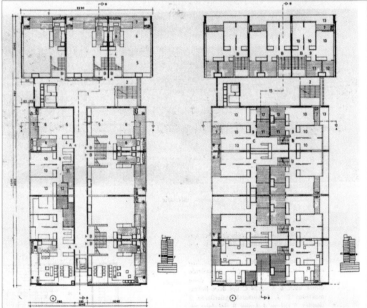

swimming pool and a perforated facade screen that casts shade on the single-loaded exterior corridors, the scheme reflects acknowledged influences not only of the Unité, but also from Lucio Costa, Oscar Niemeyer and Edward Durrel Stone.[26]

  'Architects should be aware of their rights and responsibilities . . . for the construction of an open society . . . It is the architect's debt' to

Nejat Ersin, Cinnah 19,
Ankara, 1958–60, rear
facade.

handle the housing problem.[27] 'Those who do not engage with society's problems are not architects or artists in the true sense.'[28] These comments are by Şevki Vanlı, who in the early 1960s effectively participated in the growing discourse of socially engaged architecture (*toplumcu sanat*), often demonstrating its links to the housing shortage. That half of the population lived in squatter settlements was testimony to the failure of the government as well as the architects, as he stated at a conference in Ankara in 1962.[29] Vanlı advocated the architects' direct engagement with the country's social conditions and political structures. One of his most important texts was nothing but a pre-Lefebvre declaration of the rights to the city. Unlike the majority of the urban population, Vanlı defended the rights of the new immigrants who had just arrived from rural lands, but who were deprived of city services as they were being pushed to squatter settlements. Consequently he defined the equal rights for all citizens as the right to the city (the right to immigrate to the city), the right to minimal housing, the right to use the city, the right to public services, the right to decent work spaces and the right to convenient city life.[30] The first stages of the OR-AN settlement on the outskirts of Ankara (1970–75) were an attempt to put these ideals into practice – a groundbreaking and challenging example, designed and financed mostly on the private initiative of the architect Vanlı, rather than with the financial support of the government. Deprived of the infrastructural support of the municipality, and because of its challenging location on the hills outside the master plan, OR-AN was an adamantly heroic experiment. In his memoirs, Vanlı talks about the city roads that had to be constructed to reach the houses, the malfunctioning electricity and heating system that had to be fixed constantly, and the primary school that had to be established with seven students, in order to create a new community life in an alternative neighbourhood. However, OR-AN hardly fulfilled the social ideals of Vanlı's youth: it led to his bankruptcy and culminated

Şevki Vanlı, OR-AN
Settlement, Ankara,
1970–75; photo by
Esra Akcan.

in his early resignation from the endeavour, even though the settlement was eventually completed.[31]

Ironically, the indirect influence of the OR-AN experience was to normalize capitalist housing production, rather than continue a tradition of socially committed architecture. Non-governmental housing initiatives functioned more and more in relation to profit-making business models after the 1980s, when big-budget construction firms took over the housing market (see chapter Eight). One of the first examples of this process was the establishment of the ME-SA architecture and construction firm in Ankara in 1969, which defined its mission as:

> The intention is to create a civilized environment by taking advantage of the large quantities of collective housing; to bring in the infrastructure that the municipality fails to construct; and to submit to the owners fully finished apartments that are far superior in construction quality, that have no bureaucratic obstacles but only easy payment options.[32]

By 1979 ME-SA had constructed 1,100 apartment units in Ankara, including the housing blocks of Çankaya, Gaziosmanpaşa and Batıkent, a few of which were intended as social housing. Architecturally, Güneş Settlement stands out, a collective housing scheme that combined three tall blocks

Cover of *Arkitekt*
(1979) showing MESA
Güneş Settlement,
Ankara, 1979.

and twenty houses with terraces placed on a hill, where the roofs of the
lower units are used as private gardens of the upper ones.

Despite the efforts invested in the legal, financial and intellectual
background, the production of collective housing in Turkey between
1946 and 1980 was insufficient, whether it was financed by the state or
individual endeavours. More importantly, these projects hardly served
the needs of a population that was truly in want of affordable housing.
The subsequent governments' own construction remained very limited.
Between 1950 and 1965 the Emlak Kredi Bank built only 7,200 units,
almost exclusively in Ankara and Istanbul, and hardly for the lower
income groups. These units were far more luxurious than the 30–100-
square-metre dwellings that the state itself established as the mass-
housing standard. Overall, the official institutions produced around
30,000 units in Turkey during the fifteen years of peak industrialization, a number far below the shortage, even according to the government's own calculations.[33] The number of subsidized units increased
slightly during the 1970s, when municipal aid was extended to smaller
towns such as the housing projects in Izmit and Çorum that were com-
misioned to architects Tuncay Çavdar and Altuğ & Behruz Çinici,
respectively. Yet these remained exceptions. The editor of *Arkitekt*, Zeki

Sayar, constantly warned about the inconsistencies of the social housing programmes in Turkey, and criticized both the government and the Emlak Kredi Bank, for failing to facilitate affordable cooperative houses, and the Chamber of Architects, for failing to go beyond heated disputes.[34] Such concerns were confirmed by the future studies that evaluated the effectiveness of the cooperative housing built during this time.[35] After the mid-1960s, many architects were excessively enthusiastic about socially committed architecture, but they seem to have considered their own practices as separate engagements, with occasional, albeit unfulfilled, moments of convergence. Consequently, informal practices, illegal economies and small contractors' spontaneous decisions supplied the major bulk of housing in Turkey. For better or for worse, it was not mass-housing, but squatter houses that sheltered the migrating population, and small contractors' generic apartment buildings (yap-satçı apartments) that supplied the demand for the upper middle-income families.

From Garden City to Yap-Satçı Apartments

Apartment blocks were built in Istanbul as early as the nineteenth century and more occasionally in Ankara during the early twentieth century before Jansen's master plan, and later, in spite of it. While the early Istanbul apartments were usually located in Galata, Pera and Şişli, namely in the developing European section of the city, they were built in Ankara's centre immediately outside the Citadel's walls.[36] During the post-war and Cold War periods, the city of İzmir continued developing along the coast with rows of apartment blocks, as did Istanbul's central neighbourhoods on the European side. Emin Necip Uzman was notable for his late 1940s and '50s apartment blocks in Istanbul's dense neighbourhoods, employing carefully designed plans and decent materials to create buildings that exemplify the locus of a lifestyle popularly known as the Nişantaşı bourgeoisie. In the words of the architectural historian Uğur Tanyeli, Uzman 'must have chosen to be a real bourgeois, rather than a fake national hero'.[37] A contemporary photograph from the interior of a similar Nişantaşı apartment exemplifies the choice of furniture and the domestic milieu of this group. Often constructed using a reinforced concrete frame with brick infill, the apartments had large windows covered with semi-transparent *tül* curtains, wooden floors complemented by Turkish carpets and, most likely, late nineteenth-century European-style furniture. In popular culture the apartment was most often associated with westernization; the buildings were given such names as 'Belvü' or 'Modern'. The Birkan apartments (1955–9) by Haluk Baysal and Melih

Emin Necip Uzman,
Apartment in
Nişantaşı, Istanbul,
late 1940s.

Typical furnishing in a
Nişantaşı apartment
in 1951 (architect
Ispatan Aratan).

Birsel are typical of the growing trend in Istanbul to move outside the city centre towards the hills overlooking the Bosphorus. Taking full advantage of the steep slope, Baysal and Birsel composed the two blocks at different heights so that both could take full advantage of the much sought-after view through fully transparent front facades and large balconies, made possible by the reinforced concrete frame.[38] However, the vast majority of buildings that came to be known as *yap satçı* (literally translated as 'build and sell') apartments fell far short of these exceptions.

World cities today are shaped exclusively by the proliferation of anonymous and nameless buildings, which in turn eliminates the

Haluk Baysal and
Melih Birsel, Birkan
Apartments, Istanbul,
1955–9.

designer-architect. Rem Koolhaas's observation that 'the built product of modernization is not modern architecture, but Junkspace' is confirmed by Turkish cities in the second half of the twentieth century.[39] Despite occasional examples built by professional architects, the apartment building block boosted by real-estate speculation became dominant all over Turkey, not only from its sheer quantity, but also as testimony to the elimination of the architect's voice and control over Turkish cities – an increasing complaint among professionals and a major target of criticism among the intelligentsia.[40] The legal background of this proliferation was prepared by the condominium law (*kat mülkiyeti*) and the new master plans that increased the building height to five floors or more. Due to the increasing land prices during this time, the government decided to encourage the real estate market by legalizing unit ownership, which had been employed in practice since 1954, but was officially legalized only in 1966.[41] While each building had a single owner before this law, each apartment unit could now have a separate owner. This proved to be excessively attractive for small-business contractors (*yap-satçı*) who bought the land and constructed apartment blocks, usually without commissioning an architect, and made a profit by selling units to different clients. In the words of architect and critic Ihsan Bilgin, this was a magic formula that 'brought together the owner of a small piece of land, the contractor with a small bit of capital, and the client with a small budget in a convenient and secure housing market'.[42] This market proved to be so lucrative that between 40 and 45 per cent of new housing production was financed under this procedure in major cities all over Turkey.[43] Another equally significant factor in the emergence of the small contractor as a major player on the housing scene was the rise of a domestic building industry following the adoption of import substitution policies after 1960. The cheap availability of building materials such as cement, tiles, pipes, glass and hardware was a major incentive for these entrepreneurs in ways that were not possible earlier when construction was dependent on costly imports.

The single family houses in pre-war garden city settlements that characterized the residential culture of the early republican period were completely torn down one after another to be replaced by *yap-satçı* apartments after the late 1950s. İlhan Tekeli and Selim İlkin followed the course of this transformation, leading to the eventual disappearance of Jansen's Bahçelievler cooperative housing project. With the master plan of 1957, the permitted building height was raised to five storeys on the avenues and four storeys on the streets, which seduced many families into tearing down their houses and ripping up their gardens in order to construct higher and bigger buildings with multiple apartments.

Urban fabric of
anonymous *yap-satçı*
apartments in
Istanbul; photo by
Esra Akcan.

Tekeli and Ilkin point out that the density of the building lots increased
up to sixteen times between 1938 and 1960 due to this process.[44] In 1935
there were 15,879 single houses in Ankara's four big neighbourhoods,
as opposed to 351 apartments;[45] by the end of the twentieth century the
percentage of single-family houses to apartment blocks and squatter
settlements was negligible. In no more than four decades, Ankara was
totally transformed, perhaps unavoidably so, due to the economic pressures of a developing and fast-urbanizing country. In hindsight, this
raises questions about the very appropriateness of the garden city model
itself. A model that set itself up as a solution to overcrowding in cities
as a result of immigration, but one that offers uncontrollably sprawling
low-rise, low-density settlements, and that ultimately promotes an anti-
metropolitan density was perhaps inherently unstainable for economically disadvantaged countries that had to industrialize quickly and cope
with enormous levels of immigration from the country to the city.[46]

The size, proportion and form of these apartment buildings came into
being through quite random and unintentional procedures. The dimensions of their building lots were similar to those of the Jansen-based

Erenköy, Istanbul, aerial view showing the density of urban apartments on small lots; photo by Oğuz Meriç.

master plans. Whereas Jansen had designated these dimensions for small single-family houses set in gardens, the same size lots now had to provide for multi-family apartment blocks of five storeys or more. This significantly decreased the allocated green space and preordained the proportions of the new buildings in quite unplanned ways. During the gradual transformation of the early cooperative settlements into areas with apartment buildings, the isolated individual interventions that destroyed the original houses and replaced them with taller apartments were bound to operate within building lots whose dimensions were intended for low-rise buildings.

It seems that the internal organization of developer apartments followed repetitive plan schemes, and lacked the diversity that could have responded to different family sizes and life choices. The different plan types in various cities, if any, have not been documented. In Bilgin's words, 'these schemes were not determined by the priorities of a design discipline, but by the format of a middle class life that the *yap-satçı* contractors intuitively figured out during the construction process and confirmed through the real-estate market'.[47] Almost all of the apartment buildings were built using a reinforced concrete frame and brick infill. It is a well-known 'secret' that many developers took advantage of the lack of official control to increase their profit by cheating on the structural strength of the steel hidden in the foundations or inside the poured concrete, making these buildings incredibly vulnerable to earthquakes, as has been demonstrated in recent disasters.

Gecekondu: The Human Condition of the Third World?

'Rather than mass-housing *(halk konutları)* with small units for the urgent need, big private houses and neighbourhoods for government officials were prioritized. While families were waiting without a roof over their head, homeowners were granted [social housing] credit for their second houses.'[48] The contemporary architect and editor Zeki Sayar's critique of Turkey's social housing policy in 1957 is confirmed by the examples illustrated opposite. The immigrants who had to leave their villages after the 1950s mostly due to the mechanization of agriculture, but who had neither the financial resources for available dwellings in the city, if there were any, nor the professional expertise for well-paid urban jobs, had little choice but to construct their own houses illegally. These came to be known as *gecekondu* (literally translated as 'landed-at-night'), illegally built houses that required a court order to demolish and could thus be occupied temporarily for an indefinite period of time – a specific residential type comparable to the *favelas* of São Paolo, *callejones* of Lima, *dalals* of Karachi or the shantytowns in numerous other cities. It is possible to argue that the socio-economic constraints that led to Turkey's speculative apartment boom at the hands of *yap-satçı* contractors, namely insufficient capital accumulation and the inability or unwillingness of the state to deal with the housing problem on a large scale, also produced an 'informal sector'. This was also true for urban transportation: the former resulted in the illegal, self-built squatter housing of the poorest migrants on urban fringes, the *gecekondu,* and the latter gave Turkish cities the innovative car or minibus pooling (shared 'taxis' on designated routes within the city), the so-called *dolmuş* (literally stuffed vehicle).[49]

The first *gecekondu* settlements were constructed as early as the 1940s in Ankara on the slopes just outside the Citadel walls (although the construction of illegal *baraka* houses dated from even earlier). This started around 1947 in Istanbul's Zeytinburnu, Kağıthane and today's Gaziosmanpaşa, and somewhat in İzmir on the slopes of Kadifekale after the 1950s.[50] These houses were built rapidly, using ad hoc materials from the surroundings, on land that belonged to the state or to someone else. According to official calculations, during the early 1960s approximately

Gecekondu settlements in Ankara; photo by Esra Akcan.

60 per cent of Ankara's population resided in *gecekondu*s, 53 per cent of Erzincan's, 45 per cent of Istanbul's and Adana's, and 34 per cent of İzmir's; these statistics are unreliable, however, due to the very illegality of the phenomenon and hence the indeterminacy of the numbers.[51] These illegal settlements were officially defined in 1966 in Turkish law as 'buildings erected against the legal planning and building construction regulations, on lands and lots that belong to others, without the consent of the owner'.[52] As early as the late 1940s, when the first *gecekondus* appeared on the outskirts of Istanbul, a discussion in the media started to equate these settlements with viruses contaminating the city and defining them as eyesores.[53]

According to sociological and anthropological studies of these settlements, the residents chose the specific location of their *gecekondu* house, not only based on its convenience in relation to city services and employment opportunities, but also to establish community networks. Settlers coming from similar regions of the country tended to agglomerate in the same settlement so as to benefit from the solidarity of their hometown-dwellers (*hemşeri*). The founders (*kurucular*, first settlers) worked to attract more residents by 'selling' them plots for cheap prices, knowing that their sheer numbers would make a good case in front of the government to avoid destruction and to increase their chances of legalization. New settlers also helped their relatives and hometown associates acquire homes in their own neighborhoods.[54] As a result, big cities such as Istanbul developed without master plans as a patchwork of illegal settlements where groups of the same ethnicity or those from the same home town gathered together.

Latife Tekin, who grew up in a *gecekondu* settlement, wrote one of its best fictional but emotionally revealing descriptions in her novel *Berji Kristin,* testifying to their ad hoc construction:

> They rapidly reassembled the fragments of wood, cobbled the torn *kilims* and nailed together bits of tin while the children

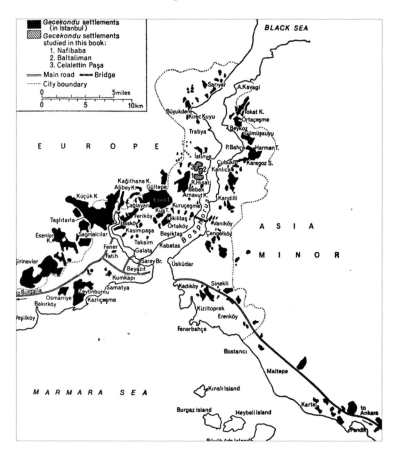

Map of *gecekondu* settlements in Istanbul (c. late 1960s); after Kemal Karpat.

collected stones, unbroken breezeblocks and bricks and piled them up. That night they erected new huts half the size of those demolished. On the roofs they spread spoils from the garbage heap, bits of plastic, tattered cotton rugs and *kilims* and, dragging fragments of broken crockery up from the flat ground below the china factory, they used them as tiles . . . But the fragments on the roof fell off one by one, the *kilims* and bits of plastic blew away and were scattered far and wide. Water seeped between the breezeblocks and formed pools in the middle of the huts.[55]

Apart from their ad-hoc construction methods, these houses were additive. They were originally built in one night as one- or two-room shelters, but became larger as new members of the family migrated to the city or as children were born. According to area studies conducted in Ankara in the 1970s, and in Istanbul in the 1950s and '60s, *gecekondu* houses ranged between 60 and 100m². Basic materials, such as adobe, wood or, if available, stone were used for walls, oilcloth or tinplate covered the roofs, and floors were left exposed without a slab.[56] As the houses expanded, residents used more durable materials that were locally manufactured, such as brick and metals, but easily changed these choices during the construction process if supplies ran out. In time, settlers built grocery stores, coffeehouses, barber shops and even real estate offices, turning the settlement into a semi-sufficient urban neighbourhood. Numerous area studies in Ankara and Istanbul during this period showed that, ironically, the physical qualities of these settlements were pretty homogenous despite their scattered and random growth. They were all low-density settlements composed of single-storey houses in gardens, built with common materials offered on the Turkish construction market.[57] Among the biggest problems in these areas, as well as their biggest toll on cities, were environmental and sanitation problems caused by the lack of infrastructure and municipal services, including the sewage system and water management, waste-collecting, transportation, electricity and drainage of rainwater. Contemporary statistics exposed that residents had numerous health problems, and the death toll in childbirth was as high as 56 per cent in some settlements.[58]

The state policy towards *gecekondu* areas stayed ambiguous between 1946 and 1980, swinging between demolition and legalization, and nothing prevented the continuing spread of these settlements. Parliament started discussing the '*gecekondu* problem' in Ankara as early as 1945.[59] Under a law of 1948, the City of Ankara was empowered to offer land to residents living in squatter houses, in order to put an end to illegal development. A law effective between 1953 and 1966 not only legalized the

Demolition of a *gecekondu*.

previously built houses all over the country, acting on the assumption that *gecekondu* was a temporary and superseded phenomenon, but also authorized municipalities to demolish any future settlements. The five-year development plans of the 1960s and '70s suggested that squatter housing should be destroyed only after the proper resettlement of residents. The law of 1966 defined three separate goals: 'improvement' of benign settlements, 'demolition' of unhealthy ones and 'prohibition' of future ones.[60] Throughout the 1970s, there were several armed battles between *gecekondu* residents and state officials over compulsory demolitions. Meanwhile copious amnesty laws in 1953, 1963, 1966 and 1976 legalized the previously built houses in specific neighbourhoods. It has not escaped the public that these amnesty laws were granted especially before elections, and that the political parties used *gecekondu* legalization as a campaign tool.

How did this happen? Were the forces of history so unavoidable that half the residents of big cities across Turkey had to live in illegal housing? Scholars have offered quite different explanations on the causes and effects of squatter settlements. *Gecekondus* have been perceived as either urban wounds or the outcome of a popular solution to the housing crises; as testimony to modern corruption or niches of self-help; as temporary structures that will disappear once immigrants are integrated into the city or as the third world's perpetual urbanization mode. Squatter settlements, coupled with anonymous contractor apartments, brought about the spontaneous growth of Turkish cities, making master plans increasingly irrelevant. The question remains: how come successive Turkish governments could not or did not prevent the growth of the *gecekondu* settlements? Was this the result of ignorance and miscalculation, even though all contemporary urban planning experts and architects were advising otherwise, or was it a conscious choice? Was the state helpless in the face of rapid modernization and urbanization, Cold War international politics, and its own citizens, who claimed land that did not belong to them? Or rather, did the state turn a blind eye to the *gecekondu* settlements' long-term impact in order to allocate the country's resources elsewhere? How can one explain why subsidized housing was used for the benefit of the upper-middle income groups, rather than rural immigrants? According to İlhan Tekeli, as self-built solutions to the workers' housing shortage, '*gecekondu* not only provided cheap labour for industry, but also reduced the resources allocated to urbanization, which could now be transferred to industrialization. *Gecekondu,* which was a problem from an urban planner's viewpoint, could hence be seen by an industrialist as a solution.'[61] Moreover, in a country where the right to the city was perceived as being given to the citizens by the state, successive governments used their authority to grant land ownership and legality in quite opportunistic ways. The illegal production of housing turned out to be quite convenient for the institutions that defined legality. In chapter Eight we will resume the account of the *gecekondu*'s transforming yet still paradigmatic effect on Turkish cities after the 1980s.

chapter six

Architecture under *Coups d'État*

Those who do not engage with society's problems are not architects or artists in the true sense.

Şevki Vanlı, 'Mimar, kişi ve toplum,' *Mimarlık ve Sanat*, 10 (1964), p. 18

The architect should know his rights and take his responsibilities in establishing the base for a new socio-economic structure and an open society.

Şevki Vanlı, 'Çevrenin Düzeni İçin,' *Mimarlık ve Sanat*, 7–8 (1963), p. 214

On 27 May 1960 a military coup interrupted the government and closed the Turkish parliament. Adnan Menderes, the first democratically elected prime minister, and two cabinet members were executed and a further fifteen politicians, including President Celal Bayar, were sentenced to death. The precarious democracy re-established in 1961 would be interrupted in 1971, and yet again nine years later with the violent military coup of 12 September 1980. The 1960s and '70s, the period squeezed between three *coups d'état*, were full of intense upheaval and accelerating battles between youth organizations motivated by the bipolar political values of the Cold War. In no other era were architects as politically engaged and as assertively vocal about their rights and responsibilities in matters of state.

Unlike the relatively submissive tone of their predecessors, a new generation of architects institutionalized the profession to raise their voice against the government. A few with busy practices stayed away from political commitment, but many architects of the time seem to have lived double lives: socialist revolutionaries in meetings of the Chamber of Architects (founded 1954) and on the streets, while also successful professionals in state-sponsored competitions and holding meetings with state officials and wealthy clients. This may be viewed as a contradiction, hypocrisy or, at best, an unresolved problem about the possibility of an architect's social commitment. Another interpretation, one that will be entertained here, may be to admit the blossoming nature of architecture in a context of debate and collective spirit. Ultimately the architects of this period could not effectively engage as much as they hoped with the problems of society as a whole, as was exposed most clearly in the accelerating

Cengiz Bektaş, Turkish Language Society, Ankara, 1973–8, interior atrium.

growth of *gecekondu* areas (see chapter Five) and the increasing social violence described below. Nonetheless, the fact that most architects enthusiastically volunteered to take responsibility for the society infiltrated their architectural values in numerous ways. This ranged from a distaste for the International Style, consciously or subconsciously associated with American cultural imperialism, to an emphasis on function that puts *human* use at the centre of architectural concerns; from an intellectualist urge to find the 'actual regional architecture', to an interest in historic preservation in the face of socio-economic trends that threatened the older fabric of cities. Placed in the perspective of the long history of modern architecture worldwide, this emphasis on the user, the context and the country's conditions might be nothing but a blending of architecture and the political spirit of the 1960s.

Critical Practice and the Politics of Organization

Despite the popular support it maintained between 1950 and 1960, many journalists, university students and faculty members criticized the Menderes government for censorship, oppression and state control. One of the architects' main dissatisfactions with the government concerned Istanbul's master plan and the accompanying excessive demolitions. In an editorial written as early as 1956, Zeki Sayar characterized the urban interventions under Menderes as an 'express demolition operation' (*yıldırım yıkma harekatı*), accusing the government of dismissing the professional expertise of architects and urban planners: 'The decision has been handed over totally from the city planner to the bureaucrat; demolitions and displacements are executed based on shallow observations on site, rather than a carefully planned project.'[1]

In this context many architects, publicly sharing their views in professional journals, supported the change of power after the coup without a hint of criticism against the interruption of democracy or against the military intervention – an intervention that would be dominant ın occasionally direct but permanently indirect ways for decades to come. As Ahmet İnsel noted, the legally secured control of the National Security Council (Milli Güvenlik Kurulu, founded in 1962) over the Parliament was nothing less than a form of military authoritarianism, despite the apparent democratic rule in Turkey.[2] Only by bracketing the paradoxes of this intrusion could the architects have hoped to put an end to the liberal capitalist tendencies of the Menderes period and to initiate the developmental ambitions of a welfare state.

The shift of power with the 1960 coup and the resulting new Constitution of 1961 redirected the emphasis towards industrialization, a self-sustaining economy and development. The challenge to manufacture the first Turkish car, the Devrim ('Revolution'), became the symbol of this new emphasis on industrialization, despite the prototype's tragic failure to operate for more than 200 metres on the day of its public launch in 1961. Even though this cancelled plans for its mass production, the Devrim project was a politically charged attempt to hold back the flood of imported cars, John Deere tractors or Mack trucks, and to prove that Turkey was capable of building a self-sufficient industry. The 1960s also witnessed the years of planned development (*planlı kalkınma*). Starting in 1963, five-year plans were institutionalized to increase Turkey's growth rate, infusing an air of conviction in progress, development, industrialization and scientific plans. Atatürk's motto 'reaching the level of contemporary civilization' (*muassır medeniyet seviyesine ulaşma*) was now rephrased as 'shaking off underdevelopment' (*az gelişmişlikten kurtulma*). Architects, too, enthusiastically took responsibility for this new state-sponsored developmental leap, even though disagreements with the actual practices of the government were soon to colour their discourses.

Many successful practising architects took full responsibility in the Chamber of Architects during this period, making the institution a major hub for intensive debates, not only on urban and architectural matters, but political subjects also. Even though they participated in the subcommittees of the State Planning Institution (Devlet Planlama Teşkilatı), which handled matters relating to architecture, the architects of the Chamber criticized the government for marginalizing their profession. Given that more than half the development plan's budget was reserved for the construction industry, they perceived themselves entitled to making more decisions about the country's future. Under the direction of Haluk Baysal, the Chamber made 'development' (*kalkınma*) its central topic in its publication *Mimarlık*, held meetings with the Prime Minister and parliament members, launched three books, more than 30 reports, four scholarly papers, seven media announcements and a photography exhibition in order to evaluate Turkey's failure in reaching her developmental targets.[3]

Should an architect directly or indirectly participate in politics? What is the professional limit of architectural engagement? Is it in designing buildings or should it rather be extended to the transformation of society's economic and political infrastructure as a whole? These questions over political commitment occupied architects throughout the 1960s and '70s in ways that had unprecedented consequences. The Chamber's regional director, Nevzat Erol, defended the association for 'proudly taking its responsibility for participating in shaking off underdevelopment . . . [since] the solutions to architectural problems were among the solutions to social, economic and cultural ones'.[4] Manfredo Tafuri's ideas on the

status of architecture under capitalism reverberated in *Mimarlık*. Even though Tafuri does not seem to have convinced Turkish architects to admit the impossibility of critical practice, as he concluded in *Architecture and Utopia*, his analysis exposing the relation between capitalism and modern architecture struck a chord.[5] For the architecture of the future, the future should have arrived; and many Turkish architects at this time were willing to participate in constructing the future society, rather than restrict themselves to the buildings of the present.

There were disagreements, however, over the level of political engagement. A group of architects around Vedat Dalokay defended more direct participation and a more severe critical tone, while Haluk Baysal rejected any direct association with a political party, and defined the association's role as a 'social service' (*toplum hizmeti*) presenting the state and the public with better architectural solu-

Cover of *Mimarlık* (professional journal of the Chamber of Architects) for the theme issue 'Turkey's Social Economy and Architecture' (1974), showing a protest march by architects.

tions within democratic principles.[6] This was ineffective and slow, according to his opponents: 'Turkish architects have to ditch being soft, throw away the sponge and take the stone, explain our mission to those who don't understand it. We have to demand our rights with force',[7] Dalokay asserted at the association's annual meeting in 1965. The polarization became even starker at the following year's meeting. Yılmaz İnkaya stood up: 'if our topic is political, we must race to it ... we cannot be happy living our sugar coated lives in this glass jar'; so did Dalokay: 'we have not fulfilled our task for the last ten years, we have always been a pushover (*pısırık*), inactive and lost in petty works'; Atilla Sorgun added: 'here, in this luxury hotel, in this congress, getting an education in respected schools with people's taxes, are we really in the service of the people? ... No, we are in the service of a privileged few.'[8] Dalokay's group finally took hold of the administration in 1966. After the mid-1960s the architects in the Chamber joined students and young professionals in embarking on a decade-long and an increasingly violent journey demanding nothing less than a socialist/communist revolution.

Revisionist Movements in Modern Form

While intense debates over the politicization of architecture and participation in social change occupied the Chamber, a new generation of architects and critics looked for alternatives to the International Style block, which had been a predominant choice during the 1950s. The discontent with the International Style proved to be a productive motivation that resulted in alternatives, which has led the architectural historian Atilla Yücel to characterize these decades as the birth of pluralism.[9]

For instance, the fragmented block, commonly known as the 'small, multi-part approach' (*küçük, çok parçalı yaklaşım*), became a common formula.[10] Nowhere is the opposition between the International Style and the fragmented block as explicitly visible as in the urban triangle on Atatürk Boulevard in Istanbul, whose three corners are held by the Municipality building (1953; architect Nevzat Erol, see chapter Four), the Manifaturacılar retail centre (1959; architects Doğan Tekeli, Sami Sisa and Metin Hepgüler), and the Zeyrek Social Security Agency (1962–4; architect Sedad Eldem). A canonic example of an International Style block asserting itself just steps away from the monumental Roman aqueduct, Erol's Municipality building was criticized for being a massive and forceful intrusion on Istanbul's historical wooden fabric. In contrast, the Manifaturacılar (small manufacturer) retail centre is composed of a series of lower-rise small blocks connected by outdoor galleries and courtyards. The courtyards open up to the Süleymaniye Mosque behind, establishing urban pedestrian links in between. The site plan and section drawings testify to a respect for the historical silhouette and an intention of infusing the large complex into its environment with small and dynamic steps. These make the building an indisputable milestone marking the departure from the canonic prismatic block in favour of a more fragmented typology and a more public-orientated urban morphology. Eldem followed the same approach in the Zeyrek Social Security Agency, just across the road from the Manifaturacılar centre. Despite the obvious stylistic differences between these two buildings, one built with flat terraces of reinforced concrete, the other with references to the 'old Turkish houses', both offer an alternative to the International Style block by fragmenting the building into smaller units that do not obstruct views of the surroundings or compete with the historical landmarks in the area. Eldem was particularly concerned about the Byzantine church of the Pantocrator (Zeyrek Camii), the Ottoman wooden houses and mosques, as it can be observed in his plan and section drawings. He designed urban paths and stairs that connect Atatürk Boulevard to the wooden houses on the slope behind, as well as a two-level inner street that joins parts of the complex to each

Doğan Tekeli,
Sami Sisa and
Metin Hepgüler,
Manifaturacılar
retail centre,
Istanbul, 1959;
two site diagrams
and a photograph.

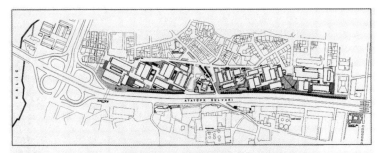

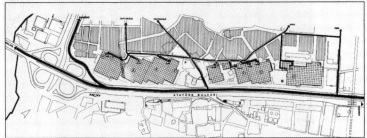

opposite: Wooden
houses and Nevzat
Erol's Municipality
building; photo
by Ara Güler.

Sedad Eldem,
Zeyrek Social
Security Agency;
Istanbul, 1962–4;
two site diagrams
and a photograph.

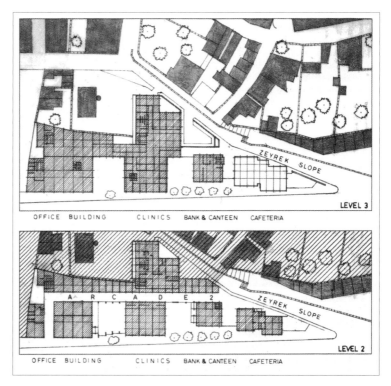

OFFICE BUILDING   CLINICS   BANK & CANTEEN   CAFETERIA

Roof detail of the
Zeyrek Social
Security Agency
at Istanbul; photo by
M. Pehlivanoğlu.

other. (The shops along the interior street were later converted to offices.) On the facade he used modular windows with precast vertical beams and tile parapets, which referred to the wooden structural frame of the 'old Turkish houses'. The flat roof detail with an extending eave both makes a historical reference to the 'old Turkish houses' and accentuates the modern horizontality of the building while not blocking the view behind. The Zeyrek building, which received an Aga Khan award in 1986, has been recognized as Eldem's contextualist turn, since the ideal, rationalized type of the 'Turkish house' transforms in conformity to a given context.[11] A similar consideration for the urban context guided Sevinç and Şandor Hadi's Milli Reasürans Complex in Istanbul, which provided a large covered public space along a busy street, while inner pedestrian walkways with retail units created shortcuts between the existing streets.

The Faculty of Architecture at the Middle East Technical University, designed by Altuğ & Behruz Çinici, stands as another memorable building composed of fragmented small blocks. After an architectural competition, the architects undertook the design of the METU campus in 1961.

Sevinç and Şandor Hadi, Milli Reassurans Complex, Istanbul, 1985–92.

This was a new state university built on the outskirts of Ankara with American support, but it soon subversively became the major locus for socialist student movements. The campus has a pedestrian spine (*alle*), 1.5 kilometres long, connecting the faculty buildings on one side and the administrative and social buildings on the other, all set back from the *alle* and dispersed in the overall area as fragmented blocks. A large pine forest of unprecedented size and microclimatic effect was also planted in the campus. While the *alle,* the carefully thought-out paths and the landscaping bring the buildings together, the buildings themselves do not give the impression of being the work of a single hand, but seem rather like experiments with diverse forms. The Faculty of Architecture extends onto the site as one or two storey fragments with square ground plans. The studios, faculty and administrative offices and generous common spaces are distributed in an ad hoc manner, without imposing a predetermined prismatic form on the programme. Circulation between the various parts is equally handled with spacious double-height common spaces that flow into each other without a dominant spine. Diffused daylight enters the space from either fully transparent walls or narrow strips of glass, skylights and courtyards. The first exposed reinforced concrete building in Turkey, the building's long spans also contributed to the progress of structural engineering.

The new generation of architects during this period secured important commissions from the state institutions through architectural competitions. Despite the sheer number of competitions, which one might have expected would open opportunities for different approaches, it is surprising to observe the lack of diversity and the dominance of the fragmented block in the winning projects and entries. The contemporary critics Zeki

Altuğ & Behruz Çinici, METU Campus, Ankara, 1961–70, photograph of the *alle*.

Altuğ and Behruz Çinici, METU Faculty of Architecture, Ankara, 1961–70; interior photograph and plan.

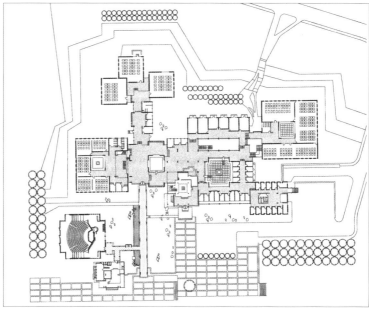

Sayar and Enis Kortan, as well as members of the Birleşmiş Mimarlar Ortaklığı (United Architects Partnership), questioned the competitions, listing such problems as unrealistic briefs, incongruity between the competition requirements and the winning projects, the dominance of the

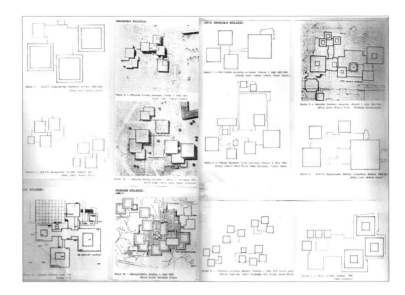

Enis Kortan's scheme showing the domineering status of the fragmented block during the 1960s.

same group of architects appearing as either jury members or competitors in different cases, and the consequent uniformity of style. This made the competitions a commission-granting power mechanism (even though some projects were not executed) that usually favoured the same group of architects and style, rather than a medium that supported research and creative leaps.[12] The explicit dominance of the fragmented block in the architectural competitions of the 1960s suggests that this approach soon became a homogenizing norm, a magic formula that was perceived fit for almost any building, regardless of the programme, climate, user or urban context.[13] Composed of blocks with square ground plans arranged on the site as an abstract composition on a grid without a prescriptive form, these projects were later ridiculed by Şevki Vanlı:

> This [design method] involved placing five to ten squares on the site plan that corresponded to the parts of the programme in a way that looked like a nice Mondrian painting. We all know how such projects were designed. First, one calculates the square metres for the halls, classrooms and studios of the given project, then one cuts out squares that corresponds to these areas, and then one starts playing to find a place for each of them so that they form a nice composition [in plan].[14]

A excessive emphasis on function (*işlev*) attracts attention in the jury reports and architects' declarations at this time. These buildings were not necessarily more or less 'functional' than their predecessors, and yet the architects' emphasis on function deserves a closer look despite, or perhaps because of, the contradictions it exposes. Behruz Çinici himself did not offer much explanation for his projects other than declaring that they were journeys into finding the best form of the building through the empirical experience of sketching.[15] 'The true value of architecture is space. The principal function is the human being', as he noted in a deceptively commonsense declaration.[16] The fragmented block was often compared to the prismatic block and advocated for its 'human scale' (simultaneously associating the American-inspired International Style block as anti-human), for its dynamism and flexibility, for its easy adaptability to nature, for avoiding boring corridors, and for generating case-specific results that emerged from the functional requirements of the programme. Beyond the fragmented block, functional concern had become an almost self-evident principle for this generation. The architect and writer Cengiz Bektaş often stressed his 'inside out' design process.[17] Contemporary critic and historian Enis Kortan exposed the contradictions in the perceived functionalism of these projects. Fragmented blocks that lost heat from many surfaces, such as were employed from Antalya to Erzurum, from Poland to Brazil, were hardly fit for all climates; the lack of open plan was hardly flexible or suitable for future extensions; square plans were not well orientated in relation to the sun; sprawling blocks on the site were not economical and lacked efficient circulation schemes; the exterior facades were hardly 'true' reflections of the architectural structure or the interior functions.[18] Nonetheless, the fragmented block seems to have been perceived as a magic formula for all projects, places and users, mainly because it gave material form to the reaction against the International Style block.

In addition to the fragmented block, a new interest in 'non-rational' and 'organic' architecture grew during this time as another way of breaking away from the prismatic block. In 1967 the architectural historian and critic Bülent Özer published an article in which he differentiated between two competing modern philosophers: Henri Poincaré, who emphasized reason and science, as opposed to Henri Bergson, who relied on intuition.[19] Özer also associated artworks and buildings with these two trajectories: the grids of Mondrian and the right-angled, universal (non-place specific) forms of Bauhaus, Loos and Mies van der Rohe expressed the 'rationality' of the first; while the free-form, case-specific buildings of Aalto, Häring and Scharoun expressed the 'non-rationality' and 'organicism' of the second. Examples of the latter trajectory that offered an alternative to the dominance of reason and science, Özer suggested, also existed in Turkey, such as Ünal Demiraslan and Ruşen

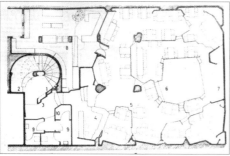

Ünal Demiraslan and Ruşen Dora. Project for the Turkish Pavilion at New York World's Fair, 1962.

Şevki Vanlı, Alpay Night Club, Ankara, 1967, plan.

Dora's project for the Turkish Pavilion at the New York World's Fair (1962) and Levent Aksüt and Yaşar Marulyalı's Dumlupınar Memorial (1963). While the former stood out with its triangular forms, acute angles and expressive roofs, the latter's modest scale and non-object orientated quality, where individuals could walk in the sculpture – an approach that would be conceptualized in Europe in the following years as a counter-monument – distinguished it from the usual state memorials.

At the same time Şevki Vanlı, a student of Giovanni Michelucci and a vocal admirer of Frank Lloyd Wright, was promoting organic architecture in Ankara as an alternative to the dominant taste, exemplifying his approach with his designs for the Tandoğan Student Dorm (1967) and the Alpay Night Club (1967), which stood out owing to their fragmented forms, and to their acute angles and circular surfaces, respectively. A group of architects and critics thus aimed to participate in the parallel debates that were taking place around organic architecture in Europe. Bruno Zevi's and Rolf Gutbrod's lectures at Istanbul Technical University in the late 1950s made an impact on the new generation.[20] Two new hotels – the Büyük Ankara Hotel (1958–65; architects Marc Saugey and Yüksel Okan) and the Istanbul Taksim Hotel (later the Sheraton, 1959–74; architects Kemal Ahmet Aru, Hande Suher, M. Ali Handan and team) – illustrated the new directions in hotel architecture, away from the two-sided prismatic block of the pervasive 'Hiltonism' of the 1950s to more angular, crystalline forms with facades facing in multiple directions. In the Maçka Hotel in Istanbul (1966; architect Yılmaz Sanlı), the soft detachment from the horizontal prism gave the opportunity to orientate each room towards the view. The Sabancı Girls' Dorm (1977; architects Fethi Dağlık and Metin Eren) was designeed to rise as a fragmented prism on the skyline of the south eastern city of Adana, where each room was expressed on the outside as a separate vertical block with tilted roofs. The Intercontinental Hotel in Taksim, Istanbul (later the Marmara, 1977; architect Tali Köprülü) was one of the last examples of skyscraper modernism. However, it was not through its architecture that the hotel made its mark on the collective memory, but it was from the

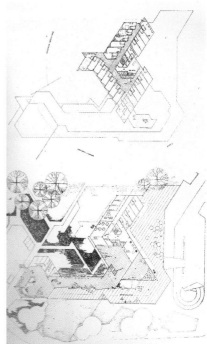

Marc Saugey and
Yüksel Okan, Büyük
Ankara Hotel, Ankara,
1958–65.

Kemal Ahmet Aru,
Hande Suher, M. Ali
Handan and team,
Istanbul Taksim Hotel
(later Sheraton),
Istanbul, 1959–74,
ground and typical
floor plans.

windows of the empty building that unidentified gunmen started the
violent killings that took place during a political rally on 1 May 1977.[21]

Architecture as an Intellectual Discipline and 'Actual Regionalism'

Architectural periodicals flourished and diversified during this period.
Arkitekt (1931–80) continued to display recent projects under Sayar's
editorship, while *Mimarlık* (1963–) became the voice of the Chamber of
Architects; *Akademi* (1964) was the platform for the Academy of Fine
Arts, and *Mimarlık ve Sanat* (1961–4) provided a forum where a group of
young scholars expanded the boundaries of the profession to an intellectual discipline. In the mission statement, the editors of *Mimarlık ve Sanat*
promised a publication that would fill in the perceived gap in intellectual
discussions and provide an informed understanding of historical and
contemporary artistic movements, as well as of Turkey's social and economic conditions.[22] In the pages of *Mimarlık ve Sanat*, Doğan Kuban and
Bülent Özer published articles on European and Turkish architectural history, while simultaneously defending a new theory of 'actual regionalism'.

'Copying forms from the West' (*kopyacılık*) had become a significant concern during this period, especially in the writings of these authors, who criticized unnamed Turkish architects for simply imitating Western forms without testing their appropriateness for the country's conditions. Özer invited architects to recognize that architecture was more than a season's fashion, and that they should stop copying forms from foreign journals.[23] Similarly, Kuban said:

> [Frank Lloyd] Wright becomes meaningful in the context of American individualism, in Whitman's, Thoreau's, Emerson's teachings; in order to evaluate Le Corbusier, one needs to be familiar with the universal abstraction of the Greco-Roman world, one needs to know cubism, the realist tradition . . . We all know these did not exist in our own architectural world. And they did not need to. However, we observe forms that are influenced from these architects in the most important commissions. In a way, we are applying nineteenth-century European eclecticism to twentieth-century forms.[24]

In a series of articles written in 1961–2, Kuban defined the new Regionalism as a response to 'environmental conditions' (*çevre şartları*), which he elaborated as a rational and candid evaluation of a country's facts.[25] He insisted that Actual Regionalism would be different from the imitation of regional forms, from historicism, folklorism and nationalism, or from any version of *a priori* formalism, a category in which he included the International Style. Kuban explained Actual Regionalism in a number of incongruous ways, including searching for inspiration in Anatolia (paradoxically similar to the metonymic regionalism he was opposing),[26] and resisting the International Style because it reduced architecture to technology and conflated sameness with universality. His justification relied on the premise of the human need to strive for difference, whether it was a regional or individual one. Even when technical advances would make climatic factors and regional materials obsolete, artistic motivation would have demanded cultural and individual difference in architecture: 'If universalism was absolute, art would not have existed.'[27]

Özer, too, defined Actual Regionalism as a third way against the formalism of both conventional regionalist tendencies and imitations of Western forms in Turkey. The former was a romantic appraisal of historical forms that failed to confront the actual problems of the region itself; the latter confused universalism with monotony and formulaic solutions (*şablonculuk*) that disseminated, to use his example, Neufert's architectural norms for the Western male to the rest of the world, regardless of physiological, psychological or environmental differences.[28] As a result he opposed a formalist 'regionalism', but advocated an 'actual regional architecture' that depended on the understanding of what he called the 'actual data' (gerçek veriler).[29]

The question of belonging never ceased to be a concern for Turkish artists and architects throughout the twentieth century. This was itself predicated on how they perceived their relation to the West and so distinguished Turkish modernism from Western. Kuban and Özer, despite their disagreements, did not advocate Actual Regionalism because they refused to learn the Western tradition, but because they embraced it as architectural historians. Treating architecture as an intellectual and conscious discipline called for a deeper understanding of its history and hence an actual regional architecture that refused to imitate it. They often launched this position as a truly modern path, rather than a blind copy of either International Style or historical forms. In that, their position was not too dissimilar to the critical regionalism advocated by Kenneth Frampton.[30]

The growing discursive practice also resulted in the birth of architectural preservation and city planning, hereafter conceptualized respectively as an architectural specialization and a separate discipline. Rapid urbanization, large-scale road construction and real estate profits had put the historical urban fabric at risk, causing the demolition of countless wooden houses and historical landmarks. While the Menderes government was the usual culprit in the architects' opinion, Kuban was one of the first to mention the necessity of architectural preservation as a specialized area.[31] The first programme in architectural preservation was established at METU in Ankara under Cevat Erder in 1964; Kuban in ITU founded the Institute of Architectural History and Restoration (MTRE) in 1974.

With the exception of Mülkiye under Ernst Reuter, the first official City Planning Department was established also at METU in 1961. In the course of the 1960s Mimarlık included an unusual number of articles about urban problems and master plans, and the Chamber organized extensive conferences and special issues on city planning including a congress on Istanbul's regional development (22–27 April 1967) and a seminar on Istanbul's planning (2–3 May 1968).[32] No other project sparked as much controversy in both architectural and public media as Turgut Cansever's urban design for Beyazıt Square. Cansever had already made a name with his regionalizing gestures in the Anadolu Club in Istanbul (with Abdurrahman Hancı, see chapter Four) and the Karatepe Open Air Museum (1957–61), where exposed concrete protective shelters were quietly inserted over the historical remnants with minimal touches. In his scheme for Beyazıt Square, Cansever prioritized pedestrian accessibility and circulation in the square, diverting vehicular traffic between Beyazıt and Eminönü to an underground tunnel and so restoring the plaza's nineteenth-century character. Conceived on three levels without a definable form, the square unified the Beyazıt Mosque and the entrance gate to the University of Istanbul. The multi-levelled informal square corrected the gateway's previous dominance over the area and restored an urban ground for the mosque, which hitherto had been isolated from the area.[33] Some criticized the project for failing to solve comprehensive traffic and parking problems, and for the lack of an identifiable architectural character,[34] while the Chamber seriously objected to it on the grounds that Istanbul's master plan should have taken priority over piecemeal decisions on Beyazıt Square. In response, the editors of *Mimarlık ve Sanat* criticized the Chamber for failing to define how a master plan could have annihilated the decisions of this particular design and, more severely, for penalizing anyone in disagreement with their own ideas.[35] The project continued to be the subject of

Turgut Cansever,
Urban Design for
Beyazıt Square,
Istanbul, 1961,
competition project.

political rivalry over zoning laws between governments.[36] The square became a locus of student protests throughout the 1960s and '70s: it was in front of the university gate that the legendary leftist student leader Deniz Gezmiş organized the student boycott in 1968 that demanded more democratic rights and student participation in university governance. Ten years later, on 16 March 1978, a bomb killed seven people and injured forty more in front of this gate, while the police watched the killings without intervening.

The Architecture of Development

In the developmentalist zeal of the 1960s and '70s many architects devoted their careers to the advancement of construction materials and techniques. The Construction Industry Centre (YEM) was founded in 1967 and has continued to contribute to architectural culture to the present day with numerous publications and exhibitions under its director Doğan Hasol. It was in these two decades that exposed reinforced concrete, large-span iron and steel construction, and prefabricated materials were first tried out in buildings. Rather than being imported, construction materials were now produced in Turkey by industrial firms such as Alarko, Koç and Sabancı, whose owners would soon become powerful businessmen and the new bourgeoisie of the following decades. National pride over producing the country's own commodities was publicly promoted in 'local goods week' (*yerli malı haftası*), and the new buildings frequently appeared in advertisements for locally produced construction materials. For instance, an Alarko advertisement reads: 'Do not hesitate about constructing your buildings in Turkey. With more than 60 engineers, 500 technicians and workers, and 17 years of experience, Alarko will certainly help you.'[37]

Many industrial buildings were designed and built in the big cities during this period, especially in Istanbul, Izmit and Adana. Those by Doğan Tekeli and Sami Sisa set the standard for Turkey's construction industry. Factories designed by the partners and built in the late 1960s for Istanbul's new industrial zones, which acted as magnets for the city's informal growth (see chapter Eight), included the Neyir Textiles Factory in Levent (1966), Northern Electrics Telephone Factory in Ümraniye, the United German Medicine Factories and the General Electrics Factory (both in Topkapı), and Corrugated Cardboard Factory in Gebze.[38] The Steel Cable and Wire Industry Factory (1968; architect Metin Hepgüler) was another example that experimented with the adoption of iron and steel as possible construction materials in Turkey.[39] These factories explored fast, efficient and affordable construction systems with standardized

DYO paint advertise-
ment with a Sheraton
Hotel image, c. 1975.

materials and repeatable procedures. Among these, Tekeli and Sisa's
Lassa Factory in İzmit, close to Istanbul (1975–7), demonstrated their
long experience and represented the highest standards of industrial
architecture in Turkey. Making use of the fastest and most economical
construction system available, the building was designed with prefabricated columns, beams and facade panels. Exposed ventilation pipes
circle the facade down to eyelevel in order to give a 'human scale' to the
factory, in the architects' own words.[40] Another architect, Aydın Boysan,
developed his characteristic factory aesthetic of the 1960s and early

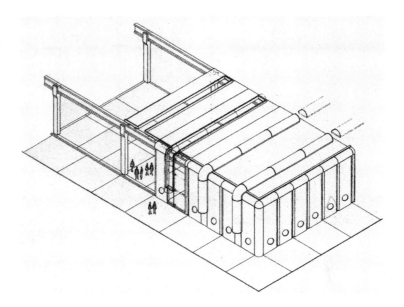

Doğan Tekeli and
Sami Sisa, Lassa
Factory, İzmit, 1975–7,
axonometric drawing.

1970s using a reinforced concrete structure with steel trusses and tubular steel space frames for the large spans of the factory floor, expressing them on the exterior as a cascading continuity of triangular roof forms like folded plates. Ample daylight is admitted into the main workspaces through the roof and through the triangular openings of the roof, as illustrated, for example, in his Arçelik Washing Machine Factory in Çayırova, Istanbul (illustrated overleaf), where brick exterior walls are used as infill between the reinforced concrete columns. The same signature aesthetic of folded plates, as used by Boysan in the İpek Paper Factory in Karamürsel, İzmit (1970), and the perforated steel beams employed for the large span of the factory floor of his Nasaş Aluminium Plant, İzmit (1970), anticipate the industrial aesthetic of 1980s High-Tech in the architectural culture at large.

In addition to these factories, new building types and a number of architectural landmarks became the tropes of national development. Hospitals, for instance, formed another ubiquitous building type, marking Turkey's commitment to self-sufficiency and social health care. At this time Yılmaz Sanlı and Yılmaz Tuncer became expert at the functional and technical requirements of hospital design, while their designs for Gülhane Hospital, Ankara (1962–), and Beyoğlu Emergency Hospital, Istanbul (1965–) are the most memorable examples. In the Agricultural Product Offices, Ankara (1964–8; architects Cengiz Bektaş, Vedat Özsan and Oral Vural), prefabricated facade elements were applied for the first

Aydın Boysan, Arçelik washing-machine factory, Çayırova, Istanbul, 1968, exterior and interior views; photos by Cemal Emden.

time in Turkey, which considerably reduced the construction time by eliminating five intermediary steps.[41] Standardization of building materials was a common concern, as Orhan Şahinler pointed out in explaining the Istanbul Trade Centre, even though the building was designed in 1963 but not completed until 1971. He advocated a Miesian curtain-wall aesthetics in order to 'build with the minimum amount of construction details'.[42] The Turkish Language Society building in Ankara (1973–8; architect Cengiz Bektaş) is also noteworthy for its extensive glass walls, which cope with the technological difficulties of a tall, free-standing glass surface without the support of slabs (see page 170). Each level of the glass surface is set back inversely to avoid leaks.

In addition to the skyscrapers mentioned above and in chapter Four, İş Bank (1976–8; architects Ayhan Böke and Yılmaz Sargın) made its mark as the tallest building in Ankara and on account of its structural ambitions. An open plan office without intruding structural columns, the elongated hexagonal building has a central core, load-bearing peripheral walls, rounded corners and perforated strips. The exposed reinforced concrete was constructed with fire-retardant materials; heat and smoke detectors were placed throughout the building in case of fire.[43] The Tercüman Newspaper Offices, Istanbul (1974; architects Çilingiroğlu and Tunca) was another daring technological statement with its unprecedented cantilevers extending in two different directions from a point

Orhan Şahinler,
Istanbul Trade Centre,
Istanbul, 1963–71.

pillar. Nowhere was the representative aspirations of a high-tech building as clearly visible, however, as in the winning entry for İzmit's shoreline competition in 1977: designed by Fatih Gorbon, Ertun Hızırlıoğlu and Yalçın Gültekin, the Congress and Exhibition Halls were conceived as a mega-structure with large trusses.

These technological ambitions were never perceived as internalizing a Eurocentric conviction about the necessity of techno-scientific progress. On the contrary, they were pursued for the sake of national prosperity, presented as 'our way of development'. For this reason, it is not uncommon to come across statements by architects in which they use regionalist or historicist references to explain progress in the construction industry. For instance, Bektaş stated that the multi-level atrium behind the tall glass wall in the Turkish Language Society building was a modern interpretation of the plan typology in traditional wooden 'Turkish houses' with outdoor *sofas*.[44] A similar tendency can be observed in the Turkish History Society building, Ankara (*c.* 1965; architects Turgut Cansever and Ertur Yener). The three-storey atrium of this building with perforated wooden screens (*kafes*) has been perceived as the quintessential example of the historicism that would be predominant in the 1980s and '90s. Admittedly this courtyard was a late addition to an originally U-shaped design for functional reasons, and it was interpreted as a historicist reference to *madrasa* plans only afterwards. In its early phases, the architects

 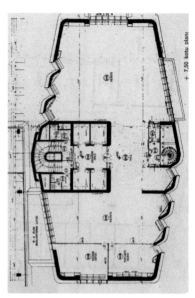

Ayhan Böke, Yılmaz
Sargın, Iş Bank,
Ankara, 1976–8,
photo and plan.

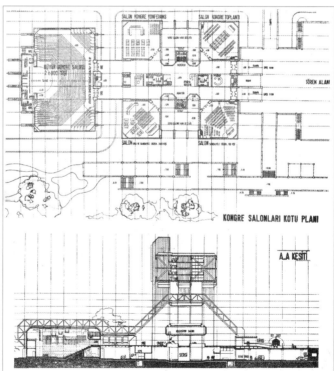

Fatih Gorbon, Ertun
Hızırlıoğlu and Yalçın
Gültekin, İzmit Shore
Line Competition
Project, İzmit, 1977,
Congress and
Exhibition halls.

rather concerned themselves with the constructional challenges of exposed reinforced concrete and decent details in stone cladding.[45]

These aspirations for developmental leaps were taking place, however, in a country that was steadily getting poorer during the late 1970s and facing violent struggles between groups with opposing views about Turkey's political future. In a country burdened by the global economic and oil crises of the mid-1970s, where no political party could reach a majority in parliament or maintain a lasting government; in a country that was experiencing up to eleven hours of blackouts a day, unable to provide heating in cold winters, and struggling with the lack of primary supplies, including basic agricultural materials, it was hard to maintain such industrial and technological ambitions. In Behruz Çinici's words, even the completion of a building's construction had to be acknowledged as a rare accomplishment in such conditions.[46] With the Soviet occupation of Afghanistan and the Islamic Revolution in Iran in 1979, the Western bloc focused more attention on the 'region'; and a committee composed of American, British, German and French delegates decided to allocate urgent economic aid to Turkey on condition that she accepted International Monetary Fund (IMF) control and adopted liberal economic procedures, a proposal that was, as expected, objected to by left-wing factions. The IMF and Turkey would soon settle on an unusually large aid plan, and the era of self-sufficient development and financial autonomy would come to an absolute close after the military coup in 1980.

Turgut Cansever and Ertur Yener, Turkish History Society, Ankara, c. 1965.

Istanbul Bosphorus
Bridge in 2011; photo
by Cemal Emden.

1968–80: A Bridge in Istanbul and a Mosque in Ankara

The military coup in 1980 would terminate much more than the years
of self-sufficient development, including an ambitious and politicized
architectural culture. In 1968, Vedat Dalokay released the annual report
of the Chamber, which contrasted the organization in the 1950s, described
as allegedly an 'introverted and passive professional organization, only
concerned with its own ego', with its current condition, which was promoted as a responsible association 'interested in the country's problems
as a whole'.[47] According to Zeki Sayar, many architects were withdrawing
from the Chamber due to this over-politicization, which resulted in the
ignorance of problems more directly related to architecture.[48] Nonetheless, a large number of professionals came together in the association to
openly support leftist movements throughout the 1970s. These architects'
commitment to 'the people' was not without its paradoxes, as was most
openly exposed in the debates concerning the Bosphorus Bridge in Istanbul and the Kocatepe Mosque in Ankara.

The Chamber mobilized all of its resources to oppose the construction
of a bridge over the Bosphorus, sending out media declarations, organizing conferences, publishing a book and even taking the issue to court
in 1968.[49] The architects and the Chamber claimed that the decision to
build the bridge was not based on a proper scientific study of Istanbul's
master plan; the construction would cost three times more than claimed;
and new bridges would soon be necessary as the first one would determine the city's growth. The Chamber seems to have been specifically
offended by being left out of the decision-making process. The controversy
soon became a heated public debate and determined the public image of

architects for years to come. While the opposition leader Bülent Ecevit and the influential leftist journalists İlhan Selçuk and Nadir Nadi vocally endorsed the Chamber's position,[50] other journalists ridiculed it: 'Unfortunately, no one listens to the bright ideas of these professionals, neither the Turkish nation, nor its legitimate representatives, nor the hundreds of truck drivers who are waiting in line to cross the Bosphorus.'[51]

Another big controversy took place over the Kocatepe Mosque in Ankara. Modern mosque design had become a sporadic concern during this period. Cengiz Bektaş's Etimesgut Mosque in Ankara (1964–8), for one, was composed of a floating flat roof, free-standing walls that let in light through narrow strips at the edges, and dynamic stairs in a rectangular perforated box that replaced the minaret. Suggested as an alternative to the 'technically and architecturally inadequate' vernacular mosques spreading across small towns and villages, Bektaş advocated more professional interest in modernizing the mosque.[52] No other mosque at this time, however, sparked controversy as much as Vedat Dalokay's design for the Kocatepe Mosque (1957). Composed of a structurally innovative shell dome standing on four corners and four spaceship-like minarets, the unconventional design was received enthusiastically by secular architects, but groups more closely associated with religion reacted otherwise. In 1967 the foundations of Dalokay's design were dynamited to be replaced by Hüsrev Tayla and Fatin Uluengin's direct replica of sixteenth-century classical mosques, most notably Sinan's Şehzade Mosque in Istanbul (see page 219). Predictably the Chamber mobilized heavy protests against the new design over copyright laws and architectural revivalism, filed ethical misconduct complaints against Tayla and Uluengin, and refused to authorize the project.[53] Doğan Kuban criticized the revivalist project as a

Vedat Dalokay,
Kocatepe Mosque
Project, Ankara, 1957.

betrayal of Ottoman architecture and Sinan himself, who always aimed at
structural innovation. Building a replica of a sixteenth-century mosque
in the twentieth century was, according to Kuban, no less than a 'culture
problem': it exposed the gap in the lives of those whose comfort level was
up to date but whose 'taste level' lingered four centuries behind.[54] The
paradox seems to have escaped the majority of secular architects that this
revivalism and 'bad taste' was the choice of the mosques' users, a concern
one would expect to be valid in the user-orientated spirit of the 1960s.

Such examples must have led the architectural critic Uğur Tanyeli to
describe this period as an age of tautological discussions:

These discussions did not try to understand, conceptualize or analyze large-scale problems by exploring new theoretical frameworks, but rather to solve the stereotypically defined problems with equally stereotypical, prearranged political standards. In other words, in the intellectual atmosphere of this period, architects believed they already knew the solutions to the problems . . . and all they had to do was to get rid of the conservative (*gerici)* obstacles that prevented the solutions . . . This also meant that between 1960 and 1980, neither architecture nor politics was truly discussed.[55]

Tautological or not, the controversy over the Kocatape Mosque was one episode in a much longer and more severe battle between *devrimci* (revolutionary/socialist) movements on the left ('communist' in their opponents' terminology) and *ülkücü* (idealist/radical nationalist) movements on the right ('fascist', according to their opponents). The increasingly violent battles, countless illegal political organizations and armed street fights divided the country into two, including the professional organizations that supported either of the ideologies. The Chamber of Architects undoubtedly placed itself on the side of the left-wing revolutionaries, supported the student protests at the universities in 1968, and joined the Revolutionary Education Front in September 1968 with a committee composed of prominent architects including Maruf Önal, Vedat Dalokay, Turgut Cansever, Demirtaş Ceyhun, Yılmaz İnkaya and Ergun Unaran.[56]

On 12 March 1971 the military intervened once again. Rather than closing the parliament as a whole, as in the last coup, members of parliament and army officials negotiated over a staged government under military supervision. The coup resulted in the arrest of the revolutionary student leader Deniz Gezmiş and two comrades, who were sentenced to death, and hanged soon after, for such comparatively minor crimes as protesting about the arrival of the US navy in Istanbul and throwing marines into the Bosphorus, for kidnapping four American soldiers who they later set free, for carrying guns that they never used to kill, and for a bank robbery – crimes that did not legally require death penalties. Rather than pacifying the leftist movements, Deniz Gezmiş's execution mobilized the students, intellectuals, song writers and poets. Author Erdal Öz's touching account describing the three men's last days in prison and moments of their execution made a deep impression in the collective memory.[57] In the poet Can Yücel's words, Gezmiş had run the best hundred metres of the long marathon to revolution; and as the fastest of them all, he was the first to face the rope.[58]

Chamber of Architects and Engineers (TMMOB) in the Political Rally of 1 May 1977 in Taksim Square, Istanbul.

After this event, the armed battles increased. Groups fought over city streets and claimed them as their own; *gecekondu* neighborhoods, which by definition were illegal in the eye of the state, became one of the main targets of this race to occupation. In 1977, when tanks rolled into the *gecekondu* settlement in Ümraniye (the name of which was later changed to Mustafa Kemal Neighbourhood), six residents were killed, hundreds were injured and countless houses were demolished. On 1 May the same year, DISK (the Revolutionary Workers' Union) organized one of the largest political rallies in Turkey's history, gathering hundreds of thousands of men, women and children in Taksim Square in Istanbul. As contemporary photos testify, the Chamber of Architects and Engineers participated on the front line of the rally, standing just in front of the AKM and holding up one of the largest, reddest banners. Soon after the rally began, unidentified gunmen started shooting from the buildings around Taksim, and turned the urban square into a war zone, leaving 34 citizens dead and hundreds injured.[59]

On 12 September 1980 the military, under the leadership of General Kenan Evren, intervened once again in an especially violent manner, ostensibly to end the rise in terrorism within the country.[60] Evren's regime imposed martial law, enforcing excessive levels of censorship and disciplinary methods. It became illegal to publish any declaration criticizing the regime, or any international news criticizing Turkey; all professional organizations, including the Chamber of Architects, were closed down; all magazines and journals, including *Arkitekt* and *Mimarlık*, were closed down (*Arkitekt*, which had been active since 1931, never resumed publication); organized sports activities were forbidden and there were also curbs on being too exuberant at weddings, going out on the streets after midnight, walking anywhere except on pavements and giving children names with leftist connotations. Soon after, universities lost their autonomy and textbooks for the entire curriculum were rewritten. The constitution that was introduced after this coup eliminated many civil rights. Overall, according to the numbers circulated today, as a result of the military coup of 1980 a total of 7,000 citizens were charged with offences that carried the death penalty, of whom 517 were sentenced to death and 50 were executed; 300 citizens died in prison, possibly following torture; 1,683,000 citizens were filed as 'suspicious'; 650,000 citizens were placed under observation; 230,000 citizens were taken to court; 30,000 were fired from their jobs; 14,000 lost their rights to citizenship; 23,677 professional organizations were closed; 937 films were banned; 400 journalists were sentenced to a total of 3,315 years in prison; newspapers were censured to publish for a total of 300 days; 39 tons of newspapers and magazines were destroyed.[61] When democracy and liberal capitalism was reinstituted with the elections that brought Turgut Özal to power three years later, an apolitical and submissive Turkey emerged from the ashes of these spirited but increasingly violent decades. It is impossible to understand and assess these decades fully when the inner workings of Cold War politics still remain hidden behind the classified documents of the state archives. It is to be hoped that future scholars will be better equipped to decipher the course of events.

chapter seven

Postmodern Landscapes in Post-Kemalist Turkey

> Money, capital, labour has no religion, nation, race or country. Money is like mercury. It flows wherever it finds a suitable channel, a secure ground for itself. If you can prepare this ground, it will come to you; otherwise it will flow somewhere else. We are determined to prepare this ground.
>
> Prime Minister Recep Tayyip Erdoğan, Speech at G-20 summit, 2009[1]

The period following the military coup of 1980 bears the legacy of the late Turgut Özal, Prime Minister and President, who initiated a spectacular transformation of Turkey along the economically neo-liberal and culturally conservative paths set by Ronald Reagan and Margaret Thatcher in the West. Labelled 'the third Republic'[2] by the historian Erik Zürcher, this period saw the dismantling of statist and protectionist economic policies in favour of full integration with global markets and an accelerated push towards Turkey's decades-old (albeit increasingly less realistic) ambition to join the EU. Perhaps best symbolized by the privatization of a national icon, the state industrial enterprises of Sümerbank (see chapter One), this era marked the end of nationalist developmentalism and import substitution policies that had dominated the Turkish economy since the early republic. Instead, it reorientated the country unequivocally towards the free market, global capitalism and export-orientated production – trends that have continued even more vigorously under the Islamist Justice and Development Party (AKP) government since 2002. Turkey's total exports increased from less than $3 billion in 1980 to $20 billion in 1990, reaching more than $100 billion in 2007. The share of manufactured goods in total exports rose from about 35 per cent of all exports in 1979 to more than 95 per cent in 2007.[3] In the same period the country's population grew from 45 million in 1980 to 56 million in 1990 and more than 75 million in 2010, with a median age of only 28.[4] Today, by all economic indicators, Turkey is among the most promising 'emerging markets' in the global economy, favourably compared with other rising economic powers like Brazil or Argentina.[5] Turkish products and businesses compete successfully in international markets, especially textiles, cement, glass and ceramic industries, as well as a robust construction

Von Gerkan, Marg und Partner with Yılmaz Gedik / Koray Construction Company, Karum Shopping Mall, Ankara, 1988–91; photo by Esra Akcan.

sector building extensively in Russia, the Middle East and elsewhere. At the same time, however, the wealthiest 20 per cent of the population took 47 per cent of gross national income in 2008, while the share of the poorest 20 per cent remained at a mere 6 per cent, with unofficial unemployment numbers estimated to be close to 20 per cent.[6] Recent research in Istanbul compellingly demonstrates that the same processes that produce new forms of wealth under neo-liberal policies (the rise in the share of the service and finance sectors in the overall economy at the expense of industry, the post-Fordist fragmentation of production and the concomitant decrease in the size and power of organized labour) are also responsible for producing new forms of poverty and urban segregation.[7] The rosy picture of Turkey painted by economic indicators is clouded by formidable problems of poverty, the unequal distribution of wealth and unemployment – issues that seem to constitute the darker side of the neo-liberal economic miracles everywhere.

As theorists of globalization and postmodernism frequently point out, contradictory tendencies of economic integration and cultural fragmentation have gone hand in hand since the 1980s. A large body of theoretical literature exists about the emergence of 'alternative', 'other', 'hybrid', 'local' or 'multiple modernities', to use some of the terms in frequent circulation, articulating the fact that emerging geographies (societies outside Western Europe and North America) are indeed becoming modern, but they are doing so in culturally specific ways not predicted by the universalist models of earlier modernization theory.[8] Turkey is, once again, an illustrative example. Since the 1980s, particularistic discourses of identity and difference have irreversibly undone the earlier republican certainties regarding modernization theories and homogeneous nation states.[9] The official ideology, cultural norms and mental habits of the old republican elite, as well as of the traditional left, have been challenged in unprecedented ways by groups ranging from liberals, feminists and civil society advocates to Kurdish activists and Islamists. In all expressions of culture (from art and architecture to literature, music and cinema) the austerity, paternalism and universalistic claims of official republican modernism have been challenged by a plurality of postmodern stylistic experiments and by diverse expressions of popular culture, such as the incorporation of vernacular and historical references in architecture or the popularity of hybrid forms like *arabesk* or Turkish-pop in music. Artists have also explored new territories in literature and painting. Accomplished examples are the 2006 Nobel laureate Orhan Pamuk in literature, whose work embodies complex cross-cultural currents between Western and Eastern sensibilities, and the late Erol Akyavaş (1932–1999) in painting, who, while solidly grounded in modernist and surrealist avant-garde currents, has looked at Islamic arts, miniature painting, calligraphy and paper-marbling as the possible philosophical and aesthetic sources of a modern Turkish art. In stark contrast to the singular voice of state broadcasting throughout most of republican history, tens of radio and TV channels have emerged, appealing to a multiplicity of tastes, classes and subcultures. Especially consequential has been the rise of political Islam as a major force, following the municipal election victories of the Welfare Party in the mid-1990s and the sweeping rise of Tayyip Erdoğan's Justice and Development Party (AKP) to national government in 2002. The increasingly pervasive (and still controversial) presence of women in headscarves in public spaces and the boom in mosque construction across the country testify to these momentous changes, to which the secularists have responded with an increasingly doctrinaire and defensive canonization of Kemalism or, as one scholar calls it, a palpable 'nostalgia for the modern'.[10] Today, the seemingly paradoxical picture is that, contrary to the predictions of postwar modernization theories, the more democratic Turkey becomes, the more 'Muslim' it seems to get.[11]

The collective impact of these developments upon the country's architectural and urban landscape has been truly dramatic. A seemingly insatiable construction boom has been transforming the physical fabric of major Turkish cities since the 1980s, following the state-sanctioned entry of trans-national finance capital, major banks, large construction and development companies and consortiums into the building market. Especially since 2002, the AKP government has been introducing further measures to make it easier for Turkish and international investors and real estate development firms to undertake large-scale commercial, residential and tourism projects. These include opening new land (formerly agricultural or forest) to construction, selling public land in prime urban locations to private real estate development companies to generate revenue, relaxing codes on taller buildings and changing zoning codes, transforming traditionally residential areas into commercial zones. As a result, the familiar spaces of trans-national capitalism have proliferated across the country, most visibly shopping malls, supermarkets, international hotel, retail and fast-food chains, office and residential towers as well as new gated suburbia, replicating global trends seen in many other parts of the world from Shanghai to São Paolo.[12] Since 2000 Turkey too has built its 'brandscapes' and 'theme parks' and continues to offer provocative material for discussions of 'transnational urbanism'.[13]

Complementing these developments, the emergence of a vibrant architectural culture, through publications, media, exhibitions, awards, conferences, graduate programmes and other means, has been instrumental in the dissemination of postmodernism, formal experimentation and theories about the autonomy of the discipline, as distinct from the activistic social and political engagement of the architectural profession in the previous era. The proliferation since the 1980s of new architectural journals and design and decoration magazines (especially *Arredamento Dekorasyon* (later *Arredamento Mimarlık*), *Tasarım*, *XXI* and *Betonart*, in addition to *Yapı* and *Mimarlık* from the previous period), the conspicuous increase in glossy architectural monographs and coffee table books that can be found in bookshops and the institutionalization of prestigious architectural awards, both national and international (most notably the National Architecture Awards given out by the Chamber of Turkish Architects since 1988 and the Aga Khan Awards, established in 1980 to recognize good design in Muslim countries), have all contributed to an unprecedented prominence of Architecture with a capital 'A', introducing new debates and opening up the profession to new influences from abroad. Architectural exhibitions (sponsored especially by major banks and the construction industry), public lectures by international star designers (including Norman Foster, Rem Koolhaas, Frank Gehry, Peter Eisenman and Zaha Hadid) and the hosting of major architectural events (such as Anytime 1998, UIA 2005 and Docomomo 2006) have followed this media explosion, with a visible impact upon the design thinking of young architects and architectural students. While basic modernist notions of functionalism, rationalism, innovation and honest expression of structure did not lose their ideological grip upon the majority of established Turkish architects, many have also celebrated what was widely perceived to be a liberation from the sterility and facelessness of modernism, in favour of new experiments ranging from high-tech expressionism to deconstructionism, or new appeals to tradition and history for postmodern image-making and/or identity construction. This new pluralist discourse was matched in practice through the availability of a vast spectrum of new digital design and drafting technologies, sophisticated construction systems, imported building materials, components, fixtures and finishes as well as their domestic versions. We can assert that, by the turn of the twenty-first century, both the theoretical and the formal assumptions of the discipline of architecture as well as its professional practice were transformed in Turkey.

What follows is a closer look at the plurality, fragmentation and re-orientation of modernity and modernism in Turkey since the 1980s, primarily alongside three major developments: the impact of integration with global markets; the rise of political Islam; and the 'postmodern turn' in Turkish architectural culture. These manifest themselves most visibly in the built environment when we turn our gaze to spaces of consumption, religion and tourism, respectively – or to the shopping centre, the mosque and the hotel/holiday resort – as the most representative architectural typologies of Turkey's post-Kemalist, postmodern shift. The other equally visible and far more pervasive mark of this era on the urban landscape involves new developments in residential architecture that will be taken up in chapter Eight.

Spaces of Global Consumption

The most paradigmatic architectural typology symbolizing the neo-liberal turn in Turkish economy and society has been the ubiquitous 'shopping centre' (*Alış Veriş Merkezi* in Turkish or AVM for short) and its more ambitious variant, the so-called 'mixed-use development' (*karma kullanım*), which combines retail shopping with luxury residences and office space. The conceptual antithesis of the modernist idea of functional zoning, the mixed-use development has emerged as a recombination of work, dwelling and recreation in a single project, all arranged around consumption, namely retail shopping, which functions as the centrepiece and generator of neo-liberal economies across the globe. With their historical origins in the great expositions, glass arcades and department stores of the late nineteenth century, contemporary shopping centres are powerful commentaries, both socially and aesthetically, on the paradigm shift from production to consumption as the defining functions of late capitalist societies. Since the 1980s, much has been written about the shopping mall as the symbol of postmodern culture par excellence, about the curious status of the mall floor as privatized 'public space' and about the evolution of the mall from a market space for the sale of commodities to commodification of experience itself.[14]

The first large AVMs appeared in Turkey in the 1990s, offering thousands of square feet of retail floor within glazed atria, displaying major international and domestic brands to a public rapidly infatuated with consumption. Of the early examples in Istanbul, Akmerkez in Etiler (1991–3) features three shopping arcades on a triangular plan, each corner marked with three glazed towers, two for offices and one for hotel-style apartments, while Capitol in Altunizade, on the Asian side of the city (1990–93; architects Mutlu Çilingiroğlu and Adnan Kazmaoğlu), sheaths its single, spacious, multi-level atrium within a solid, terracotta coloured envelope. The generic programme of these early examples (shops, supermarket, cinemas and food court) would expand in the next decade into increasingly more extravagant combinations of retail with recreation and entertainment. Since 2000 some of the newest malls prefer the term 'centre for good living' (*yaşam merkezi*) rather than just 'shopping centre'

Advertisement of
Akmerkez, Istanbul,
1991–3.

(AVM), incorporating into their designs more restaurants, sports and spa facilities and spaces for themed entertainment and live music, luring more people to spend more time inside their well-monitored perimeters. This, in effect, is an architectural confirmation of the decline of public urban space under the new neo-liberal economic regime or as Enis Öncüoğlu, a prolific architect specialized in the design and construction of AVMs in Turkey and abroad, puts it succinctly, 'AVMs can be seen as the privatization of social and cultural functions no longer provided by public authorities and municipalities'.[15]

Ankara is also illustrative in this respect. The country's first shopping mall, Atakule (1989; architect Ragıp Buluç), located on the prestigious Çankaya hill, is a slick box with facades of reflecting mirror glass and features an observation tower/rotating restaurant that quickly became an urban logo for the capital city. The Karum shopping mall, another of the earliest malls in the country (1988–91; architects Von Gerkan, Marg und Partner with Yılmaz Gedik/Koray Construction Company) stands out in Ankara's rather dreary urban fabric with its long, horizontal, sky-lit atrium enveloped by four office floors stacked upon three floors of retail and marked vertically on one end with the cylindrical tower of the Sheraton Hotel. The recipient of a Construction Award in 1994, Karum's urban context lends it a credibility lacking in many of the later malls. Located on Tunalı Hilmi Avenue, a busy shopping street, it offers the capital city a popular, easily accessible social space as well as a major urban landmark. Some ten years later the Armada centre, featuring a shopping mall, supermarket, cinemas and a 21-storey office tower of modular aluminium and glass cladding (1999–2003; architect Ali Osman Öztürk) was built on the Ankara-Eskişehir highway to the west, the major artery along which Ankara expanded rapidly, and many other new shopping centres emerged in the course of the 2000s. Accessible primarily by car, these newer and increasingly more glitzy shopping centres symbolize the gradual retreat of the urban middle classes from the experience of street shopping within the city (now enjoyed more by lower income groups and recent migrants who do not own cars) to that of driving to a suburban mall with vast car parks, the paradigmatic social space where weekends are spent and shopping is combined with entertainment. One of the latest of these, the Panora (2004–7; architect Ali Osman Öztürk) is advertised as the shopping centre with 'the largest promenade landscape' and a 'centre for good living' where, in addition to an 'indoor shopping street', there is a recreation centre, sports club, aquarium and a diverse range of restaurants.[16]

In Istanbul the same mass weekend experience of going to AVMs has numerous destinations within the city and its suburban hinterland. While the older urban malls like Akmerkez, Capitol and Cevahir continue to attract large crowds, the newer shopping mall/mixed-use developments along the Levent-Maslak axis (along the Büyükdere Caddesi highway) have given Istanbul not only a new skyline and a new urban image, but also an unprecedented prominence in the global cities discourse and in critical debates pertaining to neo-liberal urbanism.[17] Accessible by Istanbul's brand new subway line running below, this major artery along the ridge of the European land mass separates the more expensive, upper-class, Bosphorus-facing residential areas of the city in the east from the poorer neighbourhoods towards the Kağıthane valley in the west, while remaining distinct from both of these residential fabrics in terms of scale, typology and skyline. The development on Büyükdere Caddesi unequivocally marks the shift of Istanbul's big business finance and commerce further north in the city, from the old, prestigious Taksim-Nişantaşı-Şişli stretch of 'republican Istanbul' towards the new showcase of 'global Istanbul' in the Levent-Maslak direction.

Von Gerkan, Marg und Partner with Yılmaz Gedik / Koray Construction Company, Karum Shopping Mall, Ankara, 1988–91; photo by Esra Akcan.

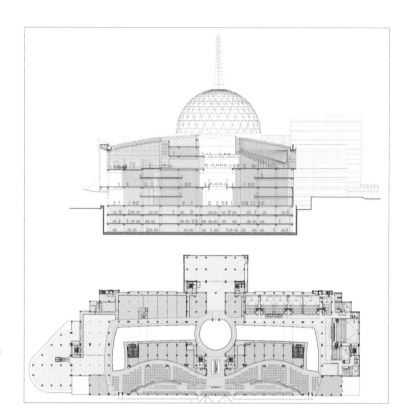

A Tasarım (Ali Osman
Öztürk), Panora
Shopping Mall,
Ankara, 2004–7,
section, plan, view.

New development along Levent-Maslak axis (Büyükdere Caddesi), Istanbul, view from the valley to the west, c. 2010; photo by Thomas Mayer.

The earliest important AVM/mixed-use development along Büyükdere Caddesi was Metrocity (1995–2003; architects Doğan Tekeli and Sami Sisa), which featured a horizontal volume for the shopping mall, pinned to the site by an office tower at the Büyükdere Caddesi end, and by two identical residential towers facing the Kağıthane valley at the opposite end (Metrocity is visible to the right in the photo above). Metrocity was followed (on an adjacent site) by the architecturally ambitious Kanyon (2002–6; architects John Jerde, John Simones, Eduardo Lopez with Tabanlıoğlu Architects in Istanbul), which was conceived as a new urban centre that claimed to avoid the 'closed box' formula and reintroduce the 'street shopping concept', albeit on four levels of open galleries with curving forms. The latter are enveloped by a curving wall containing residences with views in all directions. The project is completed by a 25-floor office tower at the Büyükdere Caddesi entrance (Kanyon is immediately to the left of Metrocity). The four levels of snaking galleries with retail units, cafes and restaurants coil around a semicircular central volume containing more shops and the inevitable multiplex cinemas, while the ground level serves as a stage set for concerts, exhibitions and activities for children – a totally controlled 'public space' that welcomes everyone who has gone through the security checks. Designed by an American firm in collaboration with Turkish architects and engineered by Arup Associates, Kanyon not only exemplifies the trans-nationalization of design and construction in Turkey (see chapter Nine), but also illustrates what commentators see as the mobilization of formal exuberance and technological innovativeness in many Asian and Middle Eastern cities, to provide an image to brand a government, corporation, city or developer.[18]

John Jerde, John
Simones, Eduardo
Lopez with Tabanlıoğlu
Architects (Murat and
Melkan Tabanlıoğlu),
Kanyon Shopping
Centre, Istanbul,
2002–6; photo by
Sibel Bozdoğan.
A plan and section
is shown opposite.

Kanyon, which was commissioned by the Eczacıbaşı Group, a leading Turkish industrial conglomerate, embodies the country's quest for 'brand-scapes', as Anna Klingman puts it.

Compared with the more generic boxy containers/glazed atria of earlier shopping centres, projects like Kanyon illustrate the renewed significance of distinctive design (and an accomplished architect) as a marketing strategy. A number of other new shopping centres in Istanbul bearing the signature of prominent international or internationally linked designers suggest that the recognition of architecture as a value generator has spread beyond the elite Levent-Maslak artery to other local developments in Istanbul's suburban hinterland catering to larger cross-sections of the social spectrum. One of these is Foreign Office Architects' Meydan Shopping Centre in Ümraniye on the Asian side of Istanbul, an award-winning project blending architecture with landscape (2007; architects Farshid Moussavi and Alejandro Zaera Polo of FOA). Meydan, literally meaning 'public square', is a notable effort to transcend the closed box convention of the AVMs in favour of a tectonic, almost 'geological' approach, 'building the site' as Kenneth Frampton would call it, and in

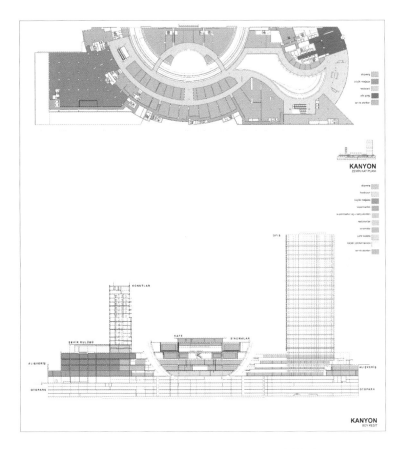

KANYON
ZEMİN KAT PLANI

KANYON
BOY KESİT

the process creating an enclosed public square available for occupation by diverse activities. To introduce some level of control over the typically chaotic and ad hoc growth of commercial spaces in suburban locations, the project anticipates possible future growth and incorporates this as an integral aspect of the infrastructural/landscape approach to the design.

Ultimately, however, it is not projects like Kanyon or Meydan but rather the more pervasive and far more generic suburban shopping malls, 'megastores' and 'hypermarkets' that make up the overwhelming metropolitan sprawl of Turkey's major cities. Initiated by large European supermarket chains such as Carrefour and Migros or giant home stores like IKEA and Habitat among others, these are the twenty-first century's 'grand bazaars' featuring a myriad of Turkish and international brands in food, fashion, toys, furniture and household goods. With their immense retail floors and vast parking lots, surrounded by brand new residential developments and ongoing construction (see chapter Eight), they constitute

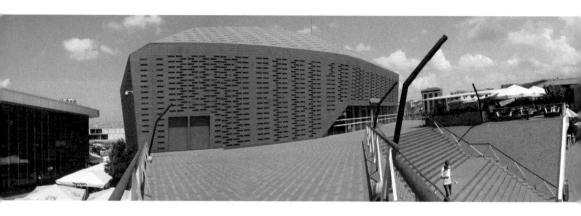

Foreign Office
Architects (Farshid
Moussavi and
Alejandro Zaera
Polo), Meydan
Shopping Centre,
Istanbul, 2007; photo
by Esra Akcan.

a chaotic landscape of new development on the suburban hinterland of large cities. Especially around Istanbul, taking advantage of cheaper land values on the city's poorer urban fringes or built on former forest or agri-cultural land newly opened to private development, these suburban out-lets have grown into vast 'edge-cities' that no longer have much to do with the historical centre of the city. The case of Ümraniye is an illustra-tive example: if we zoom out from FOA's Meydan shopping centre, we can see an immense landscape of other commercial outlets, including an IKEA superstore, endless stretches of new residential development and the construction sites of even newer shopping centres extending towards the horizon.

Even a cursory review of Arkitera, Turkey's on-line portal for archi-tecture, reveals that AVMs and commercial mixed-use developments constitute the largest group, by far, of all the building types documented in recent years. The AVMs are at least two to three times more numerous as, say, public, educational, health-related or cultural buildings.[19] More interestingly, such a survey reveals that AVM design is a distinct specializa-tion in contemporary architectural practice, with a few architectural firms designing the bulk of these often generic commercial projects, rarely men-tioned in academic circles, or recognized by prestigious awards. The ERA Architecture and Planning Office of Çiğdem Duman and Ertun Hızıroğlu is one such practice with numerous AVMs in Istanbul, İzmir and other cities, including their recent Forum shopping centre in Bayrampaşa fea-turing four commercial floors of retail shops, cinemas, recreation centre, restaurants and a concert hall (2004–9; designed with Arup Associates). Adnan Kazmaoğlu in Istanbul and Ali Osman Öztürk in Ankara are sim-ilarly prolific designers of shopping malls. The indisputable specialist of AVMs, however, is the impossibly prolific firm of Öncüoğlu+ACP (Archi-tecture, Consultancy, Planning), the partnership of Enis Öncüoğlu,

Cem Altınöz and Cumhur Keskinok, now 'an international brand' as they describe the firm. With offices in Ankara, Istanbul, Alma Ata, Moscow and Hamburg, Öncüoğlu and his team have built tens of AVMs across Turkey, in Russia and in many other parts of the former Soviet Republics, offering compelling testimony to Turkey's successful integration with global markets at professional levels (see chapter Nine).

Although the majority of AVMs follow variations of the same generic closed-box formula, the shopping mall typology has not been entirely immune to the appeal of postmodernism and accompanying discourses of identity. A number of AVMs offer 'themed environments' with vernacular or historical associations that claim to capture some aspect of local, regional or cultural identity, often contrasted with the alleged facelessness of other AVMs representing the same unsentimental efficiency and commercial rationality everywhere, the so-called 'non-places' of late capitalism.[20] How effective such ersatz environments are in restoring

Aerial view of Ümraniye, an 'edge-city' on the Asian side of Istanbul; Meydan Shopping Centre by FOA can be seen in context; photo by Cemal Emden.

local identity and a sense of place to an activity (collective consumption) that is by definition placeless and global is a contentious issue at best. Nonetheless, the populist appeal and touristic value of such projects are amply demonstrated. An early example in Ankara is Andaş Bazaar (*çarşı*), designed by Merih Karaaslan and Nuran Ünsal. Coining the term 'Anatolian collage' for their practice, the designers have placed the shops around semi-open arcades and a gated but open-to-the-sky square (*meydan*).[21] As illustrated in Karaaslan's sketch, the bazaar is composed of the postmodern interpretations of a Greek temple front and stoa, a Roman theatre and an open-air amphitheatre, a Seljuk portal (*Taç kapı*) and a village square, even though these historical references are hardly recognizable today beneath the large commercial signs of the shops. More recently a new shopping centre, Forum Bornova in İzmir (2005–6; architects Çiğdem Duman and Ertun Hızıroğlu), was designed around the concept of a Mediterranean village with streets open to the sky, courtyards and squares. This concept is further accentuated by the use of natural materials, such as stone and timber, and the incorporation of pergolas, shading devices and reflecting pools as a much-advertised critique of the mechanically acclimatized indoor atriums of other AVMS. İzmir, close to the major tourist destinations of the Aegean, is Turkey's third most important city and Forum Bornova merges the concept of the shopping mall with that of a popular theme park or holiday resort. As

Merih Karaaslan and Nuran Ünsal, Andaş Bazaar, Ankara, 1990, sketch and model.

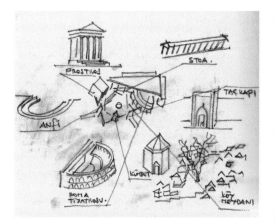

such it illustrates what we see as the post-1980, postmodern bent in Turkish architectural culture.

Political Islam, Mosque Architecture and Neo-Ottomanism

Most social scientists agree that the radical secularism of the Kemalist Republic has failed to penetrate deep within Turkish society. In every election since 1946, when the political system was liberalized and a multi-party democracy was first established in Turkey, mainstream conservative parties have courted votes with appeals to religion. A succession of openly Islamist parties have emerged since the late 1960s, finding their greatest support in the migrant populations of the urban fringes with their roots in rural and traditional values. What has been new since the 1980s, however, is a brand of Islamist politics that has successfully blended social and cultural conservatism with remarkable flexibility and openness regarding Turkey's economic and technological integration with the outside world.[22] In spite of recurrent confrontations with the staunchly secular military and judiciary and suffering a number of setbacks over the years, this more 'modern' and moderate Islam swept municipal elections in the major cities in 1994 and brought Tayyip Erdoğan's AKP to power in the national elections of 2002.

The unmistakable signs of the growing significance of Islam in Turkish society and politics have been everywhere since the 1980s. More women in headscarves and more bearded men are visible in the streets than at any time in Republican history. Religious orders, Muslim charities and Muslim businesses are thriving. Any public event, symbol or activity is a contested terrain between the Islamists (or 'conservative democrats' as they prefer to call themselves) and the hard-core secularists (who cling to the cult and iconography of Atatürk as their 'religion'). One small symbolic example is the controversial decision of Ankara's conservative mayor Melih Gökçek to change the logo of the Municipality from an ancient Hittite symbol rooted in the Kemalist nationalism of the 1930s to the domes and crescents of Islam, a decision still contested by the secularists. Similarly, in an undisguised challenge to the lavish Republic Day celebrations so dear to the country's secularists, Istanbul's Islamist municipality has been celebrating, with extravagant public ceremonies, every anniversary of the conquest of the city by the Ottomans in 1453.[23] Meanwhile, the notorious 'headscarf controversy' (the banning of headscarves on university campuses) continues to be the primary battleground of the 'culture wars' between the two groups, with passions running high on both sides.

Nowhere does the strong presence of Islam in society and public life manifest itself more visibly, however, than in the boom in mosque construction in this period, ranging from small, cheaply built and awkwardly proportioned mosques across the country to larger and more elaborate ones in major cities. That the sheer numbers of these new mosques have far exceeded the actual need for prayer space underscores the symbolic importance of this building type in marking the newly acquired political power and self-confidence of conservative parties and their followers in Turkey.[24] For example, after the 1994 municipal victory of the Islamist Welfare Party, with Tayyip Erdoğan as the mayor of Istanbul, one of the first proposals was to build a new mosque in Taksim Square, across from the Atatürk Cultural Centre, an icon of the secular modernism of the Republic. Although the proposal was strongly resisted by the secular establishment and eventually defeated when the Welfare Party was forced out of power in 1997, this and similar controversies around proposals for large mosques have become commonplace in postmodern Turkey. They mark deep divides not only between secularists and Islamists, with their competing interpretations of Turkish national identity, but also between a largely secular and (aesthetically) modernist architectural establishment and the tastes of the conservative communities that commission the mosques.

The classic example of the latter divide is the long saga of the monumental Kocatepe Mosque in Ankara (1967–87). Crowning a hill across from Atatürk's Mausoleum, arguably the holiest shrine of secular Turkish nationalism, this grand 'neo-Ottoman' mosque is probably the most provocative challenge not only to the secular republican identity of the national capital, but to Turkey's architectural profession, which considers revivalism and historicist pastiche as a rebuke of its core modernist values.[25] The story of the Kocatepe Mosque goes back to Vedat Dalokay's initial design in 1957 (see chapter Six), a modern reinterpretation of the classical Ottoman mosque in a structurally innovative, thin-shell concrete dome or tent, pitched on the four corners to cover a centralized space flooded with light – an unconventional design that even then pitted enthusiastic secular architects against religious conservatives (see page 198). In 1967, despite protests by the Chamber of Architects and the secular professional establishment, Dalokay's project was abandoned in favour of the current Kocatepe Mosque project. [26] Designed by the architects Hüsrev Tayla and Fatin Uluengin, the new project is a direct replica of Sinan's sixteenth-century Şehzade Mosque in Istanbul: a central space with a large dome supported by four half domes, and the exterior corners marked by four slender minarets with triple balconies in the manner of classical Ottoman imperial mosques. After numerous setbacks and bureaucratic hurdles, the project was realized under the sponsorship of the Religious Foundation of Turkey (Türkiye Diyanet Vakfı, established in 1975) and was completed in 1987. While the entrance facade of the mosque set on a vast plaza replicates the Ottoman tradition to the minutest detail (such as pointed arches, marble detailing and *muqarnas* column

Hüsrev Tayla and
Fatin Uluengin,
Kocatepe Mosque,
Ankara, 1967–87;
photo by Önol Soner.

capitals), the project also contains a vast supermarket/department store and parking garage in its lower levels accessed from the back. This distinctly postmodern juxtaposition of a consumer society with renewed religiosity can be viewed as an appropriate symbol of the culturally conservative and economically liberal turn that Turkey took in this period.[27]

Followed by the equally monumental Sabancı Central Mosque in Adana (1988–98) and many lesser examples in other cities, contemporary imitations of classical Ottoman precedents proliferated across the country in the 1980s and '90s. Coupled with the establishment of the generously endowed Aga Khan Architecture Awards in 1980 (with the objective of recognizing good design in Muslim countries across the world), this led to a renewed debate among architects regarding mosque design, a topic entirely neglected under the early republic. In contrast to the overt classical Ottomanism of Kocatepe, Sabancı and other similar mosques, the Parliament Mosque Complex in Ankara (1989; architects Behruz and Can Çinici) represents a non-traditional approach. An innovative combination of prayer hall and library without any recognizable markers of Islamic identity like a dome or a minaret, the project subverts the traditional architectural elements for new aesthetic effects and some degree of postmodern playfulness: the traditionally solid *qıbla* wall becomes a transparent screen overlooking a reflective pool; the traditional colonnade of the courtyard becomes a portico without the columns (except for repetitive pedestals suggestive of the absent columns); and at the junction of the prayer hall and the library, a balcony evokes the absent minaret. Although the construction of a mosque within the grounds of the Turkish Grand National Assembly is itself indicative of the shifting political landscape in post-1980 Turkey, the choice of an abstract, non-traditional design can be seen as a successful compromise, more palatable to the still predominantly secular Parliament of the time, before the rise of Islamist parties to power.

A third approach, between the neo-Ottoman revivalism of the Kocatepe Mosque and the innovative, non-traditional design of the Parliament Mosque, can be observed in Turgut Cansever's Karakaş Mosque in the Mediterranean city of Antalya (1991–8). It is a refined and well-crafted example working with the forms and materials of historical precedents in the region: the brick and masonry tradition of Seljuk and early Ottoman mosques, with tile-covered domes and a perforated wall separating the mosque from the street. A devout Muslim himself, Cansever is dismissive of recent monumental replicas of classical Ottoman mosques as shallow imitations. He is equally critical, however, of innovative modernist approaches to a traditional typology, as in the case of Vedat Dalokay's unbuilt Kocatepe Mosque project of 1957. Dalokay's project,

Behruz and Can Çinici,
Parliament Mosque
Complex, Ankara,
1989, exterior and
interior with trans-
parent *qibla* wall.

Cansever argues, 'puts the dome on the ground', thereby violating the very idea of the dome as a space cover supported on columns.[28] This kind of emphasis on timeless structural archetypes that do not change, even when materials and construction technologies change, has earned Cansever an adversarial position within Turkish architectural culture: one that places him against both the prevailing modernist belief in innovation and neo-traditionalist pastiche.

Arguably one of the most important modern Turkish architects, Turgut Cansever (1920–2009) demonstrated a deeper and more personal engagement with Islam than any other modern designer in Turkey, blending

his professional role as an architect with his personal belief system as a devout Muslim.[29] Looking at art and architecture as ontological issues belonging to the realm of religion and ethics, Cansever was a vocal and articulate critic of the instrumental rationality of the modern world and blamed the contemporary plight of architecture and urbanism on Renaissance humanism that replaced submission to divine will.[30] Arguing that two centuries of Westernization in Turkey have led to an alienation and fragmentation of the self that can only be restored by a return to Islam's holistic world-view, Cansever posits 'religion [as] the fundamental question of all cultural epochs and style [as] the formal expression of this question'.[31] To his credit, however, these ontological ruminations of 'Cansever the conservative intellectual' have not led to the prescription of an essentialist, faith-determined 'Islamic art/architecture' independent of history and context in the way other architects and critics such as Sayyed H. Nasr, Nader Ardalan or Titus Burkhardt proposed in the 1970s.[32] Nor do they claim to directly translate into Cansever's architectural work. Highly acclaimed by most critics and commentators, Cansever's oeuvre seeks to offer a critique of the over-rationalized world and restore a sense of spirituality, not so much through overt references to religion, but rather through a site-specific architecture sensitive to locality, culture, crafts and tradition.[33] The spatial, aesthetic and experiential qualities of some of his best modernist work, such as the Anadolu Club in Büyükada, Istanbul, or the Karatepe Open Air Museum cannot possibly be explained by Islam alone, displaying instead a broad range of architectural and intellectual influences from Le Corbusian tropical modernism to a phenomenologically situated 'place making' or Heideggerian 'revealing' respectively. Finding a more receptive audience to his ideas after the rise of political Islam in the 1980s, Cansever became increasingly vocal in articulating his idiosyncratic views on aesthetics, space and construction: the beauty of the built environment

Turgut Cansever,
Karakaş Mosque,
Antalya, 1991–8,
street view; photo
by Uğur Tanyeli.

in Muslim societies before the arrival of modernization and westernization, the quintessentially Islamic notions of unity (*tevhid*) and ornament-
ation (*tezyin*) as timeless guidelines for architects, and the joy of craft
skills that, he argued, are irreversibly destroyed by industrialization. He
claimed to have translated these ideas into practice in the Demir Vacation
Houses in Bodrum (1984), despite the contradictions inherent in its
purpose as a holiday resort populated by men and women in swimsuits.
Cansever's use of local stone and his sensitive site planning of these simple
cubic houses terracing down to the sea in a beautiful Mediterranean landscape earned the project considerable recognition and an Aga Khan Award
in 1992.

While the professional architectural establishment has, by and large,
remained secular and modernist, it is a fact that architects who acknowledged indebtedness to Turkish and Islamic traditions, and have system-
atically constructed their self-image around these ideas, have gained a
new visibility since 1980, parallel to the rise of identity politics. Turgut
Cansever was recognized by the Aga Khan Awards and has been the
subject of numerous publications, monographs and exhibitions, while
at the same time he has drawn criticism from the staunchly modernist
opponents of his traditionalism.[34] Regardless of its Islamist discourse,
the Demir complex has become a formal inspiration for many touristic
hotels, such as Ahmet Iğdırlıgil's Ada Hotel (1995–9), also in Bodrum,
creating a recognizable 'Bodrum style'. This testifies to the power (and
appeal) of particularistic discourses of identity, whether for Islamist
or touristic purposes, ironically at a time when the world was inti-
mately interconnected through markets, media and transnational migration – a 'modernity at large' that leaves no culture or corner of the
world unaffected.[35]

Tourism and the Paradoxes of Identity

Sporadic examples of postmodernism as a style appeared in Turkey in
the 1980s, for example with the work of Merih Karaaslan in Ankara or
Haydar Karabey in Istanbul. Yet nowhere was the postmodern style as
visible in Turkey as in the tourist complexes of the 1980s and '90s. Architects promoting postmodernism as a sincere criticism of modernism
found matching clients in the growing tourism industry who sought to
create spaces with a 'Turkish identity' for quite different reasons. Among
them, Merih Karaaslan vocally defended the 'contemporary interpretation of Anatolian architecture' as opposed to what he criticized as
placeless modern forms,[36] and designed two hotels in Cappadocia with
explicit references to the region's tufa cones known as 'fairy chimneys'.

Turgut Cansever,
Demir Vacation
Village, Bodrum,
1984; photo by
Esra Akcan.

Haydar Karabey, E-House in Cihangir incorporating the facade of a former two-storey building into the new design, Istanbul, 1994; photo by Esra Akcan.

The Ataman Hotel, Göreme (1985–95; with Ertan Ergin) was literally designed in and around the fairy chimneys by restoring some houses and inserting buildings between them that were unassertively harmonized with the context. Using *yonu* stone for both the restored and new buildings that were used as hotel rooms, the complex turned the inside of the historic caves into common areas, including the lobby, dining hall, bar and library. The Peritower Hotel, Nevşehir (1989–96; with Nuran Ünsal), on the other hand, sought to recreate a 'contemporary interpretation of Cappadocia' in a new building close by. Karaaslan suggested the accumulation of massive conic towers with 'hats' reminiscent of fairy chimneys, interior spaces easily associated with caves and underground cities in the region, and a labyrinthine circulation diagram, rather than what he called the 'rational and efficient, easily managed' international style block with a single circulation core that would have been an easier and more familiar choice in a hotel.[37] Making autobiographical references to growing up in the region, he stated:

> It was clear enough that a building in Cappadocia needed to be very different than a building designed anywhere else; besides, working in a preservation area made it mandatory to establish continuity with the regional/spatial language of the region . . . By way of discussing, feeling and reinterpreting the potentials on this piece of land, architecture is a way of making something that belongs to us, of presenting our respect to those human beings that sculpted nature in Cappadocia.[38]

Karaaslan continued promoting postmodern architectural historicism in his *oeuvre* built elsewhere, for instance, positing Cappadocia as a major, albeit abstracted, inspiration for his collective housing projects such as Sürücüler Terrace Houses and Yamaçevler in Ankara (see page 279).

One of the most distinctive voices of the 1980s in Turkey is to be found in the work of Atölye T (Tuncay Çavdar and Semra Giritlioğlu). Educated in Milan at the height of the 1960s student movements, Çavdar spent his early career translating, directing and designing stage sets for

Merih Karaaslan and
Ertan Ergin, Ataman
Hotel, Göreme,
1985–95.

Brechtian plays, co-editing the Marxist journal *Toplum ve Bilim*, and
organizing the participatory planning model of İzmit's social housing
programme with 30,000 units between 1972 and 1980.[39] The period after
the *coup d'état* of 1980 dramatically changed his client profile, albeit
paradoxically not his subversive Marxist ideals. While predominantly
building tourist complexes during this period, Çavdar theorized on what
he called the 'Eastern way of seeing' as the intellectual background of
his buildings.[40] Referring to the non-perspectival Islamic miniature tradition, and to John Berger's descriptions of the paintings of Şeker Ahmed
Paşa (1841–1907), Çavdar concluded that a different, 'Eastern' mode of
perceiving the world had been transmitted through the centuries, which
he sought to translate in architecture. Some of his observations about the
'Western way of seeing' were not too dissimilar to contemporary theories

that challenged the ocularcentric Western tradition for prioritizing perspectival vision as the sole measure of human understanding. Erwin Panofsky had already identified perspective as a symbolic form that transformed the Aristotelian conception of space to the modern Cartesian one, through which the human eye was thereafter attributed as the beholder of the correct, objective, scientific view of the world that could now be represented with mathematical exactitude.[41] Perspectival vision assumed the human eye as the centre of the universe, and the world represented by the human eye as the sole measure of truth in the modern world – or the 'age of world picture', as Martin Heidegger also analysed in his famous essay.[42] At the height of postmodern theory, both in art and architecture, many scholars questioned the consequent 'hegemony of vision' that determined the relation between the subject and object in the modern world.[43]

In translating the 'Eastern way of seeing' into architectural space, Çavdar intentionally designed vistas and objects that would create an alienation effect as in a non-perspectival Islamic painting or miniature,

Atölye T (Tuncay Çavdar and Semra Giritlioğlu), Pamfilya Hotel, Antalya, 1984, detail and, below, general view; photos by Esra Akcan.

226

Merih Karaaslan and
Nuran Ünsal,
Peritower Hotel,
Nevşehir, 1989–96.

rather than a realist scene that would now be familiar to the human eye as in a perspective painting. To that end, he deliberately fragmented buildings into an unconventional number of pieces, and increased the number of small masses that could be seen from one view point. This created a visual effect where multiple disharmonious forms were squeezed into a relatively small space, as if they were all flattened and juxtaposed on a two-dimensional surface, as in the Pamfilya Hotel, Antalya (1984), to give one example. It also facilitated a visual effect reminiscent of representations without shadows and created colour schemes that were intentionally designed as a blast of different colours springing out from the objects. Additionally, Çavdar sought to create spaces that appeared to be weightless, as if their coordinates on the Cartesian space could not be determined. To that end, heavy masses were carried by disproportionately slender columns in the Pamfilya Hotel and the Excelsior Corinthia Hotel, Side (1985–9), as if they did not touch the ground. Çavdar advocated his architectural approach stimulated by the 'Eastern way of seeing' as a humorous yet political and emancipatory stance against authority and order, against the fixed and reified rules that resulted from the hegemonic modes of perspectival vision.[44] The buildings are full of playful and surprising paths, labyrinthine and alienating circulation schemes that border on a playground for adults. However, this intellectually and politically critical endeavour was operating in one of the most conformist industries of the century and one that invested in such theme park effects for reasons that were primarily commercial – a dramatic paradox that continuously yet inconsequentially troubled Çavdar.

Atölye T (Tuncay
Çavdar and Semra
Giritlioğlu), Excelsior
Corinthia Hotel, Side,
1985–9; photo by Esra
Akcan.

The impact of postmodern commercialism on the changing habits of
travellers and the growing industry of mass tourism has been analysed
by scholars who found matching cases on the southern shores of Turkey,
particularly in the coastal towns connected to the cities of Antalya and
Muğla.[45] On the one hand, mass tourism globalizes bourgeois standards

of living. The tourists demand hot water, air conditioning, familiar codes of sanitation, king-size beds and packaged food. On the other hand, foreign tourists seem to have been attracted to Turkey in expectation of 'experiencing a different culture'. Travel brochures, which usually 'introduce the world as a supermarket', in Tom Selwyn's words, create three identities for Turkey's tourist destinations: tourists who choose to spend their holiday in Turkey are promised the sea and the sun, a palimpsest of cultures from the Hittites to the Ottomans, and authentic local lifestyles untouched by modernism. To this end, simulated Sufi rituals are performed in the open-air theatres of resort villages; the Thousand and One Nights is a favourite theme at weekly parties; Turkish coffee is served by women dressed in traditional-looking attire; industrially produced versions of traditional handcrafted objects are put on sale in hotel gift shops; gladiator schools are founded to train performers for chariot races and the gladiator fights staged for tourists in the Roman theatre at Aspendos.[46] Even though tourists are hardly ever willing to put up with the local living standards, a taste of authenticity on the building facades and entertainment activities is welcomed as complementary service. Ironically, there is little dialogue between the tourists and the local population: the resort villages are gated territories that block the local inhabitants' access to the sea, while the customers hardly ever cross the gates to experience the life existing outside. Needless to say, many of these mass tourism hotels were built by destroying the existing forests or intervening in the natural and social habitat.

Advocates of the historicist postmodern style in architecture found clients in the tourism industry, who also invested in creating spaces of 'staged authenticity', a term coined by Dean MacCanell in relation to mass tourism across the globe.[47] Many hotels incorporated architectural fragments that looked like Ottoman tombs and Seljuk portals, arched arcades and *muqarnas* decoration made out of concrete on window and door frames, with chimneys as simulated minarets, domes covered with blue tiles and fountains as blown-up Kütahya tiled vases. In the most extreme cases, the resort towns were built as exact copies of historical buildings, such as the Topkapı Palace Hotel in Antalya, which is a replica of its authentic referent in Istanbul.[48] According to its advertising, 'it is now possible to sleep in comfortable rooms that allude to *harem* buildings, eat in the palace's kitchen or Hagia Irene, cool off at the Fountain of Ahmed the Third, have a drink at the Tower of Justice with a spectacular view'.[49]

In this context, Çavdar himself increasingly reverted to dark humour and shameless irony, as was most openly exposed in the Mega Saray Hotel, Belek. Visitors are greeted by a street with a simulation of 'old Turkish

Atölye T (Tuncay Gavdar, Semra Giritlioğlu), Mega Saray Hotel in Belek, Antalya, 1992; photo by Esra Akcan.

Klüp Ali Bey Hotel, Gate, Antalya, c. 1990; photo by Esra Akcan.

Topkapı Palace Hotel, Antalya, late 1990s.

houses', before they walk along the eclectic facade of a curved building whose plan most likely refers to Alvar Aalto's MIT student campus. They can then choose to pass through a gate that looks like a Seljuk portal and walk towards the sea, where they find themselves in an open-air museum of ironic architectural references, including stepped pyramids, the Great

Wall of China, arenas, auditoriums, circular temples, tents, ruined arcades and deconstructivist follies. The Disneyfication of the resort hotel was most unapologetically displayed in the Sirene Hotel, Antalya (mid-1990), where features familiar from Disneyland were collaged together with blue Ottoman tiles and steep roofed towers reminiscent of the Orta Kapı (Middle Gate) of the Topkapı Palace. Following a legacy that was practised somewhat timidly in the interiors and details of the Istanbul Hilton Hotel by SOM and Sedad Eldem (see chapter Four), the modernized amenities of these resort hotels were complemented with historicist fragments and exotic spaces that were associated with a refurbished

Mega Saray Hotel in Belek, Antalya; photos by Esra Akcan.

Sirene Hotel, Antalya,
mid-1990s; photo by
Esra Akcan.

Turkish identity. After the 1980s tourism created one of the biggest
source of revenue for both the Turkish state and the private sector alike.
Architecture and entertainment, by their very nature, became the primary
promoters of rampant self-orientalization in this lucrative industry.

chapter eight

The Illegal City and New Residential Segregation

A gate opens at the end of a tree-lined road … Beyond it lie the sloping greens of an immaculately maintained golf course at the edges of which terracotta tile roofs, saffron yellow façades, wrought iron balconies and the glinting windows of elegant *cumba* bays can be seen. These are modern homes, with every imaginable amenity, each one carefully designed to blend in not only with their lovingly landscaped setting but with a tradition of architecture and the inspiration of the great Turkish architect Mimar Sinan.
Web advertisement for Kemer Country residential development

Global cities of the late twentieth century challenged the modernist conception that urban growth can be planned or predicted. Most architects are familiar with Rem Koolhaas's essays 'What Ever Happened to Urbanism?' and 'The Generic City', both written in 1994, where he raised doubts about urban planning's adequacy, as a profession, to respond to the tripling growth of world cities.[1] At a time when the world's urban population surpasses its rural one, cities are confronted with incalculable and unpredictable growth, and architects with the emanating difficulties or opportunities of working in a milieu of unorganized land use and ad hoc development. In the wake of rapid and random transformations, housing remains one of the major quandaries of world cities. In Turkey, urbanization and unequal distribution of wealth reached unprecedented levels after the mid-1980s. By 2008 the number of residents living in cities had reached 70.5 per cent of the overall population. Already in the mid-1990s the richest 1 per cent of the population had a family income that exceeded that of the poorest families by 327 times.[2]

The forces of globalization on the big Turkish cities brought about the legalization of slum areas, the further proliferation of anonymous apartments, the emergence of gated communities, and the implementation of new administrative and design policies for mass-housing. The search by a handful of architects for alternative residential spaces in recent years will be illustrated in chapter Nine. Together, these multiple urban residential types make up the built environment of big Turkish cities at the beginning of the twenty-first century.

A detail of Doruk Pamir, Dikmen Valley Bridge and Housing, Ankara, 1991–6; photo by Esra Akcan.

The Architecture of the Shady Real Estate

The United Nations' report *Challenge of the Slums* exposed in 2003 that almost one billion people of the world's population live in illegal housing, in an environment without adequate infrastructure, waste collection or public services. Mike Davis has rightly described the world under the global economy at the dawn of the twenty-first century as a 'planet of slums'.[3] Turkey is usually featured at the top of lists documenting the percentage of unofficial housing. The formation of squatter settlements (*gecekondu*) in big Turkish metropolises began much earlier than globalization, but it took a totally different turn with Turkey's participation in the new world economy. What marks the difference after the mid-1980s is the combination of the free market economy and the semi-legalization of the formerly illegal settlements, as well as the hybridization of the *gecekondu* and the apartment building, which were portrayed in chapter Five as the two residential types defining the urban fabric of major Turkish cities. In such a context, the definitions and the content of the legal and the illegal, the formal and the informal, were constantly in flux.

While the illegal growth of big cities is common in non-Western countries, the immensity of unofficial housing in Turkey must be explained by also taking into account the residues of the Ottoman Empire's land policies. Rights to private land ownership, which is a key prerequisite of capitalist economies, were not totally secured during the classical period of the Ottoman Empire. While farmers could cultivate the state's land for agricultural purposes as long as they paid taxes, they could not claim this land as their private property. All land belonged to the state unless it was officially affiliated with a *vakf* or a family, and even in those cases there were many historical instances where the state took over the property.[4] Land, in other words, was hardly conceived as a commodity for private ownership. There were not many significant changes in this situation during the modernization of the Ottoman Empire in the nineteenth century either; and the size of the state property increased further when the non-Muslim population perished or was forced to emigration during the wars between 1915 and 1925, resulting in a de facto transfer of their land to the state. Until very recently, two-thirds of Turkey's territory still belonged to the state, a situation now changing with the new economic structure.[5]

The scarcity of private property could in fact have been turned into an opportunity for affordable housing, if only it had been used for the sake of public services. One of the major difficulties of public housing in European and North American countries has been the provision of cheap land for residential use, which would have been less of an issue in

Turkey, since state land could have been allocated for the welfare of the lower-income groups. However, the Turkish governments and municipalities during the second half of the twentieth century neither took this opportunity, nor opened access to this land for urban development through a free market economy. Instead the unclaimed land began the big city's demise due to its illegal occupation by *gecekondu* settlements (see chapter Five). From some viewpoints, this 'Third World way' has saved the urban residents from the top-down regulations of state housing. Many examples of post-war state-sponsored mass-housing around the world have been rightly criticized for their gigantic scale, monotonous industrialized blocks and non-individualized living spaces. It would nevertheless be hard to consider illegal slums that have numerous infrastructural, economic and sanitation problems as a superior alternative to mass-housing.

With the advance of globalization and multinational capitalism after the mid-1980s, the illegal city handed over from the previous period entered a new phase. While precise statistics are unattainable due to the very illegality of settlements, the percentage of residents living in squats in relation to the overall urban population seems to have dropped, despite the continuing migration to big cities. This number had reduced to 62.5 per cent in Ankara by 2002, as opposed to the 72.4 per cent at its peak in 1980; the percentage of the urban population living in *gecekondu* settlements in Turkey in general dropped to 27 per cent by 2002, as opposed to its highest rate of 35 per cent in 1995.[6] These numbers need not imply a genuine move towards official and healthy housing, however. A series of amnesty laws (*af yasası*) throughout the 1980s gave licences to illegal buildings, and thereby upgraded them to the status of official housing. With the commoditization of land, the facilitation of access to land for private ownership, the relatively expedited building permissions and increased credits granted to individuals and private firms, it was possible for big construction corporations to invest in real estate both on new land and on previously occupied *gecekondu* areas.[7] Other individual investors replaced the flimsy and ad hoc *gecekondu* buildings with concrete apartment blocks. While many neighbourhoods are now gaining official status through this process, the new global city is being built over the foundations of the illegal city that preceded it.

A series of amnesty laws after 1980 broadened the legalization policies employed by the previous governments in consequential ways.[8] After the military coup of 1980, a new law was passed in 1983 that offered to grant legal status to *gecekondu* houses built before June 1981, unless they were located in special preservation areas. The commission that prepared the law unanimously recognized the illegal settlements as a consequence of the state's failure in providing land for urban development and in constructing public housing. 'There is a dead body,' said Abbas Gökçe, a member of parliament's consulting subcommittee on housing, 'it is ours, it is the reality of our country. It is illegal, true, but there is no other solution but to forgive it.'[9] The amnesty law introduced the following year, 1984, after the democratic process was re-established, extended the terms of the previous law even further and made it much easier for settlers to apply for a licence. This new law not only granted land ownership and building permissions to *gecekondu* settlers, but also to owners of luxury hotels, factories or apartment blocks who had erected illicit buildings. Those who owned more than one house could also claim rights to legalization, making it simple for slum profiteers to take advantage of the authorization process. Another significant consequence of the amnesty laws after 1980 was their transformative effect on the city fabric, changing it from low-rise, irregular, ad hoc *gecekondu* houses to large, anonymous apartment blocks (see chapter Five). Buildings up to four storeys high could now be constructed on the existing irregular fabric of the previously illegal areas, making the amnesty law no longer a public benefit for the urban poor who had self-built their shelters, but a new urban development strategy known as the 'rehabilitative master plan' (*ıslah imar planı*). This drastically changed the physical environment and opened *gecekondu* zones to unprecedented real estate investment. The age when a single family could occupy public land and self-build an improvised house out of ad hoc materials in one night is now over. Instead, apartment blocks erected on the irregular sites of previous *gecekondu* houses, with minimal city services, improper infrastructure, inappropriate sanitation measures and, most importantly, concrete building construction without adhering to structural regulations in high-risk earthquake zones, have proliferated in Turkish cities in what may be seen as the ubiquitous 'modern vernacular' of peripheral societies.

It is not that the illegal city of the 1970s disappeared after the 1980s, but it was now given a legitimate status and a different form. From one viewpoint, these urban development and legalization strategies unavoidably caused a sense of easy legitimization for future shady businesses and illicit deals between constructors and municipalities, creating an authorization for corruption. New and broader amnesty laws soon followed, even though each and every one of them sought public support by claiming to be the last.[10] From another viewpoint, such spontaneous strategies constituted perhaps one of the few practical ways of responding to public demand, at least quantitatively, and of avoiding extreme poverty in an age of unpredictable growth and in a country struggling to regulate its ambiguous property lines.[11] This process also proved *gecekondu* to be a

Turkey's 'modern vernacular': former *gecekondus* transformed into apartments; photo by Esra Akcan.

flexible and mutating urban form that quickly adapted to the dominant economic and political shifts. Additionally, the *gecekondu* settlers of this generation were not necessarily passive groups without organized networks to support their interests, as previous conceptual models assumed, but, on the contrary, some could benefit from bounteous opportunities for upward class mobility, albeit through ways that were outside the regular norms of modernist economic development. In any event, the process exposed the increasingly irrelevant role of conventional city planning and formal economies. It is not that master plans were not made,[12] but their influence in determining or controlling urban growth was undoubtedly smaller than spontaneous strategies and informal economies.

The quality of architecture produced as a result of these urban development strategies also needs critical reflection. To do so, one might look more closely at Istanbul's Sultanbeyli neighbourhood. Perhaps no other city was as dramatically altered by the economic policies and urban regulations of the 1980s and '90s as Istanbul. With Turkey's participation in multinational capitalism, Istanbul became the country's major candidate to function as a global city. In less than two decades, the shrinking city of the early republican period had been transformed into a booming metropolis of 12.5 million people by 2008 (20 per cent of the population of Turkey now lives in Istanbul),[13] making the lack of housing both a major investment opportunity and a liability for the city. Sultanbeyli was one of the *gecekondu* settlements that started developing on the

Sultanbeyli, Istanbul, general view: infrastructure pipes waiting to be built in after the construction; photo by Esra Akcan.

northeastern edge of the city as early as the 1950s. After the amnesty law of 1984 and the construction of the TEM highway in 1985, the area became a magnet for networks of informal economies. Sultanbeyli is a settlement with fifteen different neighbourhoods: between 1954 and 1984 there were countless lawsuits over property disputes; the population increased by 61.8 per cent between 1985 and 1990; and a total of 22,559 illegal buildings were erected by 1997, destroying the existing forest and threatening the Ömerli Dam. Sultanbeyli is a neighbourhood that lives outside the law. There is even an institutionalized, but shady, real estate market involving the preparation of fraudulent legal documents as earlier settlers on occupied land get richer by selling their illegal property to newcomers. Even though Sultanbeyli is treated here as one example out of many similar others characterizing the anonymous architecture of large Turkish cities, it is a specifically complex case due to its contested history, which involves numerous instances of religious and social hostility.[14]

As a result of the legalization processes described above, there is a mixture of *gecekondu* buildings and apartment blocks in Sultanbeyli. Earlier generations of *gecekondu* houses are either getting larger with new additions or being replaced by multi-family buildings; empty lots are being filled with new real estate. There is also a random combination of single-, two-, three- or four-storey apartment buildings, most of which have left room for expansion. 'Unfinished' is the word that best describes the built environment in Sultanbeyli. Given an air of uncertainty, where the future may bring either new building permits or court orders to destroy existing ones, developers have left steel bars jutting out of the reinforced concrete

Map of Sultanbeyli's
Fatih and Turgut Reis
neighbourhoods
prepared by Oğuz Işık
and Melih Pınarcıoğlu.

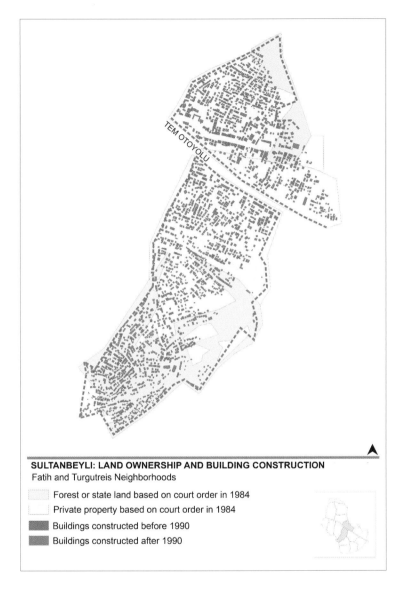

SULTANBEYLI: LAND OWNERSHIP AND BUILDING CONSTRUCTION
Fatih and Turgutreis Neighborhoods

Forest or state land based on court order in 1984

Private property based on court order in 1984

Buildings constructed before 1990

Buildings constructed after 1990

columns for a possible extension to the upper floor, regardless of the fact
that this renders the structure even more volatile to earthquake and rain
damage. Nor do the building materials and construction seem to reflect
decisions for long-term use. Architectural materials are chosen from
the most commonplace elements the construction industry can provide:
a reinforced concrete frame using the thinnest slabs and beams, most

Sultanbeyli, Istanbul: steel jutting out from concrete columns; photo by Esra Akcan.

of which may not be sufficient to withstand earthquakes, and brick infill for the walls, sometimes covered with plaster or simply left exposed for future completion. Almost all the residents look out of their apartments through a standard window frame about 1 or 1.5m wide; most have a balcony; and, if their roof is finished, it is most likely pitched. In an area without a predetermined master plan, but one that developed through a series of spontaneous decisions, multiple-lane asphalt roads with urban roundabouts connect to unfinished dirt tracks laid out on steep slopes that are inconvenient for cars or the elderly. Patches of soil and grass are left untouched next to built areas. A complex network of electrical wires serves the area, not necessarily installed with any sense of order but as an ad hoc arrangement to provide every new building with power. Since the infrastructure that carries municipal services to illegal buildings is constructed after the structures themselves, pipelines and ducts litter the streets waiting to be built in. In brief, perpetuation of the incomplete and lack of faith in the formal characterize the built environment of the shady real estate. Yet the legal collective housing schemes put in place after the 1980s are fraught with their own problems, as we discuss below.

Mass Housing Administration (TOKI) and Controversies in Social Housing

Despite notable examples, collective housing remained an exceptional residential alternative rather than the norm in Turkey before the 1980s. A new law regarding mass-housing took effect in March 1984, which facilitated the production of this residential type while simultaneously changing its definition. TOKI (Mass Housing Administration), directly connected to the Prime Ministry was founded to manage the Mass Housing Fund (Toplu Konut Fonu), which was now legally allowed to collect assets from resources other than the state's budget, and to give credit to individuals and private construction corporations. This relieved the state of the burden of providing mass-housing and helped the privatization of the housing sector as an extension of the new free market economy. The new regulations also changed the definition of mass social housing. Individuals or constructors who wished to build collective housing with units as large as 150 m² (formerly this number was 100 m²) or to build second properties and holiday homes in coastal towns were now eligible to apply for mass-housing credit.[15] As a result, more than four times as many cooperative housing projects were realized between 1984 and 1991 as had been built throughout the entire previous history of cooperative housing in Turkey.[16] Especially after the Islamist party of Tayyip Erdoğan came to power, unprecedented quantities of resources and state land were transferred to TOKI. Between 2003 and 2010 TOKI constructed 500,000 units as part of the *gecekondu* renewal projects and new social housing, not only in the three big cities of Istanbul, Ankara and İzmir, but also in Bursa, Elazığ, Erzurum, Erzincan, Gaziantep, Samsun, Şanlıurfa, Trabzon and elsewhere.[17] While these practices supplied housing for the demand, they participated in the homogenization of the built environment throughout the country, by using standardized regulations and similar residential projects. Hardly any of them explored architecturally creative ways to improve the quality of life and space.

Among the fastest growing new residential types have been sprawling high-rises with between twelve and twenty-four storeys, some even higher, often built using prefabricated techniques and rationalized construction processes unavailable to the small contractors of the previous period. Together they have formed colossal 'edge-cities' such as Ümraniye and Ataşehir on the Asian side of Istanbul, and Beylikdüzü and Bahçeşehir on the European side, arranged around giant shopping malls and international megastores. That much of the new residential construction in these edge-cities remains unfinished or empty supports İlhan Tekeli's analysis that since the 1980s the mass-production of

TOKI housing, Düzce, 2005.

TOKI high-rise blocks in Istanbul: photo by Pablo Martinez Muniz, *Bizim Evler* series, Fragmentpolis project, 2008–10.

middle and upper-middle income housing has exceeded the demand, not only reversing the picture of the previous period (when housing production was far below the demand) but highlighting the importance of *creating* demand through newer marketing and advertising techniques.[18] An almost surreal example is 'My World' in Ataşehir, a profit-generating, middle-income residential development by TOKI on the Asian side of Istanbul, covering a vast built-up landscape of 20- to 30-storey cylindrical and prismatic towers. High-rise blocks became a favourite type for private construction firms as well. On a smaller scale, albeit with greater architectural ambition for high-rise typology, are Adnan Kazmaoğlu's blocks for the Yeşil Vadi housing project in Ümraniye, Istanbul (2003), each block combining three intersecting brick-clad circular towers with large carved-in balconies.

Another of TOKI's major activities was *gecekondu* clearance, which it designated as the urban renewal initiative (*kentsel dönüşüm*) that the institution sees as part of the United Nations' HABITAT mission.[19] Under this description, however, colossal swathes of *gecekondu* were destroyed

Adnan Kazmaoğlu, Yeşil Vadi Housing, Istanbul, 2003; photo by Cemal Emden.

TOKI high-rise blocks in Ataşehir, Istanbul: photo by Pablo Martinez Muniz, *Ataşehir* series, Fragmentpolis project, 2008–10.

and massive numbers of settlers were relocated to state-built mass-housing, usually composed of smaller units miles away from the original neighbourhoods. Most of these projects were socially contested, provoking settlers to protest against the demolition of their houses. A series of laws between 2003 and 2005 gave municipalities unprecedented rights to designate *gecekondu* settlements as renewal zones and relocate the settlers, usually by buying their underpriced property and selling them state-built mass-housing units with unduly high mortgage prices.[20] In the name of the *gecekondu* renewal projects issued since 2003, TOKI planned to build 40,000 new dwellings in numerous mass-housing projects around the whole country and so enforce this new residential type on the former tenants of *gecekondu* houses.[21]

One notable example is the rehabilitation of the Protocol Road in Ankara, which connects the airport to the city centre and so greets the diplomats and visitors as they enter and leave the capital. The *gecekondu* settlements that had haphazardly spread along this highway were deemed inappropriate to bear such symbolic significance. More than 6,000 informally built houses were demolished and approximately 2,500 families relocated in mass-housing constructed from prefabricated slabs, with standardized unit plans, windows, doors and appliances.[22] Numerous *gecekondu* renewal projects have been carried out in districts of Istanbul suitable for new real-estate investment or large-scale development,[23] such as the Ayazma neighbourhood, which has been identified as a possible Olympic Village, or Maltepe, which attracts luxury housing developers due to its proximity to the main transportation routes and beautiful views of the Sea of Marmara. The displacement process usually overlooks the rights of residents without legal papers and thus causes violent disagreements between the residents and the police.[24] These *gecekondu* renewal projects of the 2000s can better be characterized as state-led gentrification rather than as public housing that should have preserved the rights of the underprivileged population.

Only a few of the *gecekondu* renewal projects were commissioned to architects who had a commitment to the creative improvement of space and the status of the profession. The first stage of construction in the Dikmen valley was an early, yet significant, example designed by Doruk Pamir and executed by the Ankara Municipality. The previous *gecekondu* settlers were given priority in purchasing apartments in the new residential blocks that replaced their houses.[25] Pamir's Dikmen Bridge and Housing (1991–6) not only provided a sanitized neighbourhood that solved major infrastructural problems such as flooding, which regularly threatened the previous settlement, but it was also more architecturally engaging than the standardized blocks usually used by the government or municipalities in other *gecekondu* renewal projects. In Pamir's project, a technologically ambitious bridge accommodating commercial and cultural activities connects the two sides of the valley as well as the high-rise residential blocks at either end, which together contain 205 units. While the bridge is an acknowledged reference to the Ponte Vecchio in Florence, the project as a whole inserts itself forcefully into the landscape without any nostalgic or pastoral pretensions, yet it preserves the natural topography of the site and opens up space for one of the largest green areas in the city.[26] Further construction in the Dikmen valley was much more controversial due its gentrification policies, but a similar site

Gecekondu renewal project for the Protocol Road in Ankara; top: Aerial view with *gecekondu* settlements before demolition; middle: Aerial view after the demolition of *gecekondu* settlements; bottom: TOKI mass-housing to relocate the previous *gecekondu* settlers; 2000s.

Doruk Pamir, Dikmen Valley Bridge and Housing, Ankara, 1991–6; photo by Esra Akcan.

planning approach was adopted and new buildings (by other architects) were erected only on the slopes at the side, while the area in between was reserved for a large-scale public park.

A few examples stand out from the mass of new affordable housing implemented by the municipalities and governmental institutions. The Eryaman project, for instance, was one of the governmental social housing initiatives constructed on the western edge of Ankara; the first stage was started in 1984 and the final stages were completed around the very end of the 1990s. Planned for a population of 210,000, organized in neighbourhoods of between 5,000 and 8,000 people, the project brings together multiple income groups (albeit usually segregated in separate sections), accommodated in mid-rise apartment blocks or houses up to three storeys high.[27] Especially during the third and fourth stages of the Eryaman housing, TOKI commissioned architects devoted to the exploration of quality-based collective housing, rather than simply a quantity-based supply to meet demand. Architects Ahmet Gülgönen, Tuncay Çavdar, Ragıp Buluç, Doruk Pamir, Erkut Şahinbaş, Ziya Tanalı and Oral Vural participated in these stages, experimenting with both stylistic and spatial alternatives that explored ways of collective living outside the regularized residential models.[28] Buluç's unadorned, purified point-blocks, Çavdar's narrow inner streets and 'streets in the air' defined by 'Turkish house' style blocks, or Pamir's massive blocks complemented by non-functional frames, contributed to the creation of a residential district with a variety of urban outdoor spaces and common green areas, as well as multiple aesthetic preferences. Architects paid attention to providing as many unit types as possible within the constraints of standardized mass-housing.

Şanlıurfa Mass Housing by the architects Erdoğan Elmas and Zafer Gülçur (begun 1996; additions by Can Elmas and Çağla Akyürek Elmas) is another architecturally significant example of state-sponsored social housing in Turkey. The ensemble is placed on a grid-iron plan with parallel rows orientated in the same direction, while the dwelling units are organized around their own private courtyards reminiscent of the local outdoor living space. Thus the project makes use of modernist mass-housing strategies, but combines them with regional space-making patterns that are appropriate for the hot and arid climate of Şanlıurfa, a city in southeastern Turkey with a substantial Kurdish population.[29] Inner circulation within the units also extends to outdoor spaces, such as arcades and terraces along the courtyard. Han Tümertekin's ATK Lodgings (near Istanbul, 1998) for textile workers in Çerkezköy is another unusual

Ahmet Gülgönen, Eryaman Housing, Fourth Stage, Ankara, 1993–6; photo by Esra Akcan.

example of mass-housing that goes against the grain of its received norms. Rather than parallel blocks in a *Zeilenbau* fashion, Tümertekin placed the two blocks in an arc so that the living spaces of the units face each other, deliberately ensuring that there would be no possibility of expansion and repeating the pattern (see overleaf). This gives the project a unique aura rather than symbolizing mass production, as is usually the case in collective social housing. The common social functions take place in the park between the blocks and inter-circulation between the units is handled along the arcade and the upper gallery at the rear side. The units range from small studio apartments to triplex units, providing maximum variety within the limits of the 6 × 9 structural frame.

There has been only sporadic interest in post-disaster housing and this has remained plainly insufficient in the face of frequent deadly earthquakes: 18,000 people died in the earthquake of 1999, for example, destroying extensive neighbourhoods in northwestern Turkey, including İzmit and Istanbul. The corrupt building industry that quickly produced low- and middle-income concrete apartment blocks without adequate

Erdoğan Elmas and Zafer Gülçur, Şanlıurfa Mass Housing, Şanlıurfa, 1996–present, plan (opposite) and model.

reinforcement was undoubtedly responsible for such massive numbers of casualties. Shigeru Ban's post-disaster shelters made of cardboard and Tabanlıoğlu's TEGV post-disaster housing were two notable responses to the earthquake in 1999. There was no change, however, in the major cause of the initial scale of the damage, namely the corrupt building industry. Despite a handful of exceptional examples cited above, it was debatable whether most of TOKI's projects improved the quality of architectural

Han Tümertekin
(Mimarlar Tasarım),
ATK Lodgings,
Istanbul, 1998,
axonometric drawing.

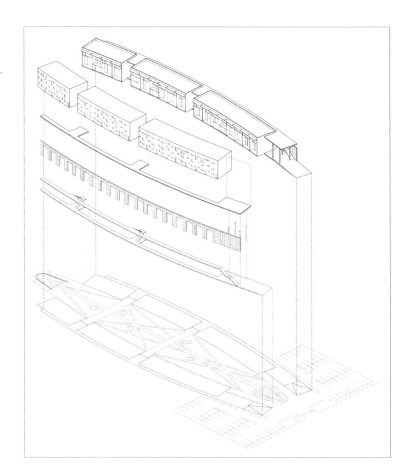

spaces for the *gecekondu* settlers and the new rural immigrants. Especially during the 2000s, TOKI, a government institution founded to provide mass-housing, was transformed into a participant in the practice of profit-orientated enterprises building urban spaces for the benefit of the financial and political elite.

New Wealth, New Suburbia and Gated Developments

The commodification of land, relatively expedited building permits and credits granted to big construction firms energized the real estate market and subsequently produced new residential patterns. Whereas the budgets of the small contractors of the 1960s and '70s were limited to constructing single apartment blocks, the big construction firms that

Shigeru Ban
Architects, paper log
houses used after an
earthquake in Turkey,
1999.

emerged after the mid-1980s, such as MESA, ENKA, TEPE and MAYA, undertook large-scale housing ensembles. Some of these attempted to carry out collective housing in small cities, such as the MESA housing projects designed by İlhan Kural and Nerkis Kural for Balıkesir, Urla and Mersin, each with a different housing typology in response to the different climates. Most of the major construction, however, took place in the bigger metropolises and usually combined multiple, but predictable, types such as high-rise blocks, mid-rise apartments and single family houses in one setting.[30]

Another outcome of the capitalist housing market after the mid-1980s was the emergence of gated communities for high-income groups, especially in Istanbul. While the construction of cooperative housing for middle-income families continued, there was a significant difference between the new gated community phenomenon and the original motivations of collective social housing. Rather than mass production for the sake of economic efficiency, buyers of houses in gated communities combined their resources to enjoy a segregated and sterilized neighbourhood that would include only people of their own economic status, and so avoid the perceived chaos of the metropolis. Istanbul's gated communities are located either close to the inner city, granting the residents views of the Bosphorus, or on the outskirts near a significant natural attraction such as a forest or a lake. Individual houses usually range between 200 m² and 500 m², but can go up to 1,000 m²; their prices may reach as high

Map of gated
communities in
Istanbul, c. 2010.

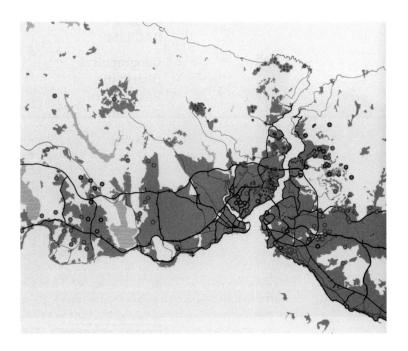

as $1.5 million, far beyond the reach of the average income.[31] Many of the communities are supplemented by deluxe amenities, including gyms and spas, indoor and outdoor pools (in addition to private pools), tennis courts, golf courses and helicopter landing pads. Sales advertisements for these houses promise luxury and escape from the metropolis. The one for Beykoz Mansions reads 'lack of parking, shortness of time, pollution or similar problems terminate at the community's gate',[32] while Acarkent, which offers villas as big as 1,200 m² for a million dollars, offers assurance that it accommodates 'those who long for a peaceful, clean-aired, modern and comfortable world, instead of the hectic life in the big metropolis'.[33] Yet these luxurious neighbourhoods are not necessarily within the legal frameworks of municipal master plans either: construction of Beykoz, Acarkent and others was started illegally in a public forest and only later were they given legal status.[34]

Typologically many of these gated communities are composed of a series of identical villas set in private gardens. Jansen's garden-city ideal has finally come true, albeit with more luxurious, segregated and ultimately anti-metropolitan attributes. The pioneering examples of gated communities employ the nostalgia of 'old Istanbul' as a marketing tool, fabricating an imaginary past of decency, elegance and sophistication, before the city became the home to immigrant 'Others' who could now be avoided by living in a neighbourhood behind closed doors. Kemer Country was an influential example of this tendency, whose design was directed by the leading new urbanist Andreas Duany, and it integrated the work of architects such as Tuncay Çavdar, Cemal Mutlu and Abdel Wahab El-Wakil. The traditional 'Turkish house' was a major formal source of inspiration here in the creation of both single-family houses in private gardens and street scenes. The 'postmodern turn' in Turkish architectural culture discussed previously manifests itself vividly in these 'Turkish style villas' and in the widespread commodification of tradition by the luxury residential market. Unlike Sedad Eldem's meticulous pro-gramme of studying, theorizing and typologically codifying the timber-frame Ottoman/Turkish houses within the nationalist context of the 1930s (see chapter Three), this new traditionalism turns tile roofs, wide overhangs, modular windows and projecting window bays into an instant identity kit applicable to a range of suburban residential typologies. A related marketing strategy involves references to traditional Ottoman *mahalles* and their idealization as the paradigm of neighbourliness, familiarity and community that Istanbul has allegedly lost in modern times, especially since the urban transformations of the 1950s.[35] Although the actual site-plans of these ultra-privatized residences (in remote sub-urban locations accessible only by car) bear no resemblance whatsoever to the narrow streets and cul-de-sacs of traditional Ottoman *mahalles*,

Andreas Duany, Tuncay Çavdar, Cemal Mutlu, et al., Kemer Country Houses, Istanbul, sketch from publicity brochure. The caption reads 'Traditional Turkish architecture inspired the houses around the square. The houses have courtyards and projection bays'.

Turkish style apartments and row houses in Göktürk residential development, Istanbul, c. mid-2000; photo by Sibel Bozdoğan.

nostalgic evocations of tradition, history and culture are strategically employed in advertisements for new gated residential developments. The names given to the projects are testimony to this strategy: from literal references to Ottoman *konaks* (such as Beykoz Konakları and Osmanlı Konakları) to allusions to closed community life (for example, Kasaba, literally 'small town').

The concept of a small town community is carried over into that of a bona fide 'theme park' by yet another gated community, Istanbul-Istanbul (1999), which is located near Kemer Country and was again developed by KORAY and designed by the French firm CMLA (Charles M. Legler Architect). Mixing different but equally luxurious residential types (duplex villas, twin villas, townhouses and studio apartments) around a picturesque landscape featuring an artificial lake and a replica of a sixteenth-century Ottoman stone bridge by Sinan, Istanbul-Istanbul is advertised as a hybrid between 'traditional Turkish architecture and a Mediterranean town'.[36] The most recent and extreme example of the gated community-as-theme park, however, is Bosphorus City at Halkalı, Küçükçekmece, some 40 km to the west of Istanbul. Financed by Simpaş Real Estate Investment Partnership and designed by an international team, the project artificially recreates the existing city (without the latter's contamination by migrants, crowds, crime, political unrest and traffic mess). Replicating the actual Bosphorus and its historical wooden *yalıs* in a totally controlled 'stage-set' environment – the

Rendering of
Bosphorus City
residential develop-
ment, Istanbul, 2010.

'Bosphorus' is a canal 720 metres long with an average depth of 1.5 m – the scheme includes a mix of waterfront villas (*yalıs*) and higher-rise apartments.

The physical transformation of the municipality of Göktürk, where both Kemer Country and Istanbul-Istanbul are located, is particularly revealing of the impact of globalization and neo-liberal policies on Istanbul's urban periphery. Initially a little-known village some 25 kilometres northwest of the city centre (with a tiny population of farmers and workers employed by the nearby brick factory and coal mines), Göktürk was incorporated into the boundaries of Greater Istanbul and became a local municipality in 1993 when development started on Kemer Country. Following the success of Kemer Country, land values increased by 500 per cent and Göktürk became a booming satellite city of numerous gated communities, ranging from villa types to other low-rise, high-density configurations. The publicity brochure produced by Göktürk's remarkably entrepreneurial municipality takes pride in the fact that 'the design quality of these [new] residences, their high prices and the quality of the infrastructure *ensures the maximum homogeneity* [our emphasis] of its inhabitants'.[37] Meanwhile the original inhabitants (the poorer farmers and industrial workers) of Göktürk are often employed as gardeners, security guards and cleaning staff by these wealthy inhabitants, underscoring both a new social segregation and a new relationship between different classes living in close suburban proximity.

It should be noted that neither the preference for villas over collective mass-housing nor garden city ideals are entirely new in Turkey, as they constituted the dominant ideological and aesthetic agenda of early republican architectural culture (see chapter Three). Yet major ideological and cultural differences separate the two periods. In stark contrast with the early republican emphasis on functional (*kullanışlı*), economical (*ucuz*) and healthy (*sıhhatli*) houses that were to be civilizing models for the entire nation, the new gated communities are primarily about exclusivity and expensiveness. New keywords like pleasure (*keyif*), quality of life (*yaşam kalitesi*), exclusiveness (*ayrıcalık*) and security (*güven*) feature most prominently in the marketing of these new villas. Since the 1990s these villas have effectively introduced the term 'lifestyle communities' to the Turkish real estate market.[38] Promising new lifestyles close to nature (with swimming pools, tennis courts, golf courses and horseback riding

Göktürk suburban
sprawl, Istanbul,
c. mid-2006;
aerial view.

among other facilities) and away from mess, environmental pollution, traffic and crime, as well as the social heterogeneity of an increasingly contested 'public space' within the city, they epitomize the global trend towards the privatization of space in general – a conspicuous retreat by the wealthy and the privileged behind well-guarded perimeters.

Even though early gated communities usually attracted 'white Turks', as they are called in popular parlance (internationally well-connected, technologically savvy and mostly young wealthy professionals), examples catering to different income levels and life choices soon emerged. Many of the new residential developments mentioned above are evidence of

258

what Richard Sennett calls 'globalization substituting alterity with a regime of differences that are non-interactive [between] populations that are diverse but have less contact with each other . . . and the result is that difference produces indifference'.[39] As Ayfer Bartu and Biray Koluoğlu have cogently observed, both the 'white Turks' of gated luxury suburbia and the poorer residents of new TOKI *gecekondu*-clearance apartment blocks on the urban periphery share a common predicament (the former by choice, the latter by poverty and absence of choice) – 'an increasing shrinking of the experience of Istanbul'.[40]

While many of these gated communities are located on the outskirts of Istanbul, there are various high-end examples in the already developed parts of the city, such as Maya Residences in Etiler and Platin Houses in Ulus, both designed by prominent international architects: SOM and Altuğ and Behruz Çinici, respectively. The Platin Houses (1992–9), for example, comprises ten identical five-storey blocks and two terraced ones, all

Behruz Çinici, Platin Houses, Istanbul, 1992–9.

Ersen Gürsel, Aktur
Houses, Bodrum,
1987–90.

organized around the common garden to enhance
the sloping land of the site. Its residents are drawn by
spectacular views of the Bosphorus, ample parking in
a relatively dense section of the city, proximity to the
metropolitan cultural attractions, and shared amenities
such as an indoor swimming pool.

The holiday home boom on the Aegean and Mediterranean coasts for upper middle-class families and
the metropolitan elite became yet another source of
revenue for architects. Many designers demonstrated
their formal statements in single-family houses located
in holiday resorts. Similarly, collective holiday housing
projects create a microcosm of stylistic tendencies in
the Turkish architectural scene, where one can find
postmodern buildings with references to traditional
'Turkish houses', purified white small cubes and spatial
experiments. A neighbourhood pattern composed of
white cubes was introduced most notably by Ersen
Gürsel in his Bodrum Aktur and Torba 83 holiday
homes, as an expression of Mediterranean identity.[41] This trend proved
to be so ubiquitous after the 1980s that it spread for miles across the slopes
of Bodrum and opened up an anonymous category popularly known as
'Bodrum houses'. In Göçek Portville, the architect Cemal Mutlu placed
villas with an 'old Turkish house' appearance along the artificial canals
on which residents take their boats for daily transportation, thereby
fabricating an unambiguous hybrid fantasy of Venice and Istanbul.

Overall, the residential culture of the period between the mid-1980s
and mid-2000s can perhaps best be characterized as productive; racing
to respond to the booming urbanization while benefiting those who
profit from housing. The production has been triangulated by informal
economies generating unplanned, spontaneous and semi-legal neighbourhoods composed of a mixture of *gecekondus* and ad hoc apartment
blocks, and by the governmental organizations producing mass-housing
and *gecekondu* renewal projects, and finally by architects working for big
construction firms and wealthy clients. The residential segregation based
on income and social status had never been so accentuated. The majority
of cities are still dominated by generic buildings, most of which are illegal
or legalized only after their construction, while architectural explorations
that open a zone for creativity within the economic and governmental
systems are few and sporadic. Even so, the possibility to design houses
collectively for bigger sites granted architects the opportunity to search
for alternative residential typologies. A number of architects from a new

generation embraced this opportunity and began working on novel residential models that set themselves apart from repetitive identical villas in a gated community, developer apartment blocks along a city street, or high-rise point blocks standing in the middle of open land. We turn to those in the next chapter.

chapter nine

The 'Young Turk Architects' of Globalization

I never believe that architects are people who can save the world . . . it is much more important to . . . produce quality jobs that please the client who demanded them.
Hasan Çalışlar [1]

On 1 May 1977 the Chamber of Architects and Engineers carried one of the largest and reddest banners in the most prestigious location of the biggest and bloodiest political rally in modern Turkish history (see chapter Six). When the architects of the 1960s and '70s are compared to the professionals of the last two decades, it is hard to believe that the two were practising in the same country only two decades apart. The identifying character of Turkish architecture at the end of the twentieth century can perhaps best be diagnosed by observing its contrast to the 1960s generation – a contrast violently instituted with the *coup d'état* of 1980 and strengthened by the global political economies after the end of the Cold War.

Post-upheaval Architecture

The exhibition 'New Explorations in Architecture/Young Turk Architects' presented a selection of works submitted for consideration in 1999.[2] From a mysteriously low number of submissions (35 projects by even fewer architects), the jury, which comprised such forceful figures as Süha Özkan (General Secretary of the Aga Khan Foundation), Haluk Pamir (the future Dean of the Faculty of Architecture at the Middle East Technical University), Michael Sorkin (head of the Urban Design department at the City University of New York), Uğur Tanyeli (editor-in-chief of the architectural journal *Arredamento Dekorasyon*, later *Arredamento Mimarlık*) and the respected architect and teacher Ziya Tanalı, selected fifteen projects by nine architectural firms.[3] Even though the terms did not pass without a sense of irony, the attributes 'new' and 'young' served as codes advocating a return to modernist aesthetics in strong opposition to the stylistically historicist tendencies of

Istanbul Modern
Museum, detail; photo
by Murat Germen.

Postmodernism that had taken the scene after the 1980s with the work of Merih Karaaslan, Tuncay Çavdar, and the contemporary work of previously established architects including Behruz Çinici and Doruk Pamir. Instead the jury underlined that the selected 'Young Turk architects' were 'expected to make a transformation in Turkish architecture at the dawn of the twenty-first century', in Özkan's words; they stayed away from 'the commoditized images of regionalism, and the clichés of ubiquitous international style', in Sorkin's words; and they were qualified for the jury's expectations to create 'new design alternatives in line with the conceptual frameworks of [world] architectural design (contextualist, brutalist, deconstructivist, minimalist, etc.)', in Pamir's words.[4] Satisfying the jury's predictions, the selected architects, with a few exceptions, made their undeniable marks on the architectural scene of the following decade, strengthening their network by participating in copious conferences, publications and professional education.

Among the architects who submitted constructed projects to the exhibition, Nevzat Sayın, Han Tümertekin and Gökhan Avcıoğlu had already made a name for themselves by advocating a shift in the ruling taste of the 1980s, and for criticizing the postmodernist tendencies of the previous generation. Nowhere was this transformation as explicitly visible as in the two phases of the Gön Leather Factory in Istanbul, designed by Nevzat Sayın. While Gön I (1990) still carried residues of the historicism and image-making tendencies found in the architect's early work, such as a monumental temple front with an abstracted pediment, colonnade and a series of round windows, Gön II (1994–5) was constructed as a minimally perforated, exposed reinforced concrete triangular box stripped of any historicist reference. In Sayın's own words, Gön II 'was a truly industrial building that came out of the first building but eliminated all of its excess; a building that contained nothing but the most necessary.'[5] In contrast to the conventional square atrium of Gön I, the atrium in Gön II was designed as a dynamic elliptic shape with free-standing concrete circular columns and i-beams crossing it in vertical and transverse directions. Sayın also oversaw the complete construction process, culminating in a tectonic sensibility for different load-bearing materials and exposed concrete eliminating any additional facade or surface treatment, as well as in a quest for precision and artful construction. This was to guide his future work, such as White House in a Void, Tekirdağ (1997), Görener House, Bandırma (1998), and the Yahşibey houses, İzmir (1999–2003). Critics were drawn to Sayın's quiet, restrained and plain forms, and his use of natural materials available or recycled on the site, in strong contrast to the bombardment of images preferred by the previous generation. During the Anyone Corporation's eighth meeting in Ankara in 1998, Serhan Ada presented Gön II to the international media as a quest for going back to the 'beginnings' when there was nothing but 'dust and wind'.[6] Tansel Korkmaz praised Sayın for 'being at peace with limits . . . avoiding the boisterousness of invasion . . . daring to bear the weight of meaning rather than the lightness of seducing.'[7]

A similar drive for tectonic sensibility and restrained expression guided Han Tümertekin's early work. The B2 holiday house in the small village of Ayvacık (2000–2001), the winner of the Aga Khan international award in 2004, was a plain rectangular prism composed of two inverted U-shaped reinforced concrete structural frames. In between were totally transparent surfaces and bamboo-filled metal-frame shutters on the front facade, and rough stone aggregate constructed by local masons on the side facades and the roof. Describing his work as a 'degree-zero architecture that necessitates a total memory loss',[8] Tümertekin's hand-drawn sketches, attention to the sectional elaboration of the interior space, interpretation of available materials, construction techniques and

Nevzat Sayın (NSMH), Gön II, Istanbul. 1994–5, two views of the atrium.

Han Tümertekin
(Mimarlar Tasarım),
B2 House, Ayvacık,
2000–2001; photo by
Cemal Emdem.

architectural types of the site captured the imagination of his colleagues and critics by way of its contrast to the established taste of the times, and soon carried his office, Mimarlar Tasarım, to international fame.[9]

In a series of residential and industrial buildings built in the late 1990s, Gökhan Avcıoğlu (Global Architectural Development/GAD), on the other hand, explored the possibilities of glass and demountable steel-frame construction. In strong contrast to the historicist facadism and solidity of buildings in the previous decade, Avcıoğlu designed totally transparent facades and underlined the expressive potential of light steel construction materials by using them as free-standing or projecting elements that created billboard effects, as in the Administration building of Yalova Elyaf Factory (1995–7), or exhibited the factory's production, as in the Aksoy Technical Research and Development Building, İzmit (1996–8). Avcıoğlu declared that the breaking of light, reflection, disappearance and illusion effects in the work of artists such as Dan Graham, Donald Judd and Robert Morris inspired him for new architectural expressions.[10] The most publicly recognized result of this approach appears in his renovation in Istanbul of the Esma Sultan waterfront house along the Bosphorus (2003). Keeping the facades but hollowing out the interior

Gökhan Avcıoğlu
(GAD), Aksoy Technical
Research and
Development
Building, İzmit,
1996–8.

as a whole, Avcıoğlu placed a glass box inside, turning the old building into a reception hall without changing the vista on the Bosphorus.

Among other practising architects, the 'Young Turk Architects' exhibition brought forward Emre Arolat and Murat Tabanlıoğlu, who both started their careers in offices established by their parents but before the age of forty had turned them into the two biggest corporate architectural firms in Turkey. In his early career, Emre Arolat had already emphasized demountable and expedited construction techniques that would 'produce alternatives to the perceived weakness of the country's construction industry'.[11] During the 1990s and 2000s Arolat and Tabanlıoğlu continued their search for technical excellence and precision through the adoption of digital technologies, construction techniques and patented building materials unavailable to previous generations. Most importantly, Arolat emphasized expanding his architectural office into 'an institution in itself', with separate partners for design, office management and public relations, and separate specialized employees for different phases and aspects of a project.[12] This new definition of the architectural profession as a corporate business and emphasis on group work, rather than the conventional conception of the architect as a solitary genius, secured Emre Arolat Architects important commissions around the world as well as in Turkey, including the İpekyol Textile Factory, Edirne (2004–6), which won the Aga Khan international award in 2010. Among other buildings, Dalaman Airport in Muğla (1999–2006), from which international tourists are taken to their holiday resorts, is composed of a reinforced concrete grid structural system covered by a steel translucent veil. A gap of 2.5 metres between the two systems regulates light and wind penetrating into the building and hence creates a microclimate. Arolat emphasized his conscious rejection of any search for architectural identity and regionalism, or any attempt at domestication and adornment, instead celebrating exposed materials.[13] Murat and Melkan Tabanlıoğlu advocated a similar professionalization and institutionalization of the big architectural office.[14] Their clients' satisfaction with the Doğan Media Printing Center, Ankara (1995–7), led to the office receiving many large-scale commissions. They have recently explored ways of improving energy performance and addressing ecological concerns in large buildings, such as the Sapphire building (2006–10), located in the new Central Business District of Istanbul. As of 2010 it was the tallest skyscraper in Turkey, accommodating business, commercial and residential functions. A buffer zone between two structural skins on the facade provides climate control, interrupted every three floors by sky-gardens.

The 'Young Turk Architects' exhibition put on the map even younger and lesser-known names, including Semra Teber, the only independent woman architect included, and Deniz Aslan / Arda Inceoğlu, who continued both professional and academic careers. After collaborating with his father Behruz Çinici, most notably in the Aga Khan prize-winning Parliament Mosque (see chapter Seven), Can Çinici embarked on housing and urban renewal projects (see below). Mehmet Kütükçüoğlu later founded Teğet Mimarlık with Ertuğ Uçar, and their Istanbul Sea Museum at Beşiktaş (2005–10) is shaping the new silhouette of the Bosphorus,

opposite:
Emre Arolat
Architects, Dalaman
Airport, Muğla,
1999–2006, interior;
photo by Ali Bekman.

Tabanlıoğlu
Architects (Murat &
Melkan Tabanlıoğlu),
Doğan Media Printing
Centre, Ankara,
1995–7; photo by
Jeroen Musch.

Tabanlıoğlu
Architects (Murat &
Melkan Tabanlıoğlu),
Sapphire Tower,
Istanbul, 2006–10;
photo by Thomas
Mayer.

opposite:
Sapphire Tower:
interior gardens;
photo by
Helene Binet.

standing at the same height as the Dolmabahçe and Çırağan palaces while abstractly alluding to their facade modulation. On the street side, the building creates a large urban piazza at the dense heart of the city, separated from a busy vehicular road by an arcade. The inner organization takes its shape from the placement of the big ships and the horizontal rows of upper-level viewing galleries. This generates a sliced fenestration on the Bosphorus facade and from the inside creates an unusual way of looking at the Bosphorus through vertical slits, rather than the ubiquitous panoramic view enabled by wall-to-wall windows.

At a time of unprecedented urbanization, ever-growing construction and property activity, and a slightly augmented demand for qualified architecture, the building boom naturally made space for many other 'Young Turk architects'. These included Şevki Pekin, who had been producing works in a restrained modernist language since the late 1970s but who started receiving recognition with national awards only in the late 1990s and early 2000s with the shift in the established taste. Among the growing practices with younger professionals in Istanbul were Kerem Erginoğlu / Hasan Çalışlar, Kreativ Architectural Office (Aydan Volkan, Selim Cengiç), Boran Ekinci, Durmuş Dilekçi / Emir Uras, while Bünyamin Derman and Cem Ilhan/Tülin Hadi made notable impressions in architectural competitions. Meanwhile, the established big architectural offices, such as Tekeli and Sisa, and Mehmet Konuralp, continued working on important sites in Istanbul. In Ankara, special mention should be made of the productive careers of Filiz and Coşkun Erkal; Erkut Şahinbaş, who designed the buildings for the Bilkent University campus; Semra and Özcan Uygur, who built many public and institutional buildings, most notably the TED College; and Hasan Özbay, Hasan Başbuğ and Baran Idil, who started work on an extension to the Ministry of External Affairs (1990–2005).

The 'Young Turk Architects' established their presence by advocating a shift in established taste and in some cases transforming the structure of the architectural office. They advocated a set of formal concerns other than the search for identity through postmodern stylistic gestures, as in the 1980s and early 1990s. These included attention to tectonics as the honest expression of construction, whether by using stone available on the site or advanced industrial materials; the employment of technological progress in the construction industry; and the use of computerized methods in the office. Many other factors remained as before, however, including the economic infrastructure, production systems and the architects' desire for good relations with the client. Uğur Tanyeli pointed out that the 'Young Turk Architects' were young in age, but not necessarily in spirit, holding professional concerns rather than experimental,

Teğet Architecture
(Mehmet Kütükçüoğlu
and Ertuğ Uçar), Sea
Museum at Beşiktaş,
Istanbul, 2005–11,
Photoshopped view
from the Bosphorus
and a rendering of
the interior.

intellectual or discursive ones.[15] It might be informative to cite an interview with Kerem Erginoğlu and Hasan Çalışlar, who won *Architectural Review*'s Best Building award in 2010 for their renovation of the saltworks warehouse in Istanbul:

> There needs to be a lot of products to be able to speak on them
> . . . Therefore, our motto has been to make buildings at all costs
> [Kerem Erginoğlu].

> I never believe that architects are people who can save the world,
> as it is constantly injected in students' minds. Did we invent the
> Internet, clone humans, can we change the world? No. We can
> only prepare packages for the changing world . . . Rather than
> saying very important things, it is much more important to deal
> with all the criteria including design, detail, finance and building
> permission in order to produce quality jobs that please the client
> who demanded them. [Hasan Çalışlar][16]

The much starker and more dramatic chronological marker that transformed the architectural profession in Turkey was not the formal

Şevki Pekin, Six Houses, Sapanca near Istanbul, 1995.

shifts initiated by the 'Young Turk architects' but the 1980 *coup d'état*. In order to understand the qualifying character of architecture after 1980, it would be more explanatory to compare it to the era that preceded it, the time when architects of the 1960s generation, despite their irresolvable contradictions, were politically charged, socially committed and critical of the system. In strong contrast to the rebellious nature of this generation, architects of post-upheaval times stayed away, perhaps unavoidably, from political engagement. As Cengiz Bektaş, a prominent architect of the previous generation, stated, those who even mentioned the term 'social responsibility' were ridiculed after the 1980s.[17] During times of forced obedience, 'Young Turk architects' pursued professional and pragmatic concerns.

Nonetheless, this post-upheaval architecture had a significant transformative power after 2000, particularly in the area of housing, when a couple of 'Young Turk architects' created collective housing projects that carved a space outside the norm. This norm had been dictated by *gecekondu* houses and small-contractor apartment buildings in the three decades following 1950, but was transformed after the 1980s as more and more *gecekondu* houses were turned into illegal/semi-legal apartment buildings, and as the real estate market was reshaped by big construction firms, the privatization of state land, and the streamlining of building permits and mortgage regulations (see chapters Five and Eight). In this context, greater numbers of large-scale gated communities were being designed than of individual small contractor apartment buildings and single-family houses.[18] Despite these changes in the housing sector, it is surprising that there was little alteration in the major housing typology until the end of the twentieth century: whether in collective housing, a gated community or an individual apartment building, most of the population continued to live in free-standing single or multi-family buildings whose size and height were regulated by similar building plot dimensions throughout Turkey. This was a norm instituted by Hermann Jansen in the 1930s for single-family houses, based on pre-war garden city principles, but when new master plan regulations were endorsed after 1955 a density about sixteen times greater in four- or five-storey buildings was squeezed into the same area. The gated communities of the 1990s, for instance, were almost always composed of rows of villas or multi-family apartment buildings placed side by side on building lots with dimensions similar to those of the last 60 years. Whether they preferred 'old Turkish house' style or elite modernist taste, the architects of these housing ensembles had not challenged the old norms or use the opportunity to design collective housing on larger plots.

It is exactly the paradigmatic nature of this housing type that makes a few recent collective housing projects critical. The social segregation introduced into the metropolitan life by gated communities remains intact, but the possibility of designing houses for bigger sites granted the architects the opportunity to search for alternative residential types. A number of architects from the new generation embraced this opportunity and began working on novel residential models that set themselves apart from repetitive identical villas in a gated community, developer apartment blocks along a city street, or high-rise point blocks standing in the middle of open ground. In a way, these architects embraced a 'post-critical' position similar to that employed by their colleagues in other countries, seizing opportunities for architectural creativity within the market and municipal regulations, rather than criticizing the capitalist system for its inability to go beyond commercialism. Manfredo Tafuri's well-known conclusion about the impossibility of critical practice, especially pertinent for social housing, cast doubt irrecoverably on architects' perceived ability to act as a critical force in society and design for the sake of the masses on whose exploitation the system depends.[19] As a result, a generation of architects after Tafuri has searched for ways to function creatively and pragmatically within the prospects of power, rather than attempting to resist or subvert reality.[20] During the 2000s a tacit or subconscious agreement with this position could be observed among the 'Young Turk architects'. After spending decades condemning authoritative zoning laws and municipal regulations for blocking architectural creativity, the new generation of architects has settled for offering piecemeal creative leaps within these economic and governmental systems of power, rather than staying outside. They have searched for zones of creativity within cracks in the systems, rather than refusing to participate in them. While such a position might have given these architects little opportunity to criticize the status quo, it has let them accomplish quality works that offer alternatives to the established residential models.

This point may be illustrated by the work of architects who addressed the concept of repetition. Some struggled with the shortcomings of repeating identical villas in a collective housing project, a common practice during this period partly because of the zoning regulations. Abdi Güzer raised an early critique of this design strategy in his article 'Extraordinary + Extraordinary = Ordinary', in which he criticized Behruz Çinici's Turkish Ministers' Housing (TBMM Housing) for disregarding the cumulative effect that the meticulously designed double houses would have when repeated in large numbers across the site.[21] To overcome the homogenizing effects of collective housing, Boğaçhan Dündaralp (of an even younger generation than the 'Young Turk architects') explored the potentials of architectural permutation in NP12 Houses, Istanbul (2003), where he devised a system that determined the stable prefabricated elements to be constructed in the first stage, and possible variations to be completed in the later stages based on residents' preferences. A matrix of fixed and variable elements provides the residents with 300 choices in six fixed building blocks.[22] The way in which repetitive holiday homes were mushrooming in the southern towns also became a major target of cultural criticism. In this context, Mehmet Kütükçüoğlu and Ertuğ Uçar experimented with novel schemes in a series of holiday housing projects in Belek, Bodrum, Alanya and Antalya.[23] The most noticeable result to this approach is the Güney Vacation Resort, Antalya (2001–5), where each white box combines double houses in an unconventional layout rather than placing them side-by-side, so enabling a diversity of outdoor spaces, such as terraces, pergolas and balconies.[24] These projects explore repetition as a design tool, rather than a liability. They conceptualize repetition in collective housing as an opportunity, rather than a problem, whose drawbacks can be redeemed by design.

A handful of architects explored new residential types that stood out from the majority of housing produced. An early example was the Sürücüler

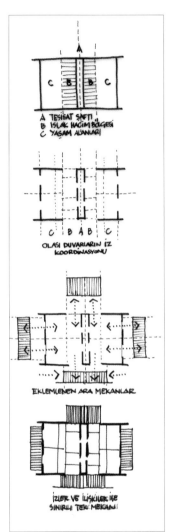

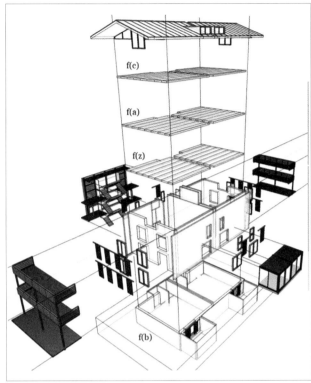

Boğaçhan Dündaralp,
NP12 Houses Istanbul,
2003, matrix of stable
and variable elements.

Terrace Houses, Ankara (1989; architects Merih Karaaslan, Nuran Ünsal and Mürşit Günday), where, by exploiting holes in the master plan's regulations, the architects managed to design terraced row houses, rather than the high-rise blocks suggested for this site. The project creates the image of an artificial hill on which terraced houses step down to the valley between them. According to Karaaslan, the natural caves of Cappadocia inspired both his formal choices and the intimate neighbourhood relations. The units are treated as colourful boxes with tilted roofs that enhance the idea of a sloping site.[25]

In the 2000s a series of collaborative projects designed by 'Young Turk architects' vitalized collective housing. Evidea Housing, Istanbul (2004; architects Emre Arolat, İhsan Bilgin, Nevzat Sayın and Mert Eyiler) stands out for its novel common outdoor space.[26] Although a periphery block encircling a big introverted garden is not an unusual scheme within the context of international collective housing, the layout had largely been blocked in Turkey by the zoning regulations. The architects of

Merih Karaaslan,
Nuran Ünsal and
Mürşit Günday,
Sürücüler Terrace
Houses, Ankara, 1989;
photo by Esra Akcan.

Emre Arolat, İhsan
Bilgin, Nevzat Sayın
and Mert Eyiler,
Evidea Housing,
Istanbul, 2004, view
from the courtyard;
photo by Ali Bekman.

Evidea had to function within the narrow constraints imposed by the developer, who had delineated fixed figures for unit sizes, number of rooms and service spaces, and had predetermined the materials; nonetheless they did everything possible to enable them to employ an unconventional site plan.[27] Doğa Meşe Park Housing, Istanbul (2005–7) is another collaborative project where Can Çinici and Boran Ekinci placed the units around an internal courtyard that functions as a communal garden for the residents.[28] In the TEPE Nar City Housing, Maltepe (2005–9; architects Nevzat Sayın and Mert Eyiler), the terracing down parallel blocks and colourful facade treatment is a comment on the *Zeilenbau* blocks of the early social housing schemes; rather than representing function, efficiency and economy, however, Nar City creates a playful Lego effect.[29] In a series of projects Emre Arolat Architects has experimented with alternative communal outdoor and indoor spaces, inter-circulation schemes as well as buffer zones between dwelling units and their communal areas.[30] Dwelling units behind fully transparent surfaces usually open onto communal outdoor spaces through buffering terraces that may be completely closed off by floor-to-ceiling shutters. Another notable example is the 35th Sokak Housing in İzmir by Teğet Architecture (Mehmet Kütükçüoğlu, Ertuğ Uçar), with its innovative site plan that creates a zigzag street and takes advantage of the site's slope to offer residents maximum proximity to gardens.

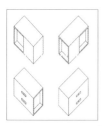

Teğet Architecture
(Mehmet Kütükçüoğlu
and Ertuğ Uçar),
Güney Vacation
Resort, Antalya,
2001–5, view from the
gardens and concept
diagram.

Nevzat Sayın and
Mert Eyiler, TEPE Nar
City, Istanbul,
2005–9; photo by
Cemal Emden.

Judged by the criteria of the 1960s generation, these projects are not 'critical': none of them aim at social transformation, political revolution or resisting the economic system. On the contrary, architects of this generation have deemed such aims as too unrealistic. In terms of the sociology and economy of housing, the projects mentioned above differ little from other gated communities, nor do they offer a real alternative to gentrification. TEPE Nar City, for example, is a luxury housing project located in a poor neighbourhood, with large units (75–300 m²), tennis courts and a swimming pool. Nonetheless something significant differentiates these projects' architectural typology from the ubiquitous residential areas. They are no longer ruled by the norms of the previous zoning regulations, seizing the opportunity to transform architecturally the prospect of major housing projects on extensive sites made possible by the policies of the large construction firms.

It did not take long, however, before architectural opportunities were transformed into a new opportunism. Daily newspapers are now adorned with countless glossy advertisements using images of these transformed residential types in order to market the investment of big construction firms. In an age where rebellion is over, 'critical architecture' seems to be sustained only through such short-lived opportunities. The pragmatic architecture of post-upheaval times thus created a professional culture that was impoverished by being too realistic.

In the context of the 'real' as a homogenizing force, unrealistic utopian paper projects gain additional significance. Paper projects, or deliberately

Emre Arolat
Architects, Göktürk
Arketip Houses,
Istanbul, 2006, plan
and view from the
courtyard; photo by
Esra Akcan.

impossible visions that envision alternative futures, have been very marginal in Turkey. This is surprising given architects' frequent complaints about oppressive municipal regulations and the allegedly uneducated taste of their clients. Among the very rare examples, one may mention the 'Linear City' (1988) by Zafer Akay, Boran Ekinci and Ahmet Ardıçoğlu, who suggested that all development should be concentrated into a linear building block connecting Ankara and Istanbul. Can Çinici's project 'City on the Highway' (1992, with Suna Konyalıoğlu) proposed drawing attention to the proliferating highways of the continuously sprawling city of

Ankara by offering a turnpike at a random point on the Ankara–Istanbul highway. They envisioned that it would be optional for drivers to take the turnpike, but if they did, that would have violated 'the road's essential desire to be as fast and as short as possible'. While utopian practices of this kind remained dormant for most of the 2000s, Boğaçhan Dündaralp devised a couple of projects that critically approach the established norms and offer idiosyncratic, impractical but alternative residential visions.[31] The 'Urban-Annex' draws attention to the impaired living conditions of the workers and ecological problems in the Tuzla Dockyard, and aims at their rehabilitation by researching the possibilities of dismantling and displacing, multiplying and subtracting, abandoning and recycling. 'Urbanecopolis', again by Dündaralp, stacks on top of each other all the

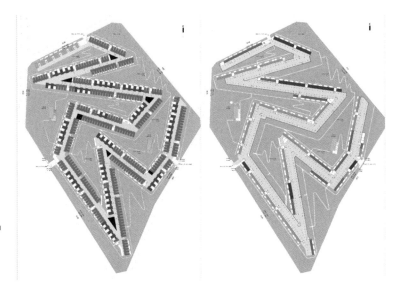

Teğet Architecture (Mehmet Kütükçüoğlu and Ertuğ Uçar), 35th Sokak Housing, İzmir, 2010, site plans and section.

Real estate
advertisement in
a daily newspaper.

Zafer Akay, Boran
Ekinci and Ahmet
Ardıçoğlu, 'Linear
City', 1988.

Can Çinici and Suna
Konyalıoğlu, 'City on
the Highway', Ankara,
1992.

layers of urban life that benefit from random convergence. Unlike early twentieth-century utopias that envisioned destroying and rebuilding the existing city, 'Urbanecopolis' hinges itself to the old as a vertical city.

Urban Renewal and Gentrification

At the opposite end of the spectrum from urban utopias, recent economic, political and cultural shifts in Turkey have ushered in a pragmatic interest in the existing city, especially in the remaining vestiges of historical fabric as potential sites of intervention and renewal. Since 2002 the uneasy but effective alliance between the AKP government and the country's powerful financial and business sector has set up favourable conditions for projects of urban renewal, rehabilitation and adaptive reuse. Although many local municipalities in major Turkish cities are catching on to this growing and lucrative trend, for a number of reasons the most notable experiments have been so far almost exclusively in Istanbul. Most obviously, as a centuries-old 'world city' with a rich historical heritage, Istanbul is a unique repository of significant historic buildings and neighbourhoods that have survived the destructive modernization and urban interventions of the mid-twentieth century. As part of the process of marketing Istanbul as a world city since the 1990s, the prospect of capitalizing upon these urban treasures has emerged as an attractive opportunity for all the players involved. To be successfully promoted as a global city – a unique and vibrant centre of arts, culture and tourism – Istanbul needed museums, galleries, hotels, restaurants, elegant shops and bars that, if they could be accommodated in retrofitted historical buildings and neighbourhoods, would give Istanbul a truly competitive edge among other global cities. This recent rise of Istanbul as 'the hot spot in Europe', as the *New York Times* called it in 2005,[32] created a demand for the rehabilitation and gentrification of the historic residential stock for a diverse clientele of artists, intellectuals, young professionals, academics, expats and foreigners. Furthermore, the flight of Istanbul's wealthy to the comfort and security of gated luxury suburbia in the 1990s has paradoxically increased their fascination with the historic city centre they left behind, especially with Galata and Beyoğlu, the throbbing heart of arts and entertainment – of excitement as well as danger.[33]

Istanbul's 'Golden Horn Urban Renewal Project', which has been underway since the 1980s as a succession of separate interventions, offers the most comprehensive vision of urban renewal and rehabilitation.[34] The Golden Horn was historically the site of factories, foundries, slaughterhouses and shipyards (including the Ottoman navy arsenal established in the fifteenth century, the imperial Feshane woollen textile factory, established in 1835, and the Silahtarağa Electricity Power Plant, established in 1911), but for most of the late Ottoman and early republican periods the area was intensively industrial and heavily polluted.[35] During the tenure of Bedrettin Dalan as Istanbul's mayor (1984–9), parallel to Turkey's switch to neo-liberal economic policies and the concomitant decline in the share of organized industry in the Turkish economy (in favour of the finance and service sectors), the extensive industrial infrastructure of the Golden Horn was dismantled. Some factories relocated to distant hinterland locations; others closed down; numerous sheds, workshops and lesser buildings were demolished and the shores of the Golden Horn were 'cleansed' into rather uninspiring parks and playgrounds serving primarily the poorer neighbourhoods on the overlooking hills.

Since the 1990s, however, under the initiative of the Istanbul Metropolitan Planning Office established by the AKP municipal government, the entire Golden Horn has been reconceptualized as a culture-education-tourism zone and turned into a major destination for Istanbulites and visitors alike. Beginning with the use of the Feshane factory as a temporary setting for Istanbul's internationally acclaimed Art Biennale (established in 1987), the conversion of the Golden Horn's historical buildings into private museums and universities has followed, sponsored largely by the country's top industrialists and businessmen, now turned into patrons of art and culture. An important symbol of this revival, coinciding with the acceptance of Turkey's candidacy to the EU, is the Istanbul Modern, which opened in 2004 as the country's first museum of contemporary art. Converted from one of the warehouses of the Galata port facilities in Tophane, a spectacular waterfront location where the Bosphorus and the Golden Horn meet, the project was carried out by Tabanlıoğlu Architects. With its spacious galleries, café and gift shop, all contained in a simple, modern industrial building with a reinforced concrete structural frame, Istanbul Modern was conceived as the first phase of what the architects envision to be a larger mixed-use development known as the Galataport Project. The latter proposes to replace the existing offices and decommissioned warehouses of the port with a mix of

Boğaçhan Dündaralp,
'Urbanecopolis',
Istanbul, 2008.

office, retail and residential spaces. Given the priceless value of this prime location by the Bosphorus, however, Galataport remains a particularly controversial case of urban renewal.

The vision of a continuous belt dedicated to art, culture and tourism running along the northern shore of the Golden Horn (from Istanbul Modern, just outside the estuary, to the new campus of Istanbul Bilgi University at its furthest western point) had its earliest boost in 1994, with the opening of the Rahmi Koç Museum of Industry and Technology. This was just one of the many philanthropic and educational investments of the powerful Koç family, Turkey's leading industrial and business enterprise, and was converted from historic buildings in the Ottoman arsenal in Hasköy. Further to the west, the Sütlüce Congress and Cultural Centre opened in 2009, featuring a cinema, theatre, concert hall and exhibition spaces on a vast waterfront site formerly containing municipal slaughter-houses and stockyards. Also along the same shore, towards the end of the estuary, Turkey's first 'architectural theme park', Minyatürk, opened in 2004 (architect Murat Uluğ; project director Cengiz Özdemir). Featuring scale models of significant architectural monuments spanning the entire history of Anatolia from prehistory to the present, Minyatürk is a visual display of the dominant Turkish nationalist narrative, not unlike its coun-terparts in China, Indonesia and elsewhere.[36] Dismissed by the art and architectural establishment as Disney-style commercialization of heritage, Minyatürk has nonetheless become a popular destination, especially for families and schoolchildren from poorer neighbourhoods of Istanbul as well as tourists from Asia and the Middle East.

The arrival of major private universities in the Golden Horn area gave a further impetus to the urban renewal project by drawing thousands of students, faculty and visitors to these formerly poor neighbourhoods, contributing to their economic and social revival. In 2002 the old Ottoman tobacco processing factory (founded in 1884) in Cibali on the southern shore of the Golden Horn was converted into the new campus of Kadir Has University (named after the industrial and business mogul who bequeathed his estate to education). The eleventh-century Byzantine cistern underneath the building was elegantly incorporated into the University's Rezan Has Museum, displaying a collection of the city's archaeological treasures and antiquities. The conversion was carried out by a team of architects and preservationists under the direction of Mehmet Alper and sought to maintain the original character of the industrial buildings (especially in its skylit atrium space with slender cast iron columns symbolic of the industrial era) and received the 2003 Europa Nostra Award for the preservation of cultural heritage.

Architecturally the most notable scheme, however, is the Santral campus and the museums of Istanbul Bilgi University, located at the very end of the Golden Horn where the freshwater Kağıthane and Alibeyköy streams join the estuary. Collectively designed by a team of young architects mentioned earlier (İhsan Bilgin, Nevzat Sayın, Han Tümertekin and Emre Arolat, 2004–7), the campus offers a skilful mix of preservation, adaptive reuse and new construction on the site of the Silahtarağa electricity power plant and distribution station (built 1911; decommissioned 1984). One of the many merits of the project is its minimally interventionist attitude to the site and to the existing industrial buildings, while accommodating a complex programme including educational buildings,

Tabanlıoğlu Architects (Murat and Melkan Tabanlıoğlu), Istanbul Modern Museum, Istanbul, 2004; photo by Murat Germen.

Mehmet Alper, et al.,
Rezan Has Museum in
Kadir Has University,
Istanbul, 2002; photo
by Murat Germen.

library, museum, cafes, restaurants and residences for visitors. Citing both Tate Modern in London and the Zeche Zollverein in Essen as recent precedents for this kind of industry-to-culture conversion, the project coordinator İhsan Bilgin explains their approach:

> Occupying two opposite ends of the spectrum of intervention, the former project completely transformed the interior space within a preserved shell, while the latter converted an old plant into a 'found object', creating an art object out of something originally not intended to function as such. In our case, various factors, including the program, the character of the site, its situation in the city and the boundaries drawn by the preservation bureaucracy forced us to seek more complex answers by exploring the 'twilight zone' between preserving the old and proposing something entirely new.[37]

Three components of the project are particularly noteworthy. The first is the Museum of Energy, the main machine hall within which turn-of-the-century turbines and generators are displayed as sublime pieces of art, viewable from the minimal, barely conspicuous galleries that Han Tümertekin has inserted into the vast, steel-framed sheds. Connected to this via a reception foyer is the four-storey prismatic block of the adjacent Museum of Contemporary Art, an entirely new building by Emre Arolat that nevertheless respects the history of the site by sitting directly on the footprint of a demolished industrial building. The four levels of the museum open on to galleries overlooking a four-storey high interior space visually connected to the surrounding urban fabric by a lattice screen facade through which light filters in atmospheric ways. The third major component of the campus involves educational

Santral Istanbul, Bilgi
University Campus,
Istanbul, 2004–7. Han
Tümertekin, Museum
of Energy; Nevzat
Sayın, Educational
Buildings; Emre
Arolat Architects,
Museum of
Contemporary
Art; photo by
Thomas Mayer.

buildings: two-storey high, long and thin blocks designed by Nevzat Sayın in a minimalist industrial aesthetic exposing the steel structure and using metal railings, perforated metal stairs and brightly coloured epoxy resin floor finishes. Three of these thin blocks occupy the perimeter of the site plan in a particularly inconspicuous and unobtrusive way, not just to pull the new construction away from the unstable soil at the centre of the campus, but also to preserve the beautiful tall trees that give the campus its unique, oasis-like charm. That the two Santral museums have become popular destinations and the campus is heavily used for concerts, youth festivals and other outside-sponsored events testifies to the big impact of a small intervention.

The transformation of old industrial sites into new cultural and commercial spaces is sure to preoccupy Turkish architects in the near future. For example, a more commercial (rather than educational) conversion in İzmir, Turkey's third largest city and a busy port on the Aegean coast, is the Konak Pier Shopping and Recreation Centre (1995–7) by Salih Zeki Pekin, coordinating a team of architects and preservationists. The badly aged nineteenth-century warehouses of the customs buildings on the pier were completely retrofitted, preserving the stone bearing walls and replacing the metal roof trusses holding up the tile, metal and glass roof covering. Meanwhile the sublime 'modern ruins' of early republican state industries and factories in major Anatolian cities such as Kayseri and Nazilli still await new initiatives of preservation and adaptive reuse.

A second category of urban renewal involving large, neighbourhood-scale residential gentrification projects has proved to be far more controversial, with Istanbul once again leading the debate under national and even international scrutiny. Since it took office in 2002, the AKP national government has passed laws that give local municipalities special permission to designate historical but derelict neighbourhoods in the city centre as 'urban renewal zones' (*kentsel dönüşüm bölgesi*). On the basis of this legislation, municipalities exercise the right to propose preservation, rehabilitation and gentrification projects for these neighbourhoods, which at present are mostly occupied by migrants, marginals and an entire spectrum of the urban poor, renting (or squatting) in very old houses belonging to mostly absentee landlords. The residents' poverty and lack of resources are put forward as the primary justification for the invitations to private investors and developers, who bid for these lucrative urban renewal jobs and hire their own design teams and consultants.

The public rhetoric employed to legitimize these projects uses arguments that are social (that the gentrified neighbourhoods will be safer, cleaner and more diverse than the current concentration of poverty and ethnic ghettoization, such as Kurds in Tarlabaşı and gypsies in Sulukule), technical (that the threat of earthquake necessitates the rehabilitation of unsafe, badly aged buildings) and aesthetic (that renewal will beautify the city and eliminate urban squalor). Although the municipalities claim to safeguard the rights of the inhabitants and require investors to negotiate with neighbourhood associations, these negotiations are often limited to property owners, excluding the poorest tenants and squatters who comprise the majority of the residents. The only choice that the latter are given is that of moving to a Mass Housing Administration (TOKI) public housing scheme outside the city (for the problems involved with these, see chapter Eight). The resistance put up by grassroots organizations and leading critics of these urban renewal schemes has so far been mostly ineffective and the inevitable result seems to be the displacement of poorer residents, followed by a subsequent transfer of gentrified property to wealthier newcomers.[38]

In two particularly high-profile cases, Istanbul's Fatih and Beyoğlu municipalities have seized this opportunity and launched the Tarlabaşı and Fener-Balat-Ayvansaray urban renewal projects in the heart of Galata-Beyoğlu and on the Golden Horn shore of the historical peninsula respectively, both neighbourhoods formerly populated during the Ottoman Empire by sizeable Greek, Jewish and Armenian communities. GAP Construction and Development Group won both contracts and invited many academics and practising architects to develop proposals.[39] These span a wide spectrum from more nostalgic, theme park-style reconstructions of imagined or idealized Ottoman *mahalles* to more modernist but site-specific interventions derived from analytical and typological studies of the existing fabric. An example of the latter can be found in Can Çinici's proposal for the waterfront sector of the Fener-Balat neighbourhood: after a meticulous study of existing subdivisions on the long and thin urban block, he proposed to combine front and back lots to create narrow but deeper lots, within which different residential typologies can be accommodated by manipulating the location of the stairwells and the number of storeys, while different social and commercial units can be inserted at street level.

In general, however, the architectural community's response to these gentrification schemes has been mixed. While the Chamber of Architects, vocal activists and many academics have been critical of the process for their disenfranchisement of the poorer residents and for the impact of neo-liberal politics on the property market in general, others have embraced the kind of postcritical pragmatism discussed above and have chosen to preoccupy themselves not so much with the urban politics surrounding these projects, but instead with the projects themselves. Designated urban renewal sites have been taken up in the design studios of major architectural schools to encourage alternative explorations and many local municipalities have elected to hold competitions, both practices helping to engage the architectural community with the challenging task of urban renewal in dense, run-down and often poorer neighbourhoods of the historic city.

The international interest in Istanbul's urban renewal agenda has also been substantial – from EU sponsorship of pilot projects (as in the case of the EU-Fatih Municipality sponsored Fener-Balat Rehabilitation Programme, which started in 2003), to academic studies, conferences and publications focusing on Istanbul (most visibly, the Urban Age Conference in Istanbul in 2009). Two high-profile urban competitions in 2006 were especially instrumental in stirring the debate and bringing international star designers to Turkey. Overseen by the Municipality of Greater Istanbul and organized by the Küçükçekmece and Kartal local municipalities respectively, and (to the annoyance of the Chamber of Architects and most Turkish practitioners) limited only to invited international designers, these competitions have exposed the loose (and for many critics, the arbitrary) nature of the concept of 'urban renewal', applied in this case to very large-scale visionary interventions beyond the historical core of the city.

The first competition, won by Ken Yeang, is a proposal for an 'ecological corridor' in Küçükçekmece, some 40 km outside the city centre, creating a blueprint for the sustainable development of the area while preserving or rehabilitating the ecology and wildlife of its lagoon lake. The extension of the concept of renewal/rehabilitation to include not only derelict historical neighbourhoods of the inner city, but also the city's entire ecology and hinterland is, without doubt, a timely recognition of the larger questions of sustainability and landscape urbanism

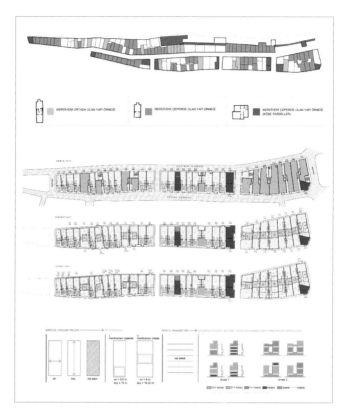

Can Çinici, Urban
Renewal in Fener-
Balat neighbourhood,
Istanbul, 2003
onwards.

Zaha Hadid, Project
for the Urban
Renewal of Kartal,
Istanbul, 2006.

that preoccupy design professionals everywhere. Nonetheless, in the
specific context of Turkish urban politics, abuse of the law and concomitant controversy are inescapable. In the same way that run-down
historic neighbourhoods have been made available to gentrification, the
law states that public land 'that has lost its formerly agricultural or forest character' can now be made available to private developers and
investors, accounting for much of the phenomenal urban sprawl of
Istanbul towards its suburban hinterland (see chapter Eight).

The second and especially contentious competition was won by Zaha
Hadid, with a visionary urban renewal project for the dense commercial, residential and industrial urban fabric of Kartal on the Asian shore
of the Sea of Marmara. Currently stalled by the inextricable difficulties
of implementation – mostly bureaucratic and legal (including competing stakeholders and fragmented property ownerships) but also technological and financial (the project being a visionary moonscape of liquid
forms characteristic of Zaha Hadid's architecture) – the project has
become the symbolic centrepiece of the ideologically charged debate
between the proponents of AKP-sponsored neo-liberal urban politics and
the angry critics of globalization and privatization. Whereas the former
tend to highlight the aesthetic, social and revenue-generating benefits of
urban renewal schemes, critics argue that most of these projects amount
to 'state-sponsored gentrification and property transfer' from the public
and the poor to wealthier private interests.

Transnational Practices

Zaha Hadid's radical scheme for Kartal's urban renewal introduces another theme that is likely to shape the future of architectural practice in the age of globalization. As discussed in the Introduction, writing the history of a nation's architecture in a global age has to overcome a contradiction. Even though the world has been divided into nation states throughout the twentieth century, and even though architecture has operated in the legal, economic and political structures that have been determined by the institutions of these nation states, a nation alone can hardly stand as a sufficient category to explain the architectural life of any place on the planet. In Turkey, too, it has been the tension between international movements and nationalist responses, as well as the cross-fertilization of architects and ideas from different nations, that have shaped modernism. Examples abound, such as the German-speaking architects, including Hermann Jansen, Ernst Egli, Clemens Holzmeister, Paul Bonatz and Bruno Taut, who designed the urban models and all of the institutional buildings for the new Turkish Republic throughout the first half of the twentieth century; Le Corbusier's master plan for İzmir, Henry Prost's for Istanbul, the collaboration between SOM and Sedad Eldem that helped change the ruling taste in the 1950s; and the solidarity with the socialist youth and the 1960s generation throughout the 1960s and '70s. With the adoption of globalization, and the World Trade Organization's definition of architectural services as globally transportable, the legal structure that facilitates this international exchange was also put in place. Transnational practice is becoming a regular occurrence: in addition to Hadid and Yeang, Aldo Rossi prepared a project for the urban design competition of Üsküdar Plaza, Istanbul (1986–7), while FOA built a shopping centre in Ümraniye, Istanbul (2007, see pages 214–15). REX designed a new headquarters for Vakko's demolished centre. Adding onto a pre-existing U-shaped structure, REX turned the building into a square within a square, with a spatially dynamic core inside, and an ultrathin sheet of glass strengthened by slumping a structural 'X' into the outside of each pane. All of the artwork from the original Vakko factory was also integrated into the design.

Globalization creates possibilities for cultural exchange, but also forecloses these very possibilities with the re-creation of neo-colonial habits. The responses of Turkish architects and critics have been diverse, analyzing both the limits and the potential for 'other' geographies in a global age unable to shake off residues of Eurocentrism.[40] The public's responses to foreign architects' projects have also been ambivalent. Despite

REX, Vakko Headquarters and Power Media Centre, Istanbul, 2010, incorporating Bedri Rahmi Eyüboğlu's sculpture from the original Vakko factory (see page 135); photo by Esra Akcan.

initial excitement, both Aldo Rossi's and Zaha Hadid's projects have disappointed many for dismissing the site's existing problems and geographical attractions, as well as for their lack of interest in the local inhabitants.[41] Professionally, globalization opens new possibilities of employment and collaboration with the centre, but competition over jobs at a global level generates anxiety about losing areas of production that local professionals once considered their own – a game they have less chance of winning due to their smaller financial resources. In this context, the fact that a collaboration between Arolat and Tabanlıoğlu Architects has secured the commission for the Zorlu Centre, after a competition that had brought in established international architects chasing for the biggest and most expansive building on one of the most prestigious hilltops of Istanbul's new Central Business District, implies that the agenda for inviting foreign architects in Turkey today may be slightly different to that current in early republican times or in contemporary Dubai and China.

Globalization is slowly generating cultural flows from East to West as well, rather than the unilateral dissemination in the opposite direction that was the case throughout the period of modernization. Many architects based in Turkey are designing buildings for places elsewhere. There were sporadic earlier examples of such a practice, most notably in the form of pavilions created for world's fairs and embassies by Sedad Eldem and Seyfi Arkan, and a few exceptional examples such as Ali Köksal's Karachi Hilton (1975), Vedad Dalokay's Islamabad Mosque (1969–87) and Şevki Vanlı's projects for post-colonial Algeria (1983–6).[42] The global-ized generation has certainly been granted more opportunities. Tümertekin designed the Shibuya Peace Monument in Japan (1990–91) and the Dutch headquarters of The Economy Bank in Amstelveen (2002–4); Arolat has projects in Tunisia, Belgium and Japan.[43] The most paradigmatic change is without doubt the emergence of a new market for Turkish architects and construction firms in the new republics of the former Soviet Union, such as Kazakhstan, Turkmenistan and Azerbaijan. The architectural offices of Enis Öncüoğlu and Cem Altınöz, Ali Osman Özturk, Günay and Sunay Erdem, Orhan Genç, Adnan Kazmaoğlu, Erginoğlu and Çalışlar have designed numerous projects in these countries, ranging from shopping malls, office buildings and hotels, to urban landmarks such as the Astana Arena (2005–9), an elliptical sports stadium designed by Tabanlıoğlu in Astana, Kazakhstan.

These are architectural offices based in Turkey designing for other countries, but yet another notable category is emerging as increasing numbers of Turkish citizens open offices in other countries or achieve responsible positions in transnational architectural firms. Ahmet Gülgö-nen in France and SOM's Mustafa Abadan in the United States were early examples. Beyhan Karahan also established her own successful practice in New York. Recently Aslıhan Demirtaş and Aybars Aşçı have found important design opportunities in I. M. Pei's office and at SOM, respec-tively. Aşçı, for one, has signed under the design of large-scale landmarks using advanced building technologies in Kuwait and Qatar. The Al Hamra Firdous Tower in Kuwait City explores passive cooling techniques by shaping the skyscraper in relation to the angle of the sun and prevail-ing winds; the project for the office headquarters in Doha, Qatar, is composed of high solid walls that curve expressively in both horizontal and vertical axes, and thereby not only function as the buildings' struc-tural bearers, but also create shadowed streets and plazas in between and underneath.

To summarize, it would not be unfair to conclude that the majority of the global Turkish architects of the 1990s and 2000s were young yet submissive, creative yet gentrifying, able to carve out possibilities from limited opportunities yet unable to criticize opportunism, competent in the transnational arena of the profession yet helpless in the face of the country's own daunting problems. Meanwhile, Turkey itself is under-going radical transformations both by local and global forces. In the absence of a strong and popular opposition to the Islamist Justice and Development Party (AKP), the new conservative trend in Turkish culture and politics is fast becoming mainstream rather than an aberration. Curbing the traditional power of Turkey's staunchly secular military

Aybars Aşçı for SOM, Project for Office Headquarters, Doha, 2008.

and judiciary while forging new ties with Turkey's traditionally neglected neighbours in the Middle East and Asia, the AKP is in the process of taking Turkey to uncharted new territories. It is likely that future historians will treat the turn of the twenty-first century as the beginning of an entirely new era of Turkish modernity.

References

Introduction

1   In addition to numerous recent books on modern architectures in individual countries like Turkey, Japan, China, India, Iran, Brazil and Indonesia, broader and comparative regional studies have challenged the Eurocentric biases of canonic histories of modern architecture. Especially relevant among recent publications are Mark Crinson, *Modern Architecture and the End of Empire* (London, 2003); Sandy Isenstadt and Kishwar Rizvi, eds, *Modern Architecture and the Middle East* (Seattle, WA, 2008); Jilly Traganou and Miodrag Mitrasinovic, eds, *Travel Space and Architecture* (Burlington, VT, 2009); Duanfang Lu, ed., *Third World Modernism: Architecture, Development and Identity* (London and New York, 2010); J. F. Lejeune and Michelangelo Sabatino, eds, *Modern Architecture and the Mediterranean* (New York, 2010); Mark M. Jarzombek, Vikramaditya Prakash and Francis D. K. Ching, *A Global History of Architecture*, 2nd edn (Hoboken, NJ, 2011).

2   Duanfang Lu, *Third World Modernism*, p. 11.

3   In our earlier work we have addressed the 'nationalization' of modernism in early Republican Turkey (Bozdoğan) and the 'translations' and cross-cultural encounters between Turkish and German-speaking architects during the same period (Akcan). See Sibel Bozdoğan, *Modernism and Nation-Building: Turkish Architectural Culture in the Early Republic* (Seattle, 2001) and Esra Akcan, *Architecture in Translation: Germany, Turkey and the Modern House* (Durham, NC, 2012).

4   An important precedent is Uğur Tanyeli, *Istanbul, 1900–2000: Konutu ve Modernleşmeyi Metropolden Okumak* (Istanbul, 2004), in which, taking issue with writing the history of modern Turkish architecture primarily from the official and canonic examples of early republican Ankara, he argues that there is another, lesser-known Turkish modernism for which we must turn to the metropolitan experience of Istanbul since the late Ottoman period and look primarily at the residential work of anonymous designers and developers – namely, apartment buildings from turn-of-the-century Art Nouveau to 1950s modernism.

5   See also H.-J. Henket and H. Heynen, eds, *Back from Utopia: the Challenge of the Modern Movement* (Rotterdam, 2002), p. 398.

6   For example in the titles of Cemal Kafadar, *Between Two Worlds: the Construction of the Ottoman State* (Berkeley, 1995) and Stephen Kinzer, *Crescent and Star: Turkey between Two Worlds* (New York, 2008).

7   Of these, Inci Aslanoğlu, *Erken Cumhuriyet Dönemi Mimarlığı, 1923–1938* (Ankara, 1980; reprint 2001) is still the standard reference.

8   For example the work of Ipek Akpınar, Bülent Batuman, Gülsüm Baydar, Cana Bilsel, Ali Cengizkan, Elvan Ergut, Murat Gül, Ela Kaçel, Zeynep Kezer, Uğur Tanyeli, Bülent Tanju, Ipek Türeli and Haluk Zelef. We would also like to include our previous works in this list.

9   For recent examples of such interdisciplinary volumes, see Sibel Bozdoğan and Resat Kasaba, eds, *Rethinking Modernity and National Identity in Turkey* (Seattle, WA, 1997); Deniz Kandiyoti and Ayse Saktanber, eds, *Fragments of Culture: the Everyday of*

Modern Turkey (New Brunswick, NJ, 2002); Orhan Pamuk, *Istanbul: Memories and the City* (New York, 2005); Resat Kasaba, ed., *The Cambridge History of Turkey: Turkey in the Modern World* (Cambridge, 2008); Kerem Öktem et al., eds, *Turkey's Engagement with Modernity* (Basingstoke, 2010); Deniz Göktürk, Levent Soysal and Ipek Türeli, *Orienting Istanbul: Cultural Capital of Europe?* (New York, 2010).

10 Something also articulated recently in Maiken Umbach and Bernd Huppauf, eds, *Vernacular Modernism: Heimat, Globalization and the Built Environment* (Stanford, CA, 2005).

11 For 'anxious modernism' in the post-war period see Sarah Williams Goldhagen and Rejean Legault, eds, *Anxious Modernisms: Experimentation in Postwar Architectural Culture* (Cambridge, MA, 2000). For two classic texts of modernization theory, see Daniel Lerner, *The Passing of Traditional Society* (New York, 1958) and Cyril Black, *The Dynamics of Modernization* (New York, 1966).

12 David Harvey, *The Condition of Postmodernity: An Enquiry into the Origins of Cultural Change* (Malden, MA, 1990); Fredric Jameson, *Postmodernism or the Cultural Logic of Late Capitalism* (Durham, NC, 1991); Appadurai Arjun, *Modernity at Large: Cultural Dimensions of Globalization* (Minneapolis, 1996).

13 See especially Arif Dirlik, 'Architectures of Global Modernity: Colonialism and Places', *Modern Chinese Literature and Culture*, XVII/1 (Spring 2005), pp. 33–61, and Anna Klingmann, *Brandscapes: Architecture in the Experience Economy* (Cambridge, 2007).

chapter one: Architecture of Revolution

1 For an interdisciplinary discussion of how new challenges to this foundational ideology appeared after the 1980s see Sibel Bozdoğan and Reşat Kasaba, eds, *Rethinking Modernity and National Identity in Turkey* (Seattle, WA, 1997).

2 Erik Zürcher treats 1908–1950 as a single unit in Erik J. Zürcher, *Turkey: A Modern History* (London, 1993). Feroz Ahmad characterizes the Constitutional Revolution of 1908 as 'the opening of the 20th century for Turkey', the marker of the historical transition from empire to nationhood, in Ahmad, *The Making of Modern Turkey* (London, 1993), p. 3

3 Mary Matossian, 'Ideologies of Delayed Development', in *Nationalism*, ed. John Hutchinson and Anthony D. Smith (Oxford, 1994), pp. 218–25.

4 For a comprehensive account of this historical overlap, see Sibel Bozdoğan, *Modernism and Nation Building: Turkish Architectural Culture in the Early Republic* (Seattle, WA, 2001).

5 David Crowley, 'National Modernisms', in *Modernism: Designing a New World*, ed. Christopher Wilk (London, 2006), pp. 341–60.

6 On the making of the modern architectural profession in Turkey, see Gülsüm Baydar, 'The Professionalization of the Ottoman-Turkish Architect', PhD diss., University of California, Berkeley, 1989, and Sibel Bozdoğan, *Modernism and Nation Building*, Chapters 1 and 4.

7 See especially Ahmet Ersoy, 'Architecture and the Search for Ottoman Origins in the Tanzimat Period', *Muqarnas,* XXIV (2007), pp. 117–39.

8 Most significantly by Şerif Mardin; see his *Religion and Social Change in Modern Turkey,* (Albany, ny, 1989) and his 'The Just and the Unjust', *Deadalus*, 3 (Summer 1991), pp. 113–29.

9 On the 'nationalization' and 'Turkification' of Ottoman heritage see Sibel Bozdoğan, 'Reading Ottoman Architecture through Modernist Lenses: Nationalist Historiography and the New Architecture in the Early Republic', *Muqarnas*, 24 (Autumn 2007), pp. 199–221.

10 Ahmet Haşim, *Gurabahane-i Laklakan* [1928] (Ankara, 1981), pp. 154–7.

11 İsmail Hakkı Baltacıoğlu, 'Mimaride Kubizm ve Türk Ananesi', *Darülfünun İlahiyat*

Fakültesi Mecmuası (Istanbul, 1929), pp. 118–21.

12 Celal Esat Arseven, *Türk Sanatı* (Istanbul, 1970), p.182.

13 Celal Esat [Arseven], *Yeni Mimari* (Istanbul, 1931), adapted from André Lurçat, *L'Architecture* (Paris, 1929).

14 Project for the Grand National Assembly competition by Joseph Vago, published in *Arkitekt*, 4 (1938), p. 110.

15 For a compelling discussion of the 'programmatic' versus 'transient' dimensions of modernity, see Hilde Heynen, *Architecture and Modernity: a Critique* (Cambridge, MA, 1999).

16 *La Turquie Kemaliste*, 47 (1943), pp. 38–9.

17 See Bernd Nicolai, *Moderne und Exil: Deutschsprachige Architekten in der Türkei, 1925–1955* (Berlin, 1998) and Esra Akcan, *Architecture in Translation: Germany, Turkey and the Modern House* (Durham, NC, 2012).

18 See Ali Cengizkan, *Ankara'nın İlk Planı: Lörcher Planı 1924–25* (Ankara, 2004) and 'Ankara 1924–25 Lörcher Planı: Bir Başkenti Tasarlamak ve Sonrası', in *Modernin Saati* (Ankara, 2002), pp. 37–59.

19 See Esra Akcan, *Architecture in Translation* for a detailed historical and theoretical account of the 'translation' of the Garden City idea from Europe and Germany to Turkey.

20 Lörcher was incensed at not being invited and accused Jansen of stealing his design. His attempt to sue Jensen in Berlin failed because Jansen had carefully reworked the plan to obliterate any obvious connections to Lörcher's design. Ali Cengizkan, 'Ankara 1924–25 Lörcher Planı', p. 56.

21 Ernst Egli, 'Mimari Muhit', *Turk Yurdu*, XXX/224 (June 1930), pp. 32–6 and his later *Die neue Stadt in Landschaft und Klima* (Zürich, 1951).

22 Cited in Aslıhan Demirtaş, 'Artificial Nature: Water Infrastructure and Its Experience as Natural Space', Master's Thesis, MIT, 2000.

23 S. Süreyya, 'Beynelminel Fikir Hareketleri Arasında Türk Nasyonalizmi', *Kadro*, 20 (August 1933), p. 13.

24 Zeynep Uludağ, 'Cumhuriyet Döneminde Rekreasyon ve Gençlik Parkı Örneği', in *Bilanço '98: 75 Yılda Değişen Kent ve Mimarlık*, ed. Yıldız Sey (Istanbul, 1998), pp. 65–74.

25 Designed primarily to serve as the main reservoirs of the elaborate water management system of regulating dykes, canals, conduits and pumps, the plans of these pools reproduced the exact contours of the actual seas they were named after. This symbolic simulation was carried to such a remarkable level of detail that even the islands, bays and peninsulas of the real shores were reproduced. See Demirtaş, 'Artificial Nature'.

26 These were, of course, the same themes that mobilized other modernizing nation states or nationalist movements of the time, from the Tennessee Valley Project of New Deal America to the draining and settling of the Agro Pontino marshes in Fascist Italy or the Zionist utopia of redeeming and settling the land of Palestine. For the relationship between the high-modernist projects of nation states and the taming, ordering and controlling of nature, see James C. Scott, *Seeing Like a State: How Certain Schemes to Improve the Human Condition have Failed* (New Haven, 1998), especially Chapter 1.

27 Editorial in *Ülkü*, I/1 (1933), pp. 1–2. In his comprehensive work on Peoples' Houses, Anıl Çeçen traces the ideological sources of the organization to the Jacobin clubs of the French Revolution and the *narodnik* movement in Tsarist Russia, thereby highlighting the 'revolutionary' premises of the concept. Anıl Çeçen, *Halkevleri* (Ankara, 1990).

28 On the architecture of the Peoples' Houses, see Neşe Gürallar Yeşilkaya, *Halkevleri, İdeoloji ve Mimarlık*, (Istanbul, 1999).

29 Ibid., p. 80.

30 For example, a new village with 10,500 houses was constructed in 1938 in Thrace to settle some 80,000 immigrants from Bulgaria, Romania and Yugoslavia. 'L'Immigration en Turquie', *La Turquie Kemaliste*, 23–24 (April 1938), pp. 15–18.

31 Abdullah Ziya, 'Cumhuriyette Köy Yapımı', *Ülkü*, II/10 (1933), pp. 333–6, and Nusret Kemal, 'Köy Misyonerliği', *Ülkü*, II/8 (1933), p. 150.

32 For the case of Italy see especially Annibale Folchi, *I Contadini del Duce: Agro Pontino, 1932–1941* (Rome, 2000). Both Mussolini and Atatürk posed for photographs operating a tractor or harvesting grain with the farmers and both leaders capitalized upon the metaphor of the sword and the plough, highlighting the heroism of battling not only with an actual enemy, but also with the forces of nature.

33 Zeki Sayar, 'İç Kolonizasyon', *Arkitekt*, VI/2 (1936), p.47.

34 Abidin Mortaş, 'Köy Projesi: Mimar Burhan Arif', *Arkitekt*, V/11–12 (1935), p. 320.

35 Ziya, 'Cumhuriyette Köy Yapımı', p. 333.

36 Abdullah Ziya, 'Köy Mimarisi', *Ülkü*, I/8 (1933), p. 38. An even more remarkable example of the diagrammatic approach to village architecture is Kazım Dirlik's 1933 project for an 'ideal republican village' (*ideal cumhuriyet köyü*), laid out in perfect concentric zones for residential units, for health, educational and sports facilities and for commerce and light industry, all radiating from the centre of the circular plan, evocative of such nineteenth-century precedents as Ebenezer Howard's garden city diagrams or the 'disciplinary environments' of Jeremy Bentham's Panopticon.

37 See Gülsüm Baydar Nalbantoğlu, 'Silent Interruptions: Urban Encounters with Rural Turkey', in *Rethinking Modernity and National Identity in Turkey*, ed. Sibel Bozdoğan and Reşat Kasaba (Seattle, WA, 1997), pp. 192–210.

38 Cited in Y. Tezel, *Cumhuriyet Döneminin Iktisadi Tarihi 1923–1950* (Ankara, 1986), p. 128.

39 Y. Kastan, 'Atatürk Döneminde Sanayileşme ve Karabük Demirçelik İşletmeleri', *Kastamonu Eğitim Dergisi*, II/2 (October 2003), p. 488.

40 For example, Yakup Kadri Karaosmanoğlu, 'Kültür ve Medeniyet', *Kadro*, 15 (1933), p. 25.

41 Şevket Süreyya Aydemir, *Ikinci Adam*, V/2 (Istanbul, 1999), pp. 445–6, cited in Y. Kastan, 'Atatürk Döneminde Sanayileşme ve Karabük Demirçelik İşletmeleri', pp. 492–3.

42 Leo Marx, *The Machine in the Garden: Technology and the Pastoral Ideal in America* (New York, 1964).

43 For a comparative discussion of Soviet and Turkish state-owned industrial complexes, see Özlem Arıtan, 'Sosyalist Modernleşme, Sovyet Sanayii Yerleşkeleri ve Türkiye'deki Devlet Yerleşkeleri', *Arredamento Mimarlık* (November 2006), pp. 120–27.

44 We are grateful to Jean-Louis Cohen for making available to us the Russian-language monograph, *Ivan Nikolaev, 1901–1979* (Moscow, 2002) and for translating relevant parts from the book.

45 See especially Burak Asıliskender, 'Cumhuriyet'in İlk Yıllarında Modern Kimlik Arayışı: Sümerbank Kayseri Bez Fabrikası Örneği', master's thesis, Istanbul Technical University, 2002; and his '1930'ların Modern Yapıtının Günümüzdeki Yalnızlığı', *Tol Mimarlık Kültürü Dergisi* (Winter 2003), pp. 46–51. Also see Özlem Arıtan, 'Sümerbank Yerleşkeleri: Ideolojik ve Mekansal bir Okuma', *Arredamento Mimarlık* (January 2005), pp. 102–9.

46 In the Kayseri project, workers' housing consisted of different typologies of reinforced concrete apartment units. Four two-storey blocks containing 64 two-bedroom units were reserved for married workers and their families; a three-storey block with a 350-bed capacity housed the unmarried workers; eight duplex units and sixteen three-bedroom apartments were given to supervisors and their families.

47 On the architecture of industrial buildings in Turkey, see Sibel Bozdoğan, 'Industrial Architecture and Nation-Building in Turkey: a Historical Overview', in *Workplaces: the Transformation of Places of Production*, ed. M. Al-Asad (Istanbul, 2010), pp. 17–40.

48 This typology, traceable to Peter Behrens's work for the AEG factories in Berlin at the turn of the century, was first introduced to Turkey by the Germans in the construction of the Silahtarağa Electricity Power Plant in Istanbul in 1911 during the final years of

the Ottoman Empire. In the case of Turhal sugar factory, a number of modern buildings were added in the mid-1930s by the German architect Fritz August Breuhaus, who also proposed a plan for factory housing.

49   See, for example, Abdullah Ziya, 'Yeni Sanat', *Mimar*, II/4 (1932), pp. 97–8.
50   On the question of the avant-garde in early republican culture, see Sibel Bozdoğan, *Modernism and Nation Building*, pp.148–52.

chapter two: **Building for the Modern Nation State**

1   Benedict Anderson, *Imagined Communities: Reflections on the Origins and Spread of Nationalism* (London, 1983), p. 11.
2   See especially Christiane C. and George R. Collins, 'Monumentality: A Critical Matter in Modern Architecture', *Harvard Architecture Review*, IV (Spring 1984), pp. 15–35.
3   Lewis Mumford, *The Culture of Cities* (New York, 1938), p. 438.
4   See Lawrence Vale, *Architecture, Power, National Identity* (New Haven, CT, 1992)
5   For a recent compilation of the Armenian architects of the later Ottoman Empire, see Hasan Kuruyazıcı, ed., *Batılılaşan İstanbul'un Ermeni Mimarları*. [Armenian Architects of Istanbul in the Era of Westernization] (Istanbul, 2010).
6   For political and economic relations between Germany and Turkey, see especially Rıfat Önsoy, *Türk-Alman İktisadi Münasebetleri (1871–1914)* (Istanbul, 1982); Cemil Koçak, *Türk-Alman İlişkileri (1923–1939)* (Ankara, 1991); Ulrich Trumpener, *Germany and the Ottoman Empire* (Princeton, NJ, 1968); Sean McMeekin, *The Berlin-Baghdad Express: The Ottoman Empire and Germany's Bid for World Power* (Cambridge, 2010).
7   For German-Turkish relations in architecture and visual arts during the Republican period, see Bernd Nicolai, *Moderne und Exil. Deutschsprachige Architekten in der Türkei* (Berlin, 1998); Burcu Doğramacı, *Kulturtransfer und nationale Identität. Deutschsprachige Architekten, Stadtplaner und Bildhauer in der Türkei nach 1927* (Berlin, 2008); Arnold Reisman, *Arts in Turkey: How Ancient Became Contemporary* (Charleston, SC, 2009); Esra Akcan, *Architecture in Translation: Germany, Turkey and the Modern House* (Durham, NC, 2012).
8   A number of these buildings were also constructed by German firms, such as Lenz & Co., Brüder Redlich und Berger.
9   Horst Widmann, *Exil und Bildungshilfe: Die deutschsprachige akademische Emigration in die Türkei nach 1933* (Frankfurt, 1973); Regine Erichsen, 'Die Emigration deutsch-sprachiger Naturwissenschaftler von 1933 bis 1945 in die Türkei in ihrem sozial- und wissenschaftshistorischen Wirkungszusammenhang', in *Die Emigration der Wissenschaften nach 1933*, ed. Herbert Strauss and others (Munich, 1991); Stanford J. Shaw, *Turkey and the Holocaust: Turkey's Role in Rescuing Turkish and European Jewry from Nazi Persecution* (London, 1993); Kemal Bozay, *Exil Türkei: Ein Forschungsbeitrag zur deutschsprachigen Emigration in die Türkei (1933–1945)* (Münster, 2001).
10 Oya Atalay Franck, 'Ernst Egli: Erken Cumhuriyet Dönemi Mimarı ve Eğitimcisi. 1930–1936', *Arredamento Mimarlık* (March 2004), pp. 110–19; see also Nicolai, *Moderne und Exil*, and Doğramacı, *Kulturtransfer und nationale Identität*.
11 Sibel Bozdoğan, 'Against Style: Bruno Taut's Pedagogical Program in Turkey, 1936–1938', in *The Education of the Architect: Historiography, Urbanism and the Growth of Architectural Knowledge*, ed. Martha Pollak (Cambridge, 1997), pp. 163–92; Bernd Nicolai, 'Bruno Taut's Akademiereform und sein weg zu einer neuen Architektur für die Türkei', in *Atatürk için Düşünmek. İki Eser: Katafalk ve Anıtkabir. İki Mimar: Bruno Taut and Emin Onat* (Istanbul, 1997), pp. 37–43.
12 Johannes Glasneck, *Türkiye'de Faşist Alman Propagandası*, trans. Arif Gelen (Istanbul, 1978); Anne Dietrich, *Deutschsein in Istanbul. Nationalisierung und Orientierung in der deutschsprachigen Community von 1843 bis 1956* (Opladen, 1998).

13 Jansen continued to work in Germany after 1933 and won the Goethe Medal in 1939; Bonatz designed bridges and autobahns for the regime, and brought the National Socialist propaganda exhibition *New German Architecture* to Turkey.

14 Particularly the Salzburg Festspielhaus (1926), individual houses in different small towns, as well as collective housing projects in Vienna, including *Volkswohnhaus* (people's apartments, 1924–6), the Werkbund Housing Exhibition (1932) and an unrealized project for Karl Marx-Hof (eventually built by Karl Ehn). See especially *Clemens Holzmeister: Bauten, Entwürfe und Handzeichnungen* (Salzburg and Leipzig, 1937); Joseph Gregor, *Clemens Holzmeister: Das architektonische Werk* (Vienna, 1953); Clemens Holzmeister, *Architekt in der Zeitenwende: Selbstbiographie* (Salzburg, 1976); Georg Rigele and Georg Loewit, *Clemens Holzmeister* (Innsbruck, 2000).

15 Uğur Tanyeli, *Mimarlığın Aktörleri. Türkiye 1900–2000* (Istanbul, 2007), pp. 426–30.

16 For instance, Atatürk's choice of Holzmeister as architect of his own presidential residence, as well as the Ministries, was described as the end of an era by both Sedad Eldem and *Arkitekt*'s editor Zeki Sayar. The same sentiment was expressed by the Austrian Ambassador Norbert von Bischoff. Moreover, at a meeting from which Kemalettin Bey left with tears in his eyes, the Ministry of Education openly demanded the elimination of arches and domes, favouring Ernst Egli for the task of building schools. Sedad Eldem, *50 Yıllık Meslek Jübilesi* (Istanbul, 1983), p. 49; Norbert von Bischoff, *Ankara: Eine Deutung des Neuen Werdens in der Türkei* (Vienna, 1935), pp. 101–02; Ilhan Tekeli and Selim Ilkin, eds, *Mimar Kemalettin'in Yazdıkları* (Ankara, 1997).

17 Carl Lörcher, 'Stadtbaufragen in der Türkei', *Bauwelt* (1925), pp. 6-8; Hemann Jansen, 'Izahname', *Ankara Şehrinin Profesör M. Jausseley, Jansen ve Brix taraflarından yapılan plan ve projelerine ait izahnameler* (Ankara, 1929); Hermann Jansen, 'Der Generalbebauungsplan von Ankara', Manuscript of 17 September 1936, Nachlaß Hermann Jansen, ZR ABK 785, Folder: B7, Germanisches Nationalmuseum, Nürnberg.

18 Nicolai, *Moderne und Exil*, pp.18-20, Ali Cengizkan, 'Robert Oerley: Söylemsel Dönüşümler Döneminde Ankara'da Viyanalı Bir Mimar', *Modernin Saati* (Ankara, 2002), pp. 71-91; Kıvanç Kılınç, 'Öncü Halk Sağlığı Projelerinin Kamusal Mekanı Olarak Sıhhiye', in Güven A. Sargın, ed., *Ankara'nın Kamusal Yüzleri* (Istanbul, 2002), pp. 119-56.

19 See for instance: Michel Foucault, *Discipline and Punish. The Birth of the Prison*, 2nd edn (New York, 1995); Anson Rabinbach, *The Human Motor: Energy, Fatigue, and the Origins of Modernity* (Berkeley, 1990); Tim Armstrong, *Modernism, Technology and the Body* (Cambridge, 1998); In the case of visual arts one can think of Futurism, Constructivism and Cubism.

20 The building was featured in *La Turquie Kemaliste* (October 1934), pp.1-5, along with articles that emphasized the importance of health reform.

21 Nicolai, *Moderne und Exil*, p.18; Kılınç, 'Öncü Halk Sağlığı Projelerinin Kamusal Mekanı Olarak Sıhhiye', p. 126.

22 See especially Werner Aebli, Rolf Meyer and Ernst Winkler, eds, *Stadt und Umwelt: Festschrift zum siebzigsten Geburstag von Ernst Egli* (Zurich, 1964). For Egli's work in Turkey, see Nicolai, *Moderne und Exil*; Oya Atalay Franck, 'Politik und Architektur: Ernst Egli und die Suche nach einer Moderne in der Türkei', PhD diss., ETH, Zürich, 2004; Bernd Nicolai, 'Ernst Egli and the Emergence of Modern Architecture in Kemalist Turkey', in 'Intertwined Histories. Turkey and Central Europe', ed. Esra Akcan, *Centropa*, VII/2 (May 2007), pp. 153–63.

23 Aebli, Meyer and Winkler, eds, *Stadt und Umwelt*; Atalay Franck, 'Politik und Architektur'.

24 Ernst Egli, *Climate and Town Districts: Consequences and Demands* (Erlanbach, Zürich, 1951); Ernst Egli, *Sinan: Der Baumeister osmanischer Glanzzeit* (Erlanbach, Zürich, 1954); Ernst Egli, *Şehirciliğin ve Memleket Planlamasının Esasları* (Ankara, 1957); Ernst Egli, *Geschichte des Städtebau*, 2 vols (Zürich, 1959–62). He also published

articles on the 'Turkish house'. For more discussion, see Esra Akcan, 'Modernity in Translation. Early Twentieth Century German-Turkish Exchanges in Land Settlement and Residential Culture', PhD diss., Columbia University, New York, 2005, Chapter 6.

25 Yael Navoro-Yaşın, 'Evde Taylorizm: Türkiye Cumhuriyeti'nin ilk yıllarında evişinin rasyonelleşmesi (1928–1940)', *Toplum Bilim*, 84 (Spring 2000), pp. 51–74.

26 Nicolai, *Moderne und Exil.*

27 Nicolai notes that the Turkish delegation established close contacts with Mendelsohn's staff, and the Technical University in Berlin-Charlottenburg regularly served as a consultant to the Turkish government. Nicolai, 'Ernst Egli and the Emergence of Modern Architecture in Kemalist Turkey', p.157.

28 Celal Esat [Arseven], *Yeni Mimari* (Istanbul, 1931).

29 Ernst Egli, 'Mimari Muhit', *Türk Yurdu* 4–24, nos 30–224 (1930), pp. 32–6 [34, 35].

30 Ibid., p. 36.

31 Taut's report to the Ministry of Education, Manfred Speidel Archive. For Taut's work in Turkey, see İnci Aslanoğlu, 'Dışavurumcu ve Usçu Devirlerinde Bruno Taut (1880–1938)', *METU Journal of Architecture*, II/1 (1976), pp. 35–47; Kristina Hartmann, 'Bruno Taut im Türkischen Exil', *Der Architekt*, 2 (January 1992), pp. 111–17; Manfred Speidel, 'Naturlichkeit und Freiheit. Bruno Tauts Bauten in der Turkei', in *Ankara 1923–50: Bir Baskentin Olusumu* (Ankara, 1994), pp. 52–65; Manfred Speidel, 'Bruno Taut: Wirken und Wirkung', in *Atatürk için Düşünmek. Iki Eser: Katafalk ve Anıtkabir. Iki Mimar: Bruno Taut and Emin Onat* (Istanbul, 1997), pp. 54–62.

32 Bruno Taut, 'Türk Evi, Sinan, Ankara', *Her Ay*, no. 2 (1938), pp. 93–4.

33 For more discussion, see Akcan, *Architecture in Translation.*

34 Bruno Taut, Letter to Tokugen Mihara, undated, Nachlaß Taut, BT–Slg–01–145/2, Baukunst Sammlung, Akademie der Künste, Berlin.

35 Especially see Bruno Taut, *Mimari Bilgisi,* trans. A. Kolatan (Istanbul, 1938); Bruno Taut, 'Nippon, mit europäischen Augen gesehen', Manuscript of 1933, Nachlaß Taut, Baukunst Sammlung, Akademie der Künste, Berlin; Bruno Taut, *Fundamentals of Japanese Architecture* (Tokyo, 1935); Bruno Taut, *Japans Kunst* (Tokyo, 1936); Bruno Taut, *Houses and People of Japan*, 2nd edn (Tokyo, 1958, original 1937).

36 Taut, *Japans Kunst*, p. 206.

37 Akcan, *Architecture in Translation.*

38 For more conceptual discussion, see Akcan, *Architecture in Translation.*

39 For Eldem's trip to Europe, see Akcan, 'Modernity in Translation', Chapter 5; Uğur Tanyeli and Bülent Tanju, eds, *Sedad Eldem*, vol. 1 (Istanbul, 2007). For Burhan Arif Ongun, see Tanyeli, *Mimarlığın Aktörleri,* pp. 64–78.

40 Doğramacı, *Kulturtransfer und nationale Identität*, pp. 59–76. For Arkan's education in Germany, see Esra Akcan, 'Ambiguities of Transparency and Privacy in Seyfi Arkan's Houses for the New State', *METU Journal of Architecture* (Spring 2006), pp. 25–49.

41 Tanyeli, *Mimarlığın Aktörleri,* pp. 292–5, 84–6.

42 B. Sabri and B. Hamdi, 'Turk Inkilap Mımarısı', *Mimar*, III/9–10 (1933), p. 266.

43 The prize-winning competition project was published in 'Sergi Binası Müsabakası', *Mimar*, III/5 (1933), pp. 131–7.

44 See, for instance, the description in Maruf Önal, *Anılarda Mimarlık* (Istanbul, 1995), pp. 63–4.

45 Elvan Altan Ergut, 'Sergievi'nden Opera'ya: Bir Dönüşüm Üzerine Notlar', *Doxa* (2006).

46 The editor of *La Turquie Kemaliste*, Vedat Nedim Tör, called for photographs to be published in the journal and selected Othmar Pflerschy, who was starting a studio in Istanbul in the tradition of the nineteenth-century Orientalist photographers, as the proper artist who would disseminate the regime's architectural ambitions both to the international and national public. Almost all of the contemporary photographs used in propaganda and publicity media, and reproduced here, were most probably by Pflerschy. See Vedat Nedim Tör, *Kemalizmin Dramı*, 2nd edn (Istanbul, 1983). Also

see Engin Özendeş, ed., *Cumhuriyet'in Işığında: Othmar Pferschy Fotoğrafları*, exh. cat., Istanbul Modern (Istanbul, 2006).

47 For a visual testimony to these affinities, see S. Bertaux, *Projecting the Nation: European States in the 1920s and 1930s*, exh. cat. (Istanbul, 2006).

48 Aptullah Ziya, 'Inkılap ve San'at', *Mimar*, III/9–10 (1933), pp. 317, 318.

49 For example, Aptullah Ziya, 'Sanatta Nasyonalizm', *Mimar*, IV/2 (1934), p. 53.

50 Sedad Çetintaş, 'Inkılap Mimarisi Isteriz!', *Yapı*, no. 6 (1942), p.19. Also see Sedad Çetintaş, 'Inkılap Mimarisi Isteriz!', *Yapı*, no. 5 (1942), pp. 9, 19; no. 6 (1942), pp. 15, 19; no. 7 (1942), pp. 12–13; Sedad Çetintaş, 'Kendimizi Nasıl Bulalım?', *Yapı*, no. 39 (1943), pp. 15–16; Bedri Uçar, 'Mimarlığımızı Yaşatalım, Mimarlığımızı Tanıtalım', *Mimarlık*, no. 1 (1944), p. 2; 'Büyük Davamız', *Mimarlık*, no. 2 (1944), pp. 1, 4.

51 For example, the architectural journal *Mimarlık* held a survey on the definition of 'national architecture' to which many architects responded by voicing the necessity of state support. Adil Denktaş, no. 2, *Mimarlık* (1944), p. 4; Sedad Eldem, no. 4 (1944), pp. 3, 8; Feridun Kip, no. 4 (1944), p. 6. For Turkish architects' hostile statements against their foreign colleagues, see Gürhan Tümer, *Cumhuriyet Döneminde Yabancı Mimar Sorunu* (İzmir, 1998).

52 'DDY Umumi Idare Binasi', *Arkitekt*, XI/11–12 (1941), p. 241.

53 See Michael Meeker, 'Once There Was, Once There Wasn't: National Monuments and Interpersonal Exchange', in *Rethinking Modernity and National Identity in Turkey*, ed. Sibel Bozdoğan and Reşat Kasaba (Seattle, WA, 1997), pp. 157–91; *Atatürk için Düşünmek* (Istanbul, 1998); Christopher Wilson, 'Representing National Identity and Memory in the Mausoleum of Mustafa Kemal Atatürk', *Journal of the Society of Architectural Historians*, LXVIII/2 (June 2009), pp. 224–53.

54 Zeki Sayar, 'Anıt-Kabir Müsabakası Münasebetiyle', *Arkitekt*, XIII/1–2 (1943), pp. 1–21.

55 Emin Onat and Orhan Arda, 'Anıt-Kabir', *Arkitekt*, xxv/2 (1955), pp. 55–9. For an excellent discussion of the construction of Anatolian civilizations as the basis of nationalist historiography, see Can Bilsel, 'Our Anatolia: Organicism and the Making of Humanist Culture in Turkey', Sibel Bozdoğan and Gülru Necipoğlu, eds, *Muqarnas*, 24 (Autumn 2007), pp. 223–41.

56 See especially Friedrich Tamms, *Paul Bonatz: Arbeiten aus den Jahren 1907 bis 1937* (Stuttgart, 1937); Matthias Roser, *Paul Bonatz: Wohnhäuser* (Stuttgart, 1992).

57 Paul Bonatz, 'Noch einmal die Werkbund Siedlung', *Schwäbische Kronik*, 5 March 1926.

58 Paul Bonatz and Bruno Wehner, *Reichsautobahn–Tankanlagen* (Berlin, 1942).

59 Albert Speer, 'Introduction', *Neue Deutsche Baukunst – Yeni Alman Mimarisi* (Berlin, 1942).

60 Paul Bonatz, 'Yeni Alman Mimarisi' [1], *Arkitekt*, nos 3–4 (1943), pp. 73, 74; 'Yeni Alman Mimarisi' [2], *Arkitekt*, nos 5–6 (1943), p. 119.

61 Ibid., p. 75.

62 Abidin Mortaş, 'Yeni Alman Mimarisi Sergisi', *Arkitekt*, nos 3–4 (1943), pp. 67–70.

63 Behçet Ünsal, 'Eminönü Halkevinde Açılan Alman Mimari Sergisi Dolayısıyla. Yeni Bir Mimariye Doğru', *Yapı*, nos 43–44, no. 45, nos 48–49 (1943).

64 For more discussion, see Zeynep Çelik-Hinchliffe, 'Rootedness Uprooted: Paul Bonatz in Turkey, 1933–1954', in Esra Akcan, ed., 'Intertwined Histories. Turkey and Central Europe', *centropa*, VII/2 (May 2007), pp. 180–96.

65 Paul Bonatz, 'Yeni Alman Mimarisi' [1], p. 74.

66 'Güzel Sanatlar Akademisi,' *Mimar*, no. 1 (1931), p. 25; 'GSA Yüksek Mimarlık şubesi. Diploma Müsabakası', *Arkitekt,* nos 5–6 (1943), pp. 151–63.

67 'Istanbul Radyo Evi Proje Müsabakası', *Arkitekt*, nos 7–8 (1945), pp. 143–57; nos 9–10 (1943), pp. 204–13. 'Adana Adalet Sarayı Proje Müsabakası', *Arkitekt*, nos 1–2 (1946), pp. 25–31; 'Istanbul Adalet Sarayı Proje Müsabakası', *Arkitekt*, nos 5–6 (1947), pp. 103–15.

68 Paul Bonatz, *Leben und Bauen* (Stuttgart, 1950).

1   Hermann Jansen, 'Der Generalbebauungsplan von Ankara', Manuscript of 17
    September 1936, Nachlaß Hermann Jansen, ZR ABK 785, Folder: B7, Germanisches
    Nationalmuseum, Nuremberg, p.10.

2   In addition to Ankara, he prepared master plans for İzmit, Adana, Ceyhan, Tarsus,
    Mersin and Gaziantep.

3   Hermann Jansen, 'Angora', Manuscript of 11 June 1929, Nachlaß Hermann Jansen, ZR
    ABK 785, Folder: B6a, Germanisches Nationalmuseum, Nuremberg, p. 5.

4   See also Esra Akcan, 'Modernity in Translation: Early Twentieth Century German-
    Turkish Exchanges in Land Settlement and Residential Culture', PhD diss., Columbia
    University, New York, 2005, translated as Çeviride Modern Olan (Istanbul, 2009); Esra
    Akcan, Architecture in Translation: Germany, Turkey and the Modern House (Durham,
    NC, 2012).

5   Jansen, 'Der Generalbebauungsplan von Ankara', p. 3.

6   For instance, the Austrian ambassador in Ankara described at length the differences
    between this house and other statesmen's palaces. Norbert von Bischoff, Ankara: Eine
    Deutung des Neuen Werdens in der Türkei (Vienna, 1935), pp. 101–2.

7   This was how the house was introduced in foreign magazines. Howard Robertson,
    'Two Villas for Kemal Atatürk and his Sister', Architect and Building News, no. 133
    (March 1938), pp. 362–4. Arkan also referred to the fact that the house was designed
    for a woman in one of his three articles on this house. Seyfi Arkan, 'Villa Projesi',
    Arkitekt, no. 6 (1935), p. 167.

8   For more discussion, see Akcan, Architecture in Translation.

9   4 August 1936, 24 September 1937. Niyazi Ahmet Banoğlu, Atatürk'ün Istanbul'daki
    Hayatı (Istanbul, 1974), pp. 201, 336.

10 Sibel Bozdoğan, Modernism and Nation Building: Turkish Architectural Culture in the
    Early Republic (Seattle, WA, 2001), Chapter 5.

11 Yedigün, no. 177 (1936), p. 8.

12 Hermann Jansen, 'Erläuterungsbericht für die Emlak Bankası Kooperatifi', Manuscript
    of 9 September 1937, Nachlaß Hermann Jansen, ZR ABK 785, Folder: B7, Germanisches
    Nationalmuseum, Nuremberg.

13 İlhan Tekeli and Selim İlkin, Bahçelievlerin Öyküsü (Ankara: KentKoop, 1984); Esra
    Akcan, 'Modernity in Translation', Chapter 3.

14 Allaettin Cemil Topçubaşı, 'Yapı Kooperatifleri ve Ucuz Ev', Parts I–II, Karınca
    (March 1936), pp. 4–5, Karınca (June 1936), p. 33; 'Uzgören'den Gelen Cevap',
    Karınca (March 1936), pp. 62–76.

15 Of these, twenty-two were in Ankara, eight in Istanbul, twenty in Aydın, Adana,
    Antalya, Balıkesir, Burdur, Denizli, Diyarbakır, İzmir, Tarsus Tekeli and İlkin,
    Bahçelievlerin Öyküsü, p. 106.

16 For documentation on these housing cooperatives, see Ali Cengizkan, 'Discursive
    Formations in Turkish Residential Architecture: Ankara, 1948–1962', PhD diss., METU,
    Ankara, 2000.

17 Zeki Sayar, 'Mesken Davası', Arkitekt, nos 3–4 (1946), pp. 49–51; Arkitekt, no. 7–8
    (1946), pp. 149–50; Martin Wagner, 'Şehircilikte Sermayenin Yanlış İdaresi,' Arkitekt,
    no. 7 (1936), pp. 187–8.

18 Burak Asıliskender, 'Cumhuriyet'in İlk Yıllarında Modern Kimlik Arayışı: Sümerbank
    Kayseri Bez Fabrikası Örneği', Master's Thesis, Istanbul Technical University, Istanbul,
    2002.

19 For more information, see Bozdoğan, Modernism and Nation Building, Chapter 2;
    Akcan, 'Modernity in Translation', Chapter 8.

20 Akcan, 'Modernity in Translation', Chapter 7.

21 Zeki Sayar, 'İnşaatta Standard', Mimar, no. 1 (1931), pp. 10–11.

22 Zeki Sayar, 'İç kolonizasyon', parts 1–2, *Arkitekt*, no. 2 (1936), pp. 46–51 [48]; *Arkitekt*, no. 8 (1936), pp. 231–5.

23 Behçet Ünsal, 'Zamanımız mimarlığının morfolojik analizi', *Arkitekt*, no. 7 (1937), pp. 201–4 [202]; *Arkitekt*, no. 8 (1937), pp. 219–22.

24 Akcan, 'Modernity in Translation', Chapter 8.

25 Yakup Kadri Karaosmanoğlu, *Ankara* [1934], 4th edn (Istanbul, 1972), p. 11.

26 Martin Wagner, Letter to Walter Gropius, 20 August 1935; quoted in Nicolai, *Moderne und Exil*, p. 127.

27 Behçet Ünsal, 'Mimarlıkta Gerçeklik', *Arkitekt*, no. 4 (1935), pp. 116–20.

28 Abidin Mortaş, 'Evlerimiz', *Arkitekt*, no. 1 (1936), pp. 24, 27.

29 See, for instance, Behçet Ünsal, 'Kübik Yapı ve Konfor', *Arkitekt*, nos 3–4 (1939), pp. 60–62.

30 Peyami, Safa, 'Bizde ve Avrupa'da Kübik', *Yedigün*, no. 188 (1936), pp. 7–8 [7].

31 For the impact of the 'Turkish house' on modern architecture in Turkey, see (in addition to the books about Turkish architecture in general in the Bibliography) Sibel Bozdoğan, Süha Özkan and Engin Yenal, *Sedad Eldem Architect in Turkey* (London, 1987); Sibel Bozdoğan, 'The Legacy of an Istanbul Architect: Type, Context and Urban Identity in Sedad Eldem's Work', in *Modernism and the Mediterranean*, ed. Jean-François Lejeune and Michelangelo Sabatino (London and New York, 2010), pp. 141–56; Gülsüm Baydar Nalbantoğlu, 'Between Civilization and Culture: Appropriation of Traditional Dwelling Forms in Early Republican Turkey', *Journal of Architectural Education*, XLVII/2 (November 1993), pp. 66–74; Sibel Bozdoğan, 'Vernacular Architecture and Identity Politics: The Case of the "Turkish house"', *Traditional Dwellings and Settlements Review*, VII/2 (1996), pp. 7–8; Carel Bertham, 'The Turkish House, an Effort on Memory', PhD diss., University of California, Los Angeles, 1998; Uğur Tanyeli, 'Türkiye'de Modernleşme ve Vernaküler Mimari Gelenek', in Zeynep Rona, ed., *Bilanço 1923–1998*, vol. I (Istanbul, 1999), pp. 283–90; Uğur Tanyeli and Bülent Tanju, eds, *Sedad Eldem*, 2 vols (Istanbul, 2007–8).

32 Sedad Eldem, Sketchbooks, Book 6, Berlin, 1929. Property of Edhem Eldem. Also see Edhem Eldem, 'Mimar Sedad Eldem'in Gençlik Yazıları (1928–1929)', in *Aptullah Kuran için Yazılar: Essays in Honor of Aptullah Kuran*, ed. Çiğdem Kafesçioğlu and Lucienne Thys-Senocak (Istanbul, 1999), pp. 519–42; Tanyeli and Tanju, eds, *Sedad Eldem*, vol. I; Akcan, *Architecture in Translation*, Chapter 2.

33 For a comparison of Eldem's and Egli's different theories on the origin and development of the 'Turkish house', see Esra Akcan, 'Eldem, Arseven, Egli ve "Türk Evi" Tezinin Algılanan Nesnelliği', in *Sedad Eldem*, ed. Uğur Tanyeli and Bülent Tanju, vol. II (Istanbul, 2008).

34 The list of books defining the traditional 'Turkish house', especially those written after the 1950s, would be impossible to document here. For a comprehensive bibliography, see *Türk Evi ve Biz* (Istanbul, 1993).

35 Sedad Eldem published his research in a number of essays and books. The most significant may be listed as: Sedad Eldem, 'Anciennes maisons d'Ankara', *La Turquie Kemaliste* (June 1935), pp. 10–12; Sedad Eldem, 'Türk Odası', *Güzel Sanatlar Dergisi*, no. 5 (1944), pp. 1–27; Sedad Eldem, *Türk Evi Plan Tipleri* (Istanbul, 1955); Sedad Eldem, *Istanbul Yalıları*, 2 vols (Istanbul, 1993–4); Sedad Eldem, *Türk Evi*, 3 vols (Istanbul, 1984–7).

36 Eldem, *Türk Evi Plan Tipleri*, p. 12.

37 For more discussion, see Akcan, *Architecture in Translation*.

38 For his manifesto-like essays, written during this period, see especially Sedad Eldem, 'Milli mimari meselesi', *Arkitekt*, nos 9–10 (1939), pp. 220–23; Sedad Eldem, 'Yerli Mimariye Doğru', *Arkitekt*, nos 3–4 (1940), pp. 69–74; Sedad Eldem, 'Milli ve Yerli Davamız', *Mimarlık*, no. 4 (1944), pp. 2–5, 8.

39 Sedad Eldem, 'Elli Yıllık Cumhuriyet Mimarlığı', *Mimarlık*, nos 11–12 (1973), p. 6.

40 Sibel Bozdoğan, 'Reading Ottoman Architecture through Modernist Lenses: Nationalist Historiography and the New Architecture in the Early Republic',

Muqarnas, no. 24 (Autumn 2007), pp. 199–221.

41 See also Bernd Nicolai, *Moderne und Exil;* Akcan, 'Modernity in Translation', Chapter 8; Zeynep Çelik-Hinchliffe, 'Rootedness Uprooted: Paul Bonatz in Turkey, 1933–1954', in 'Intertwined Histories: Turkey and Central Europe', ed. Esra Akcan, *centropa*, VII/2 (May 2007), pp. 180–96.

42 Paul Bonatz, 'Şükrü Saraçoğlu Stadtteil in Ankara', undated manuscript (*c.* 1945), Peter Dübers Personal Collection, Stuttgart. Daily newspapers and professional journals underlined exactly this aspect. Fatih Metigil, 'Milli Mimariye Doğru', *Ulus*, 20 (November 1945), pp. 1, 4; Orhan Alsaç, 'Saraçoğlu Mahallesi', *Mimarlık*, no. 6 (1945); Zeki Sayar, 'Saraçoğlu Mahallesi', *Arkitekt*, nos 3–4 (1946), pp. 56–9, 86.

chapter four: Populist Democracy and Post-war Modernism

1 Cited in R. Kasaba, 'Populism and Democracy in Turkey, 1946–1961', in *Rules and Rights in the Middle East* (Seattle, WA, 1993), p. 56.

2 Especially in Daniel Lerner, *The Passing of Traditional Society* (New York, 1958); Cyril Black, *The Dynamics of Modernization* (New York, 1966); and Bernard Lewis, *The Emergence of Modern Turkey* (London and New York, 1961).

3 Fredric Jameson, 'Notes on Globalization as a Philosophical Issue', in Fredric Jameson and Masao Miyoshi, eds, *The Cultures of Globalization* (Durham, NC, 1998), pp. 54–77.

4 On this dimension of modernity, see especially Marshall Berman, *All That is Solid Melts into Air: The Experience of Modernity* (New York, 1982) and Hilde Heynen, *Architecture and Modernity: A Critique* (Cambridge, MA, 1999).

5 See Cana Bilsel, 'İzmir'de Cumhuriyet'in "Modern" Kentine Geçişte Şehircilik Deneyimi ve Model Transferi Sorunu: Danger-Prost Planı ve Le Corbusier'nin Nazım Plan Önerisi', in Esra Akcan, ed., *Küreselleşme Sürecinde 'Öteki' Coğrafyalar. Domus M* (Feb–March 2001), pp. 42–6.

6 See Pierre Pinon and Cana Bilsel, eds, *From the Imperial Capital to the Republican Modern City: Henri Prost's Planning of Istanbul, 1936–1951* (Istanbul, 2010) and Murat Gül, *The Emergence of Modern Istanbul* (London and New York, 2009).

7 Dr. Lütfü Kırdar, as quoted in *Güzelleşen Istanbul* (Istanbul, 1943).

8 Burak Boysan, 'Politik Hummanın Silinmeyen İzleri: Halkla İlişkiler Stratejisi olarak İstanbul'un İmarı', *İstanbul Dergisi*, 4 (January 1994), pp. 84–9. For a revisionist account challenging Menderes's critics, see Gül, *The Emergence of Modern Istanbul*, especially pp. 157–71.

9 *Havadis*, 26 February 1957, cited in ibid., p. 140.

10 Flights between Ankara and Istanbul started in 1933 but it took another 20 years to turn this airstrip into Istanbul's first airport designed according to an agreement between the Turkish Government and the Westinghouse International Electric Company and the J. G. White Engineering Corporation in 1947; *Ulaşımda 50 Yıl* (Ankara, 1974), p. 85.

11 See Sarah Williams Goblhagen and Réjean Legault, eds, *Anxious Modernisms: Experimentation in Post-war Architectural Culture* (Cambridge, MA, 2000). The feelings of 'optimism' and 'imagination' that are central to modernization theory deserve more attention than they typically receive in critical histories of modern architecture, especially as a counterweight to the term 'anxiety' that Goldhagen and Legault have employed to characterize post-war modernism. It is only when one looks beyond the West, towards the decolonizing and modernizing nation states of the Middle East, Asia and Latin America, that one sees the brief moment of optimism attached to the aesthetic and ideological precepts of international style, precisely at the same time that these were beginning to be questioned in Europe and the US.

12 The events of 5–6 September 1955, when nationalist thugs vandalized non-Muslim businesses in Istanbul, was the last of a series when minorities were harassed after the

imposition of a heavy 'wealth tax', exclusively on the minorities, in the 1940s. As a result of these events, most of the non-Muslim bourgeoisie left Turkey and Istanbul's population changed from 75.3 per cent Muslim and 26 per cent non-Muslim in 1935 to 90 per cent Muslim and only 10 per cent non-Muslim in 1960. Devlet İstatistik Enstitüsü, various years.

13 See Zeki Sayar's editorial to *Arkitekt*, nos 9–12 (1954) on the occasion of the establishment of the Chamber of Turkish Architects, with 720 members.

14 Enis Kortan, *1950'ler Kuşağı Mimarlık Antolojisi* (Istanbul, 1997).

15 For example in Uğur Tanyeli, 'Haluk Baysal – Melih Birsel', *Arredamento Mimarlık* (April 1998), pp. 72–9.

16 Ela Kaçel, 'Intellectualism and Consumerism: Ideologies, Practices and Criticisms of Common Sense Modernism in Postwar Turkey', PhD diss., Cornell University, 2009.

17 See recent monographs: *Abdurrahman Hancı – Buildings/Projects 1945–2000* (Istanbul, 2008); Müge Cengizkan, ed., *Haluk Baysal – Melih Birsel* (Ankara, 2007); Uğur Tanyeli and Atilla Yücel, eds, *Turgut Cansever: Düşünce Adamı ve Mimar* (Istanbul, 2007).

18 Kortan, *1950'ler Kuşağı Mimarlık Antolojisi*, p. 29.

19 For more discussion, see Kaçel, 'Intellectualism and Consumerism'.

20 G. Holmes Perkins even prepared the first proposal for the campus plan of METU in Ankara in 1959, but the project was later commissioned to the Turkish architects Altuğ and Behruz Çinici. See A. Payaşlıoğlu, *Barakadan Kampusa, 1954–1964* (Ankara, 1996).

21 A number of architectural theorists have located the post-war roots of 'critical regionalism' in the tropicalized modernism of the 1950s: see Liane Lefaivre, Alexander Tzonis and Bruno Stagno, *Tropical Architecture: Critical Regionalism in the Age of Globalization* (New York, 2001); Liane Lefaivre and Alexander Tzonis, *Critical Regionalism: Architecture and Identity in a Globalized World* (Munich, 2003).

22 Şevki Vanlı, *Bilinmek Istenmeyen 20. YY Türk Mimarlığı: Eleştirel Bir Bakış* (Ankara, 2006), p. 211.

23 See especially *Building Diplomacy: the Architecture of American Embassies* (Ithaca, NY, 2004); Jane Loeffler, *The Architecture of Diplomacy* (New York, 1998); Annabel Wharton, *Building the Cold War: Hilton International Hotels and Modern Architecture* (Chicago, IL, 2001).

24 Wharton, *Building the Cold War*, p. 22.

25 'Hilton's Newest Hotel', *Architectural Forum* (December 1955), p. 123. The hotel was also published in 'Hotel in Istanbul', *Architectural Review* (December 1955), pp. 290–96.

26 Esra Akcan, 'Amerikanlaşma ve Endişe. İstanbul Hilton Oteli', *Arredamento Mimarlık* (November 2001), pp. 112–19.

27 *Atatürk Kültür Merkezi* (Istanbul, 1979); and Hayati Tabanlıoğlu, 'Istanbul Opera Binası', *Arkitekt*, 324, no. 4 (1966), pp. 161–9.

28 The saga of the AKM took a new twist in 2007. After an initial proposal to tear down the aged building led to vocal protests, Murat Tabanlıoğlu, the son of the original architect, secured the commission to rework the building with minimal changes, such as the widening of the entrance and lobby areas for a more inviting public space and the inclusion of a roof restaurant.

29 Vanlı, *Bilinmek Istenmeyen 20. YY Türk Mimarlığı*, pp. 207 and 211. The original article in which he coined the term Hiltonism is 'Hiltonculuk', *kim Haftalık Haber Dergisi*, 28 November 1958, pp. 21–2.

30 Sedad Eldem, '50 Yıllık Cumhuriyet Mimarlığı', *Akademi Mimarlık ve Sanat*, 8 (July 1974), p. 11.

31 An article on this topic by Frederick Gibberd, 'Expression in Modern Architecture', *Architects' Journal*, no. 115 (24 January 1952), pp. 118–24, was published in Turkish translation in *Arkitekt*, 1–4 (1953), pp. 53–61, and was received with great interest. See Ali Cengizkan, *Modernin Saati* (Ankara, 2002), pp. 219–27.

32 Semra Germener, 'Türk Sanatının Modernleşme Süreci', *Modern ve Ötesi* (Istanbul, 2007), p. 11.

33 See especially the theme issue 'Art and Architecture', *Docomomo International Journal*, 42 (Summer 2010) and the original historical debate published as 'A Symposium on how to Combine Architecture, Painting and Sculpture', *Interiors*, 10 (May 1951), pp. 100–105. In Turkey the architect Utarit İzgi has written on the topic in *Mimarlıkta Süreç: Kavramlar, İlişkiler* (Istanbul, 1999), pp. 214–21.

34 Particularly illustrative of this point is the mosaic panel that Bedri Rahmi Eyüboğlu designed for the Hilton's famous Karagöz Bar, named after the traditional *karagöz* puppet theatre, with obvious orientalist connotations.

35 See Sibel Bozdoğan, 'Turkish Pavilion in Brussels Expo '58', in *The Architecture of Expo '58*, ed. Rika Devos and Mil DeKoonig (Brussels, 2006), pp. 198–213; for a shorter version, see 'A Lost Icon of Turkish Modernism: Expo '58 Pavilion in Brussels', *Docomomo International Journal*, 35 (September 2006), pp. 62–70.

36 For example, Iran's pavilion for the Brussels Expo 1958 featured a tall portico derived from the traditional *talar* motif of Safavid architecture, while that of Thailand was a gilded temple on a podium. Sedad Eldem's 'Turkish Pavilion' for the 1939 New York World's Fair was a replica of one of the ornate pavilions in Topkapı Palace.

37 İzgi, *Mimarlıkta Süreç*, pp. 214–21.

38 Ela Kaçel, 'Fidusyer: Bir Kollektif Düşünme Pratiği', in *Haluk Baysal – Melih Birsel*, ed. Müge Cengizkan (Ankara, 2007), pp. 7–31; see also 'Vakko Turistik Elişi Eşarp ve Konfeksiyon Fabrikası', *Arkitekt*, IV/340 (1970), pp. 159–66.

39 Ali Cengizkan, 'Bedri Rahmi'nin Bilinmeyen bir Mozaiği: Mimarlık ve Duvar Resmi', *Modernin Saati* (Ankara, 2002), p. 237. For a reconstruction of the story of the lost mosaic panels, see Johann Pillai, *The Lost Mosaic Wall: from Expo '58 to Cyprus* (Nicosia, 2010).

40 See, for example, D. C. Tipps, 'Modernization Theory and the Comparative Study of Societies: A Critical Perspective', *Comparative Studies in Society and History*, 15 (1973), pp. 199–226.

41 Daniel Lerner, 'Turkey: From the Past', in *The Turkish Administrator: A Cultural Survey*, ed. J. R. Hopper and R. I. Levin (Ankara, 1968).

42 Murat Gül attributes this critique to secular, republican critics while in the more conservative Muslim circles, it is Henri Prost's plans and early republican interventions that are blamed for Istanbul's loss of character. See Gül, *The Emergence of Modern Istanbul*.

chapter five: **Housing in the Metropolis**

1 Orhan Pamuk, *Black Book*, trans. G. Gün (New York, 1994), pp. 181–2.

2 For the governments' legal and financial initiatives to handle the housing shortage, including the five-year development plans between 1963 and 1980, see İlhan Tekeli, *Türkiye'de Yaşamda ve Yazında Konut Sorununun Gelişimi* (Ankara, 1996); Ruşen Keleş, *Kentleşme Politikası*, 10th edn (Istanbul, 2006).

3 Utarit İzgi, 'Haluk Şaman Villası', *Arkitekt*, 296, no. 3 (1959), pp. 94–8; Utarit İzgi and Mahmut Bir, 'Muammer Arıtan Villası', *Arkitekt*, 298, no. 1 (1960), pp. 16–21; Utarit İzgi and Mahmut Bir, 'Çiftehavuzlar'da Bir Villa', *Arkitekt*, 303, no. 2 (1961), pp. 56–7; Utarit İzgi, Asım Mutlu and Esat Suher, 'Adnan Kunt Villası', *Arkitekt*, 332, no. 1 (1968), pp. 151–3.

4 Birleşmiş Mimarlar, 'Barlas Yalısı (Yeniköy)', *Arkitekt*, 322, no. 2 (1966), pp. 66–9; Haluk Baysal and Melih Birsel, 'Hami Çon Villası', *Arkitekt*, 340, no. 4 (1970), p. 172; Haluk Baysal and Melih Birsel, 'Şevket Saatçioğlu Villası', *Arkitekt*, 340, no. 4 (1970), p. 173.

5 Muhteşem Giray, 'Uzunoğlu Villası', *Arkitekt*, 325, no. 1 (1967), pp. 8–9; Muhteşem Giray, 'Özgür Villası', *Arkitekt*, 325, no. 1 (1967), pp. 10–11.

6 Ercüment Bigat and İlhan Bilgesu, 'Mühendis Arif Saltuk Villası', *Arkitekt*, 291, no. 2 (1958), pp. 55–60.

7   Abdurrahman Hancı, *Abdurrahman Hancı. Yapılar Projeler 1945–2000* (Istanbul, 2008).

8   For more examples from this generation, see Enis Kortan, ed., *1950ler Kuşağı Mimarlık Antalojisi* (Istanbul, 1997).

9   The following articles were written by Nezahat Arıkoğlu: 'Mimari Hakkında Bir Konuşma', *Arkitekt*, 317, no. 4 (1964), pp. 160–61; 'Ofis Binaları (U.S.A)', *Arkitekt*, 318, no. 1 (1965), pp. 14–16; '165 Daireli Bir Apartman', *Arkitekt*, 321, no. 1 (1966), pp. 10–11; 'Le Corbusier', *Arkitekt*, 321, no. 1 (1966), pp. 37–8; 'Whitney Müzesi Mimarları', *Arkitekt*, 325, no. 1 (1967), pp. 21–2; 'ABD'de ev', *Arkitekt*, 326, no. 2 (1967), pp. 53–5; 'Nursing Homes', *Arkitekt*, 329, no. 1 (1968), pp. 27–8; *Arkitekt*, 331, no. 3 (1968), p. 137; 'Bir Ofis Binası', *Arkitekt*, 336, no. 4 (1969), p. 141–2.

10 Cemil Gerçek, ed., *Sedad Hakkı Eldem: Büyük Konutlar* (Ankara, 1982); Sibel Bozdoğan, Süha Özkan and Engin Yenal, *Sedad Eldem. Architect in Turkey* (Singapore, 1987); Uğur Tanyeli and Bülent Tanju, eds, *Sedad Eldem*, 2 vols (Istanbul, 2007–8).

11 Gerhard Kessler, 'İstanbul'da Mesken Darlığı, Mesken Sefaleti, Mesken İnşaatı', trans. E. Zadil, *Arkitekt*, nos 5–6 (1949), pp. 131–4.

12 For a more detailed discussion of these experts' reports, see Tekeli, *Yaşamda ve Yazında Konut*, pp. 98–106. The Ministry of Reconstruction and Settlement published 17 Turkish books on housing and a further 25 appeared in translation between 1962 and 1969. *50 Yılda İmar ve Yerleşme, 1923–1973* (Ankara, 1973), p. 108. See also Bernard Wagner, 'Türkiye'de Mesken Meselesi', *Arkitekt*, 284 (1956), pp. 78–92, 94; Bernard Wagner, 'Türkiye'de Mesken Meselesi II', *Arkitekt*, 285 (1956), pp. 119–39.

13 Skidmore Owings and Merrill, *Construction, Town Planning and Housing in Turkey*, report prepared for the Minister of Public Works in Ankara, Turkey, 1951, p. 78. They also cited in full the Declaration of National Housing Policy from the United States Housing Act of 1949, so that 'Turkey can take advantage of the U.S. experience in this problem'. Ibid., pp. 83–4.

14 Türk Mimarlar Odası, *Bildiri 1960. Yurdumuzda İmar Çabaları* (Ankara, 1960), pp. 25–6.

15 *Konut Paneli I–IV* (Istanbul, 1961–5).

16 *50 Yılda İmar ve Yerleşme, 1923–1973* (Ankara, 1973). For assessment about the intentions and results of these governmental initiatives, see Tekeli, *Yaşamda ve Yazında Konut*, pp. 67–88; Keleş, *Kentleşme Politikası*; Yıldız Sey, 'Cumhuriyet Döneminde Konut', in *75 Yılda Değişen Kent ve Mimarlık*, ed. Yıldız Sey (Istanbul, 1998), pp. 273–300; Yıldız Sey, 'To House the New Citizen', in *Modern Turkish Architecture*, ed. Renata Holod and Ahmet Evin (Philadelphia, 1984).

17 *II. İmar Kongresi (1962). Sosyal Mesken Standartları* (Ankara, 1963); Tekeli, *Yaşamda ve Yazında Konut*, pp. 76–7.

18 For documents of these housing projects, see 'İmar ve İskan Bakanlığı. Mesken Genel Müdürlüğü', *Şehir ve Kasabalar için Proje Çalışmaları, 1962–1965* (Ankara, 1965).

19 For a list of housing projects carried out by Emlak Kredi Bank until 1973, and a list of housing cooperatives in Ankara established between 1950 and 1958, see Tansı Şenyapılı, 'Baraka'dan Gecekonduya. Ankara'da Kentsel Mekanın Dönüşümü (Istanbul, 2004), pp. 286, 337.

20 See the articles by Abidin Mortaş in *Arkitekt* and Mithat Yenen in *İller ve Belediyeler Dergisi*. See also Ali Cengizkan, 'Discursive Formations in Turkish Residential Architecture. Ankara, 1948–1962', PhD diss., METU, Ankara, 2000.

21 Kemal Ahmet Aru, 'Levend Mahallesi', *Arkitekt*, nos 9–10 (1952), pp. 174–81; '4. Levent', *Arkitekt*, 285 (1956), pp. 140–53.

22 'Ataköy Sitesi', *Arkitekt*, 2/291 (1958), pp. 61–6; Ertuğrul Menteşe, 'Ataköy Sitesi Hakkında Rapor', *Arkitekt*, 2/291 (1958), pp. 79–82.

23 'İstanbul Belediyesi T. Emlak Kredi Bankası Blok apartmanları- Atatürk Bulvarı', *Arkitekt*, 286 (1957), pp. 12–15 (12).

24 Vedat Erdener, 'Berlin'de Yabancı Mimarlar', *Arkitekt*, 3/288 (1957), pp. 126–9.

25 Haluk Baysal and Melih Birsel, 'Hukukçular Sitesi', *Arkitekt*, 4/305 (1961), pp. 163–72.

26 Ali Cengizkan, *Modernin Saati* (Ankara, 2002), p. 177.

27 Şevki Vanlı, 'Çevrenin Düzeni İçin', *Mimarlık ve Sanat*, 7–8 (1963), pp. 213–14 [214].

28 Şevki Vanlı, 'Mimar, kişi ve toplum', *Mimarlık ve Sanat*, 10 (1964), pp. 17–18.

29 Şevki Vanlı, 'Toplum Düzeninin Şehir ve Yapıya Etkisi,' *Arkitekt*, 4/309 (1962), pp. 175–81.

30 Vanlı, 'Toplum Düzeninin Şehir ve Yapıya Etkisi', p. 180.

31 Şevki Vanlı, *Mimarlık Sevgilim* (Istanbul, 2000).

32 'me-sa toplu konut A.Ş.nin bir kaç uygulaması', *Arkitekt*, 1/373 (1979), pp. 47–51 [47].

33 Tekeli, *Yaşamda ve Yazında Konut*, pp. 96–7.

34 See, for instance, Zeki Sayar, 'Hatalı bir Iskan Işi', *Arkitekt*, nos 5–8 (1952), pp. 101–2; Zeki Sayar, 'Bizde Mesken Finansmanı', *Arkitekt*, nos 5–8 (1952), pp. 165–6; Zeki Sayar, 'Mesken Davasında Teşkilat', *Arkitekt*, nos 11–12 (1952), pp. 213–14; Zeki Sayar, 'Şu Mesken Davamız', *Arkitekt*, nos 1–2 (1956), pp. 3–4; Zeki Sayar, 'Imar Vekaletinden Beklediklerimiz', *Arkitekt*, 290/1 (1958), pp. 3–4; Zeki Sayar, 'Mesken Davası!', *Arkitekt*, 305/4 (1961), pp. 151–2.

35 See, for instance, Şule Özüekren, 'Konut Kooperatiflerinde Örgütsel Özellikler ve Başarı Göstergeleri Arasındaki İlişkiler', in *Konut Araştırmaları Sempozyumu* (Ankara, 1995), pp. 109–45; Gülden Berkman, 'Türkiye'de Konut Kooperatiflerinin Konut Üretimine Katkısı ve Başarı ve Başarısızlıklarının Değerlendirilmesi', in *Konut Araştırmaları Sempozyumu* (Ankara, 1995), pp. 147–80.

36 Yıldırım Yavuz, 'İkinci Meşrutiyet Döneminde Ulusal Mimari Üzerindeki Batı Etkileri', ODTÜ *Mimarlık Fakültesi Dergisi*, II/1 (Spring 1976), pp. 9–34; Afife Batur, Atilla Yücel and Nur Fersan, 'İstanbul'da Ondokuzuncu Yüzyıl Sıra Evleri Koruma ve Kullanım için Bir Monografik Araştırma', *odtü Mimarlık Fakültesi Dergisi*, V/2 (Autumn 1979), pp. 185–205; Gülsüm Baydar Nalbantoğlu, 'An Architectural and Historical Survey on the Development of the 'Apartment Building' in Ankara, 1923–1950', Master's thesis, METU, Ankara, 1981; Zeynep Çelik, *The Remaking of Istanbul: The Portrait of an Ottoman City in the Nineteenth Century* (Berkeley and Los Angeles, 1986).

37 Uğur Tanyeli, 'Bir "İstanbul Mimarı": Emin Necip Uzman', *Arredamento Dekorasyon* (September 1995), pp. 71–3 [73].

38 'Birkan Apartmanları', *Arkitekt*, 294/1(1959), pp. 4–10.

39 Rem Koolhaas, 'Junkspace', in Chuihua Judy Chung, Jeffrey Inaba, Rem Koolhaas and Sze Tsung Leong, *Harvard Design School Guide to Shopping* (Cologne, 2002), pp. 408–21. Also published in *Content* (Cologne, 2004), pp. 162–71.

40 See, for instance, Ayşe Öncü, 'The Politics of the Urban Land Market in Turkey: 1950–1980', *International Journal of Urban and Regional Research*, XII (1988), pp. 38–64; Oktay Ekinci, 'Kaçak Yapılaşma ve Arazi Spekülasyonu', in *75 Yılda Değişen Kent ve Mimarlık*, ed. Yıldız Sey (Istanbul, 1998), pp. 191–8; İhsan Bilgin, 'Modernleşmenin ve Toplumsal Hareketliliğin Yörüngesinde Cumhuriyet'in İmarı', in *75 Yılda Değişen Kent ve Mimarlık*, ed. Yıldız Sey (Istanbul, 1998), pp. 255–72.

41 Tekeli, *Yaşamda ve Yazında Konut*, pp. 85–93.

42 İhsan Bilgin, 'Anadolu'da Modernleşme Sürecinde Konut ve Yerleşme', in *Tarihten Günümüze Anadolu'da Konut ve Yerleşme*, ed. Yıldız Sey (Istanbul, 1996), pp. 472–90 [482].

43 Ibid., p. 483.

44 İlhan Tekeli and Selim İlkin, *Bahçelievlerin Öyküsü* (Ankara, 1984), pp. 106–11.

45 Tansı Şenyapılı, *'Baraka'dan Gecekonduya. Ankara'da Kentsel Mekanın Dönüşümü* (Istanbul, 2004), p. 280.

46 For more discussion, see Esra Akcan, *Architecture in Translation: Germany, Turkey and the Modern House* (Durham, NC, 2012).

47 Bilgin, 'Anadolu'da Modernleşme Sürecinde Konut ve Yerleşme', p. 483.

48 Zeki Sayar, 'İmar Vekaleti Teşkili Münasebetiyle', *Arkitekt*, 288 (1957), pp. 97–8 (97).

49 İlhan Tekeli, Yiğit. Gülöksüz and Tarık Okyay, *Gecekondulu, Dolmuşlu, Işportalı Şehir* (Istanbul, 1976).

50 Tansı Şenyapılı, 'Cumhuriyet'in 75. Yılı, Gecekonudunun 50. Yılı', in *75 Yılda Değişen Kent ve Mimarlık*, ed. Yıldız Sey (Istanbul, 1998), pp. 301–16.

51 Kemal Karpat, *The Gecekondu: Rural Migration and Urbanization* (Cambridge, 1976), p. 59.

52 The law, which has been cited on numerous occasions, was published in *Resmi Gazete*, no. 12362, 30 July 1966.

53 For example in newspaper articles such as 'Gecekondularımız', *Her Hafta*, 16 July 1949; 'Gecekondu ve Gecekonduculuk', *Cumhuriyet*, 19 June 1955.

54 For research on Zeytinburnu, see: C.W.M., *Zeytiniburnu Gecekondu Bölgesi*, trans. N. Saran (Istanbul, 1969); for Hisarüstü, Baltalimanı and Celalettin Paşa settlements in Istanbul, see Karpat, *The Gecekondu*; for Ümraniye, see Semra Erder, *Istanbul'a Bir Kent Kondu. Ümraniye* (Istanbul, 1996).

55 Tekin, *Berji Kristin* (London, 1993), p. 19.

56 For the most comprehensive urban history of *gecekondu* especially in Ankara, see: Şenyapılı, 'Baraka'dan Gecekonduya.

57 Ibid., pp. 248–51.

58 Ibid., pp. 264–5.

59 Ibid.

60 Keleş, *Kentleşme Politikası*, pp. 595–620. See also Şenyapılı, 'Baraka'dan Gecekonduya.

61 Tekeli, *Yaşam ve Yazında Konut*, p. 63.

chapter six: Architecture under *Coups d'État*

1 Zeki Sayar, 'Istanbul'un Imarında Şehirci Mimarın Rolü', *Arkitekt*, 285 (1956), pp. 97–8 (97).

2 Ahmet Insel, 'Cumhuriyet Döneminde Otoritarizm', *Bilanço 1923-1998* (Istanbul, 1999), pp. 35–45.

3 *Mimarlık*, 42/4 (1967). For details of some of these endeavours, see *Mimarlık*, 1964-7. These venues often asserted that current Turkish development was insufficient (the 7 per cent growth rate target was never accomplished), uneven (resources were not evenly distributed to the regions) and unplanned (the State Planning Institution's principles were not followed); and criticized the government for failing to mobilize technical expertise in the construction industry. '1967 Oda Genel Kurul Toplantısı', *Mimarlık*, 42/4 (1967).

4 Nevzat Erol, 'Şube Başkanı Nevzat Erol'un Genel Kurul Açılış Konuşması', *Mimarlık*, 28/2 (1966), p. 28.

5 See, for instance, Sait Kozacıoğlu and Ali Artun, 'Kapitalist Toplumda İşbölümünün Gelişimi ve Mimarlar', *Mimarlık*, no. 3 (1976), pp. 50–56.

6 Haluk Baysal, 'Oda Başkanı Haluk Baysal'ın 12. Genel Kurulu Açılış Konuşması', *Mimarlık*, 29/3 (1966), p. 2–3.

7 Vedat Dalokay, 'Mimarlar Odası XI Genel Kurulu', *Mimarlık*, 17/3 (1965), p. 10.

8 These quotations were recorded by Firuzan Baytop at the Annual Meeting of the Chamber of Architects. Firuzan Baytop, 'Mimarlar Odası Genel Kurulu izlenimleri', *Mimarlık*, 30/4 (1966), pp. 8–12 [İnkaya, p. 9; Dalokay, p. 10; Sorgun, p. 12].

9 Atilla Yücel, 'Pluralism Takes Command: The Turkish Architectural Scene Today', in *Modern Turkish Architecture*, ed. Renata Holod and Ahmet Evin (Philadelphia, PA, 1984), pp. 119–52.

10 Enis Kortan, *Türkiye'de Mimarlık Haraketleri ve Eleştirisi (1960-1970)* (Ankara, 1974).

11 Sibel Bozdoğan, Suha Özkan and Engin Yenal, *Sedad Eldem: Architect in Turkey* (Singapore, 1987), p. 92.

12 Zeki Sayar, 'Proje Müsabakaları Hakkında', *Arkitekt*, 308/3 (1963), p. 100; 'Birleşmiş

Mimarlar Ortaklığı', *Arkitekt*, 308/3 (1963), pp. 110–16; Enis Kortan, 'Yaratıcı Ruh', *Mimarlık*, 22/8 (1965), pp. 7–8; Enis Kortan, 'Yarışmalar ve Jüriler Üzerine', *Mimarlık*, 57/7 (1968), pp. 8–9.

13 The following competition-winning designs all employ a variation of the 'small, multi-part approach': the School of Higher Education Teachers in Ankara and the Turkish Council in New Delhi (1960, 1962; architects Tekeli, Sisa and Hepgüler), the Ministry of Education in Ankara and the iron and steel factory in Ereğli (1962; architects Sanlı, Tuncer and Özsan), Ataköy Primary School in Istanbul (1963; architect Giray), Antalya Museum (1964; architects Arolat and Arolat), the Turkish Council in Lisbon (1964; architects Şahinler, Şensoy and Türkmen), Istanbul Harbiye Museum (1964; architects Özer and Eraman), Government Centre in Edirne (1965; architects Taftalı and Çakılcı), Beykoz High School in Istanbul (1965; architects Taşçıoğlu, Öncüoğlu, Altaylı and Onrat), Faculty of Dentistry in İzmir (1965; architect Talu), Turkish Council in Brazil (197; architects Ural and Ural), Turkish Council in Warsaw (1967; architects Taftalı and Cömertoğlu), the Erzurum Municipality (1967; architects Aran and Pamir, 1967), Diyarbakır University (1971; architect Aru).

14 Şevki Vanlı, 'Arayış ve Uygulamanın Kırk Yılı: 6olı Yıllar', *Arredamento Dekorasyon* (January 1995), pp. 94–5.

15 Architecture critic Uğur Tanyeli has thus interpreted Çinici's position as 'improvisation'. Uğur Tanyeli, 'Behruz Çinici', *Behruz Çinici* (Istanbul, 2001), p. 8.

16 *Behruz Çinici* (Istanbul, 2001), p. 86.

17 Uğur Tanyeli, 'Cengiz Bektaş ile Söyleşi', *Cengiz Bektaş* (Istanbul, 2001), pp. 8–26.

18 Enis Kortan, *Türkiye'de Mimarlık Haraketleri ve Eleştirisi (1960–70)*.

19 Bülent Özer, 'İfade Çeşitliliği Yönünden Çağdaş Mimariye bir Bakış', *Mimarlık*, 41/3 (1967), pp. 12–42. Özer had already developed some of these ideas in his 'Rejyonalizm, Üniversalizm ve Çağdaş Mimarimiz Üzerine Bir Deneme', PhD diss., Istanbul Technical University, 1964.

20 Yücel, 'Pluralism Takes Command', p. 122.

21 Mehmet Ali Birand, *12 Eylül Belgeseli,* nine-part documentary film series (Istanbul, 1998).

22 *Mimarlık ve Sanat*, 1 (1961), pp. 7–8.

23 Bülent Özer, 'Mimaride Üslup, Batı ve Biz', *Mimarlık*, 25/11 (1965), pp. 17–28.

24 Doğan Kuban, 'Gelecek Açısından Günümüz Mimari ve Şehircilik Uygulamalarının Eleştirisi', *Mimarlık*, 57/7 (1968), pp. 13–17 (14).

25 Doğan Kuban, 'Bizde Rejyonalizm Üzerine', *Mimarlık ve Sanat*, 1/1 (1961), pp. 14–15; Doğan Kuban, 'Modern mimarinin gerçek yolu: çevre şartlarının değerlendirilmesi veya rejyonalizm', *Mimarlık ve Sanat*, 2 (1961), pp. 57–8; Doğan Kuban, 'Benzerlikler ve Farklar', *Mimarlık ve Sanat*, 6 (1962), pp. 211–13.

26 'What exists in us and continues to exist is there . . . the building that gives meaning and introduces the soul is in Anatolia.' Kuban, 'Bizde Rejyonalizm Üzerine', p. 15.

27 Kuban, 'Benzerlikler ve Farklar', p. 213.

28 Bülent Özer, 'Mesken mimarisinde evrensellik ve bölgesellik üzerine', *Mimarlık ve Sanat*, 7/8 (1963), pp. 13–15; Bülent Özer, 'Rejyonalizm, Üniversalizm ve Çağdaş Mimarimiz Üzerine Bir Deneme', *Mimarlık*, 12/6 (1964), p. 5; Bülent Özer, 'Mimarimiz ve Araştırma', *Mimarlık*, XIV/8 (1964), pp. 5–6.

29 Özer, 'Rejyonalizm, Üniversalizm ve Çağdaş Mimarimiz Üzerine Bir Deneme', p. 5.

30 Kenneth Frampton, 'Towards a Critical Regionalism: Six Points for an Architecture of Resistance,' in *Anti-Aesthetic: Essays on Postmodern Culture*, ed. Hal Foster (Seattle, WA, 1983), pp. 16–30.

31 Doğan Kuban, 'İstanbul'da Tarihi Çevrenin Bir Kısmı Ortadan Kalkıyor', *Mimarlık*, XXIV/10 (1965), pp. 20–21.

32 See, for instance, *Mimarlık*, 20/6 (1965); 23/9 (1965); 30/4 (1966); special issue 37/11 (1966); 39/1 (1967); 53/3 (1968); 55/5 (1968).

33 Turgut Cansever, 'Beyazıt Meydanı', *Mimarlık ve Sanat*, 2 (1961), pp. 74–8.

34 Zeki Sayar, 'Beyazıt (Hürriyet) Meydanı', *Arkitekt*, 302/1 (1961), p. 1.
35 'Yankılar: Beyazıt Meydanı', *Mimarlık ve Sanat*, 2 (1961), pp. 55–6. *Mimarlık* denied the charges raised in this article.
36 Turgut Cansever later narrated several anecdotes: Uğur Tanyeli and Atilla Yücel, *Turgut Cansever: Düşünce Adamı ve Mimar* (Istanbul, 2007), pp. 94–8.
37 *Arkitekt*, 342/2 (1971).
38 *Arkitekt*, 335/3 (1969), pp. 101–12; *Mimarlık*, 38/12 (1966), pp. 22–4; *Arkitekt*, 328/4 (1967), pp. 149–51.
39 *Arkitekt*, 329/1 (1968), pp. 9–11.
40 *Tekeli-Sisa* (Istanbul, 2001), pp. 26–7
41 Vedat Özsan, Orhan Vural and Cengiz Bektaş, 'Toprak Mahsülleri Ofisi Genel Müdürlük Binası', *Mimarlık*, 61/11 (1968), pp. 37–42.
42 Orhan Şahinler, 'Istanbul Ticaret Odası Sarayı', *Arkitekt*, 342/2 (1971), pp. 57–62.
43 'Türkiye İş Bankası A.Ş Genel Müdürlük Binası', *Arkitekt*, 369/1 (1978), pp. 4–6.
44 Uğur Tanyeli has pointed out the contradiction between the building and architect's statement. Uğur Tanyeli, '1950'lerden Bu Yana Mimari Paradigmaların Değişimi ve "Reel" Mimarlık', *75 Yılda Değişen Kent ve Mimarlık*, ed. Yıldız Sey (Istanbul, 1998), pp. 235–54.
45 Tanyeli and Yücel, *Turgut Cansever: Düşünce Adamı ve Mimar*, pp. 160–74.
46 Behruz Çinici, 'Mimar Kendisini Anlatıyor', *Behruz Çinici* (Istanbul, 2001), p. 88. Çinici reprinted these words from his first monograph published in 1970.
47 Vedat Dalokay, 'Mimarlar Odası 1968 Yılı Çalışma Raporu Üzerine', *Mimarlık*, 55/5 (1968), pp. 13–14 (13).
48 Zeki Sayar, '1968'de Mimarlar Odası', *Arkitekt*, 333/1 (1969), p. 3.
49 Gülten Kazgan, Nejat Erder, Tuğrul Akçura, Remzi İlker and Turgut Cansever participated as speakers. The court appeal was on 8 October 1968. These activities were reported in several issues of the Chamber's journal. *Mimarlık*, 53/3 (1968); 58/8 (1968).
50 *Cumhuriyet*, 3 September 1968.
51 Dündar Engin. News report, *Haber*, 4 September 1968.
52 Cengiz Bektaş, 'Etimesut Camii, Ankara', *Arkitekt*, 351/3 (1973), pp. 124–5. See also 'Şikago'da Bir Cami Projesi', *Arkitekt*, 335/3 (1969), pp. 118–19.
53 *Mimarlık*, 47/9 (1967), p. 3; *Mimarlık*, 48/10 (1967), p. 6.
54 Doğan Kuban, '20. Yüzyılın ikinci yarısında 16.yy stilinde cami yapmayı düşünenlere', *Mimarlık*, 48/10 (1967), pp. 7–8.
55 Tanyeli, '1950'lerden Bu Yana Mimari Paradigmaların Değişimi ve "Reel" Mimarlık', pp. 242–3.
56 The meeting took place on 4–8 September 1968. *Mimarlık*, 59/9 (1968), p. 2.
57 Erdal Öz, *Gülünün Solduğu Akşam* (Istanbul, 1986).
58 *En uzun koşusuysa elbet Türkiye'de de Devrim*
    O, onun en güzel yüz metresinin koştu
    En sekmez lüverin namlusundan fırlayarak . . .
    En hızlısıydı hepimizin,
    En önce göğüsledi ipi . . .
    Acıyorsam sana anam avradım olsun
    Ama aşk olsun sana çocuk, AŞK olsun.
59 In the late 1970s individual killings were replaced by massacres spreading out to the towns of Maraş, Çorum and Sivas. By 1980 between 20 and 25 people per day were being murdered for ideological reasons. For more detailed information on the political battles during this long decade, see Birand, *12 Eylül Belgeseli*.
60 Evren justified the coup with the explanation that '5,241 people were murdered, 14,152 were injured due to terrorism in the last two years'; http://www.belgenet.com/12eylul/12091980_08.html, accessed 16 August 2011.
61 http://www.belgenet.com/12eylul/12092000_01.html, accessed January 2010. For more

documents, see http://www.belgenet.com/12eylul/12eylul.html, accessed January 2010; 'Darbenin Bilançosu', *Cumhuriyet* (12 September 2000).

chapter seven: Postmodern Landscapes in Post-Kemalist Turkey

1   See http://www.nethaber.com/Ekonomi/96662/Tayyip-Erdogan-Paranin-dini-irki-vatani-olmaz, accessed 2009.
2   Erik Zürcher, *Turkey: A Modern History* (London and New York, 1993), pp. 292–322.
3   Şevket Pamuk, 'Globalization, Industrialization and Changing Politics in Turkey', *New Perspectives on Turkey*, no. 38 (2008), p. 268; Pamuk also argues that Turkey's 'third wave of industrialization' since the 1980s has also led to the emergence of a new generation of industrial elites in Anatolian cities, the so-called 'Anatolian tigers', out of predominantly rural, merchant societies politically leaning towards the AKP (p. 271).
4   See http://www.belgenet.com/arsiv/nufus.html and World Bank figures 2009.
5   Special 14 page report on Turkey, *The Economist*, 23–29 October 2010.
6   *Income and Living Conditions Survey*, 2008, Turkish Statistical Institute, Prime Minister's Office, Republic of Turkey, Press release, no. 130, 29 July 2010. Available at www.turkstat.gov.tr.
7   See especially Ayfer Bartu and Biray Kolluoğlu, 'Emerging Spaces of Neoliberalism: A Gated Town and a Public Housing Project in Istanbul', *New Perspectives on Turkey*, no. 39 (2008), pp. 5–46.
8   See especially Arjun Appadurai, *Modernity at Large: Cultural Dimensions of Globalization* (Minneapolis, MN, 1996); Dilip Gaonkar, ed., *Alternative Modernities* (Durham, NC, 2001); Nezar Al-Sayyad, ed., *Hybrid Urbanism: On the Identity Discourse and the Built Environment* (London, 2001).
9   Sibel Bozdoğan and Reşat Kasaba, eds, *Rethinking Modernity and National Identity in Turkey* (Seattle, WA, 1997). See also Sibel Bozdoğan and Reşat Kasaba, 'Turkey at a Cross-road', *Journal of International Affairs*, 54 (Fall 2000), pp. 1–20.
10   Esra Özyürek, *Nostalgia for the Modern: State Secularism and Everyday Politics in Turkey* (Durham, NC, 2006).
11   As noted by many foreign observers. See, for example, Christopher Caldwell, 'Bordering on What?', *New York Times Magazine*, 25 September 2005, pp. 46–51, and the special 14-page report on Turkey, *The Economist*, 23–29 October 2010.
12   An empirical documentation of which can be found in Ricky Burdett and Deyan Sujic, eds, *Endless City* (London, 2007) and *Living in the Endless City* (London, 2011).
13   See especially Anna Klingmann, *Brandscapes: Architecture in the Experience Economy* (Cambridge, 2007); David Harvey, *Spaces of Global Capitalism* (London, 2006); Anthony D. King, *Spaces of Global Cultures: Architecture, Urbanism, Identity* (London and New York, 2004); and Michael P. Smith, *Transnational Urbanism: Locating Globalization* (Oxford, 2001).
14   Margaret Crawford, 'The World in a Shopping Mall', in *Variations on a Theme Park: The New American City and the End of Public Space*, ed. Michael Sorkin, 2nd edn (New York, 1999), pp. 3–30. Also pioneering the discussion is William S. Kowinsky, *The Malling of America* (New York, 1985).
15   *Arkitera* interview, March 2010.
16   See www.arkitera.com.
17   See, for example, *Istanbul: City of Intersections*, Urban Age Newspaper, 2009, http://www.urban-age.net/conferences/istanbul/.
18   Kanyon is mentioned in this context in Alejandro Zaera Polo, 'High-Rise Phylum 2007', *Harvard Design Magazine* (Spring/Summer 2007), p. 17.
19   Istanbul alone had 57 AVMs in 2008 and an estimated 122 in 2010 with a total floor space of nearly 4 million m². Bartu and Kolluoğlu, 'Emerging Spaces of Neoliberalism', p. 16.
20   As theorized most famously in Marc Auge, *Non-Places: An Introduction to an*

Anthropology of Supermodernity (London, 1995).

21 Merih Karaaslan, *Merih Karaaslan. Yapıtlar Anılar 1* (Ankara, 2001), pp. 89–100. The architects carried a similar collaged approach to the design of other bazaars around Anatolia, including those in Afyon and Niğde, and of public buildings such as the Municipality Buildings in Ankara, Iskenderun and Zonguldak.

22 See Richard Tapper, ed., *Islam in Modern Turkey* (London, 1991); Jenny White, *Islamist Mobilization in Turkey* (Seattle, WA, 2002).

23 See Alev Çınar, 'National History as a Contested Site: The Conquest of Istanbul and the Islamist Negotiations of the Nation', *Comparative Studies in Society and History*, XLIII/2 (April 2001), pp. 364–91.

24 Although official numbers are hard to come by, given the illegal construction of many smaller mosques in the urban periphery, architectural historian Doğan Kuban suggests that about 1,500 new mosques were built per year during the early 1990s. Doğan Kuban, 'Türkiye'de Çağdaş Cami Tasarımı', *Arredamento Dekorasyon* (October 1994), pp. 80–83.

25 See Sibel Bozdoğan, *Muqarnas*, 24. For a discussion of Kocatepe Mosque and Anıt-Kabir in terms of their politics and identity implications, see Michael Meeker, '"Once there was, once there wasn't": National Monuments and Interpersonal Exchange', in *Rethinking Modernity and National Identity in Turkey*, ed. Sibel Bozdoğan and Reşat Kasaba (Seattle, WA, 1997), pp. 157–91.

26 A different version of the project was subsequently built for the King Faisal Mosque, Islamabad, Pakistan (1969–87).

27 A more recent example of this neo-liberal Islamism can be seen in the Şakirin Mosque in Istanbul (2009; Zeynep Fadıllıoğlu, interior designer in collaboration with painters, sculptors and stained glass artists), which features a single spherical dome touching the ground on four points, just like Dalokay's unbuilt Kocatepe Mosque project of 1957, albeit in slick, polished materials with a reflecting pool and glittering decorative wall panels that can best be characterized as 'postmodern chic'. It also illustrates what a special issue of the *New York Times Magazine* described as 'Empire Strikes Back', that is how, after being banished from modern Turkish culture for most of the twentieth century, all manifestations of Ottomania have returned with a vengeance: from architecture and interior design to fashion, tourism and culinary culture (*New York Times Magazine*, 2001).

28 Turgut Cansever, *Kubbeyi Yere Koymamak* (Istanbul, 2007).

29 A devout Muslim holding a PhD in Art History and profoundly interested in philosophical and ontological questions, Turgut Cansever was a rare example of a practising architect who was also a conservative intellectual, albeit without any direct overlap between the two roles. This was articulated extensively in an exhibition and the catalogue, Uğur Tanyeli and Atilla Yücel, eds, *Turgut Cansever: Mimar ve Düşünce Adamı* (Istanbul, 2007).

30 See the interview with Cansever in *Dergah* (July 1991).

31 Turgut Cansever, *Islamda Şehir ve Mimari* (Istanbul, 1997), p. 78.

32 Sayyed H. Nasr, *Islamic Art and Spirituality* (Albany, NY, 1987); Nader Ardalan and Leila Bakhtiar, *The Sufi Tradition in Persian Architecture* (Chicago, IL, 1973); Titus Burckhardt, *The Art of Islam: Language and Meaning* (London, 1976).

33 Tanyeli and Yücel, eds, *Turgut Cansever*; Halil Ibrahim Düzenli, *Idrak ve Inşa: Turgut Cansever Mimarlığının İki Düzlemi* (Istanbul, 2009).

34 Şevki Vanlı, 'Dönemin mimarisi, yirminci yüzyıl sorumluluğu', *Yapı*, 248 (2002), pp. 59–61, followed by polemical debates with Süha Özkan, the Deputy Secretary General of the Aga Khan Awards. Similarly, Cansever's talk about his Islamic world-view as the basis of a critical architecture was dismissed by Cengiz Bektaş as religious propaganda: Symposium on Contemporary Architectural Currents and Turkish Architecture, Ankara, 11–15 December 1989; cited in Uğur Tanyeli, *Mimarlığın Aktörleri: Türkiye, 1900–2000* (Istanbul, 2007), p. 192.

35 Appadurai, *Modernity at Large.*
36 Merih Karaaslan, 'Anadolu'nun Çağdaş Yorumu', *Tasarım* (December 1991), pp. 56–81.
37 Merih Karaaslan, *Merih Karaaslan. Yapıtlar Anılar 1* (Ankara, 2001), pp. 143–4.
38 Ibid., pp. 137, 129.
39 For instance, Çavdar translated and staged Brecht's *Die Dreigroschenoper*: Bertolt Brecht, *Üç Kuruşluk Opera*, trans. Tuncay Çavdar (Istanbul, 1964). For the İzmit project, see Tuncay Çavdar, 'Bir Katılımsal Tasarım Uygulamasının Ardından', *Mimarlık*, 1 (1982), p. 8.
40 Tuncay Çavdar, 'Turizm Hizmetindeki Dört Yapı', *Tasarım* (July–August 1990), pp. 40–56; Atilla Yücel-Tuncay Çavdar Interview, *Arredamento Dekorasyon*, 72 (July–August 1995), pp. 56–62; Esra Akcan, 'İmgenin İki Yüzü', ibid., pp. 73–6. Doğan Kuban, 'Tuncay Çavdar'ın turistik yapılarındaki mimari imgeler', ibid., pp. 69–70; Uğur Tanyeli, 'Çavdar'ın Dramatik İkilemi', ibid., pp. 71–2.
41 Erwin Panofsky, *Perspektive als symbolische Form* (Hamburg, 1927).
42 Martin Heidegger, 'The Age of World Picture', in *The Question Concerning Technology and Other Essays* (New York, 1977), pp. 115–54.
43 D. M. Levin, ed., *Modernity and the Hegemony of Vision* (Berkeley, 1993); Hal Foster, ed., *Vision and Visuality*, Dia Art Foundation Discussions in Contemporary Culture 2 (Seattle, WA, 1988); Alberto Perez-Gomez, *Architecture and the Crisis of Modern Science* (Cambridge, 1983).
44 Esra Akcan–Tuncay Çavdar Interview, 26 May 1995, Office Atölye T, Istanbul; Atilla Yücel–Tuncay Çavdar Interview.
45 See especially John Urry, *The Tourist Gaze*, 2nd edn (London, 2002); Dean MacCannell, *The Tourist. A New Theory of the Leisure Class*, 2nd edn (Los Angeles, CA, 1999); Tom Selwyn, *The Tourist Image: Myth and Myth Making in Tourism* (New York, 1996); Valene Smith, ed., *Hosts and Guests: An Anthropology of Tourism* (Philadelphia, PA, 1989).
46 For gladiator schools, see http://haber.mynet.com/detay/guncel/aspendos-gladyator-okulu-acildi/540946, accessed 17 August 2011.
47 Dean MacCannell, 'Staged Authenticity', *American Journal of Sociology*, LXXIX/3 (November 1973).
48 References were not limited to Turkey. Along the same Mediterranean shore, close to the Topkapı Palace Hotel, tourists can find the Kremlin Palace Hotel and the Venice Hotel, with full replicas of St Basil's Cathedral and San Marco, respectively.
49 'Temalı Otellerde İlginç Bir Tatil Deneyimi', *Hello Antalya* (16–22 July 2006), p. 14.

chapter eight: **The Illegal City and New Residential Segregation**

1 Rem Koolhaas, 'What Ever Happened to Urbanism?', *S,M,L,XL* (New York, 1998), pp. 961–71; 'The Generic City', *S,M,L,XL* (New York, 1998).
2 http://www.tuik.gov.tr Devlet İstatistik Enstitüsü, 1994 Yılı Gelir ve Tüketim Harcamaları Anketi (State Institution of Statistics, Income and Consumption Questionnaire of 1994).
3 Mike Davis, *Planet of Slums* (London and New York, 2006).
4 Halil Inancık, *The Ottoman Empire: The Classical Age* (New York, 1973).
5 Çağlar Keyder, 'The Housing Market from Informal to Global', in *Istanbul: Between the Global and the Local*, ed. Çağlar Keyder (Lanham, MD, 1999), p. 145.
6 Ruşen Keleş, *Kentleşme Politikası*, 10th edn (Istanbul, 2006), pp. 583–4.
7 Keyder, 'The Housing Market from Informal to Global', pp. 143–59.
8 For a more detailed discussion of the Amnesty Law no. 2805 of 1983, and no. 2981 of 1984, see Keleş, *Kentleşme Politikası*, pp. 616–20; Erdoğan Bayraktar, *Gecekondu ve Kentsel Yenileme* (Ankara, 2006), pp. 155–67. For the economic and social consequences of the series of amnesty laws throughout the 1980s, see Tansı Şenyapılı,

'Cumhuriyet'in 75. Yılı Gecekondunun 50. Yılı', in *75 Yılda Değişen Kent ve Mimarlık*, ed. Yıldız Sey (Istanbul, 1998), pp. 301–16.

9 Bayraktar, *Gecekondu ve Kentsel Yenileme*, p. 159.

10 As an example of the writings of a committed public critic, see Oktay Ekinci, 'Kaçak Yapılaşma ve Arazi Spekülasyonu', in *75 Yılda Değişen Kent ve Mimarlık*, ed. Yıldız Sey (Istanbul, 1998), pp. 191–8; Oktay Ekinci, *Istanbul'u Sarsan On Yıl. 1983–1993* (Istanbul, 1994). See also Ayşe Buğra, 'The Immoral Economy of Housing in Turkey', *International Journal of Urban and Regional Research*, xxii/2 (1998), pp. 303–17.

11 Oğuz Işık and Melih Pınarcıoğlu assess a positive outcome to this process and argue that the informal real estate market in Turkey after 1980 has, for better or worse, 'increased the benefits for a large section of the population and enlarged the overall cake', and thus 'prevented poverty from reaching dimensions that would threaten the system'. They challenge the bipolar definitions of the formal and the informal, and demonstrate the economic transformative effect of *gecekondu* neighbourhoods, which complicates the conventional definition of the urban poor as an unorganized, homogenous and static group. Oğuz Işık and Melih Pınarcıoğlu, *Nöbetleşe Yoksulluk. Sultanbeyli Örneği* (Istanbul, 2001), pp. 43, 77. As another example of the second viewpoint, one might consider the concluding assessment in İlhan Tekeli, 'Türkiye'de Cumhuriyet Döneminde Kentsel Gelişme ve Kent Planlaması', in *75 Yılda Değişen Kent ve Mimarlık*, ed. Yıldız Sey (Istanbul, 1998), pp. 1–24, see esp. p. 24. Even though it is not particularly on illegal settlements but on the dominant reactionary opposition to Istanbul's metropolitization, one might also see as another example of the second viewpoint: Uğur Tanyeli, 'Türkiye'de Metropol Kavrayışı: İstanbul Üzerinden Bir Oku(ya)ma(ma) Denemesi', *Arredamento Mimarlık* (October 2002), pp. 89–92.

12 For information on several master plans of Istanbul from 1836 to the present, see Mete Tapan, 'İstanbul'un Kentsel Planlamasının Tarihsel Gelişimi ve Planlama Eylemleri', in *75 Yılda Değişen Kent ve Mimarlık*, ed. Yıldız Sey (Istanbul, 1998), pp. 75–88.

13 See http://www.tuik.gov.tr.

14 The numerical facts on Sultanbeyli in this chapter are from Işık and Pınarcıoğlu's research, which constitutes the most comprehensive study on the settlement. According to their area studies, there is a common myth among the Sultanbeyli residents that the area was previously owned by a Jewish person who planned to establish a Jewish state on this land. On the other hand, Sultanbeyli residents themselves are usually treated in derogatory terms in popular and academic publishing, as a gathering of threatening radical Islamic groups or as a provincial population corrupting Istanbul's 'high culture'. Işık and Pınarcıoğlu, *Nöbetleşe Yoksulluk* (for the religious and social conflict, see pp. 191–220).

15 Keleş, *Kentleşme Politikası*, pp. 549–65.

16 While 140 co-operations were founded per year before 1984, this number increased to 2787 per year during 1984–1991. Gülden Berkman and Sevin Osmay, *1984 Sonrasında Konut Kooperatifçiliği* (Ankara, 1996), pp. 3–5.

17 Bayraktar, *Gecekondu*, pp. 208–34. See also Tuna Kuyucu, 'Bir Mülkiyet Transferi Aracı olarak TOKİ ve Kentsel Dönüşüm Projeleri', in *Osmanlı Başkentinden Küreselleşen İstanbul'a: Mimarlık ve Kent 1910-2010*, ed. İpek Akpınar (Istanbul, 2010), pp. 122–34.

18 Ilhan Tekeli, 'Türkiye'de Konut Sunumunun Davranışsal Nitelikleri ve Konut Kesiminde Bunalım', *Konut '81* (Ankara, 1982), pp. 91–2.

19 Ibid., pp. 235–8.

20 Even though it is too early to be conclusive, it is doubtful that the ex-*gecekondu* residents in Istanbul will be able to pay their mortgages; *La Turquie en Marche* (Paris, 2004).

21 For a list of projects and the number of relocated units, see Bayraktar, *Gecekondu*, pp. 251–2.

22 These numbers are taken from ibid., pp. 251, 255–8.

23 Projects have been undertaken with the municipalities of Küçükçekmece/Halkalı, Tuzla, Kadıköy, Şişli/Kuştepe, Kartal, Fatih, Avcılar, Maltepe. Ibid., p. 252.

24 Kuyucu, 'Bir Mülkiyet Transferi Aracı olarak TOKİ ve Kentsel Dönüşüm Projeleri'.

25 However this policy could not be maintained during the later stages of the Dikmen Valley Rehabilitation project designed by other architects. The fourth and fifth stages especially provoked social unrest after changes in the regulations no longer protected the previous settlers, but favoured the area's gentrification. As a result, the residents of the Dikmen Valley often protested against the new projects that replaced their *gecekondu* houses with luxury apartment blocks. See http://dikmenvadisi.org/index.php?option=com_content&task=view&id=30&Itemid=37, accessed 19 August 2011.

26 *Doruk Pamir. Yapılar Projeler 1963–2005* (Istanbul, 2006), pp. 84–5; Aydan Balamir, 'Dikmen Vadisi Köprüsü', in *1950ler Kuşağı Mimarlık Antolojisi*, ed. Enis Kortan (Istanbul, 1997), pp. 159–61.

27 The density of the area was projected as 175 people per hectare. Semih Eryıldız, *Batıkent* (Istanbul, 2002).

28 Ali Cengizkan, 'Toplu Konut İdaresi (TOKİ): Bir Tasarım Deneyi: Eryaman 3. Etap ve 4. Etap Konutları', *XXI Mimarlık Kültürü Dergisi*, 4 (September–October 2000), pp. 136–43.

29 The project was intended to create 1,500 low-rise housing units, but due to the changes during the process, half of the units were placed in mid-rise blocks. There are seven types of blocks and two different unit types. The users are lower-income groups, mostly expected to be first-generation immigrants to the city from rural areas. Erdoğan Elmas, 'Şanlıurfa Toplu Konut Projesi', in *1950ler Kuşağı Mimarlık Antolojisi*, ed. Enis Kortan (Istanbul, 1997), pp. 84–7.

30 Numerous projects by Yeşim Hatırlı (some with Nami Hatırlı), such as Sebla Houses, stand out because they exemplify a rare case where a woman architect sees through the design and construction of a large-scale corporate project.

31 For a list of gated communities in Istanbul with their sizes and sales prices, see Işık and Pınarcıoğlu, *Nöbetleşe Yoksulluk*, pp. 144–5. For a critique of the gated community phenomenon in Istanbul, see Ayşe Öncü, 'İdealinizdeki Ev' Mitolojisi Kültürel Sınırları Aşarak İstanbul'a Ulaştı', in *Mekan, Kültür İktidar*, ed. Ayşe Öncü and Petra Weyland (Istanbul, 2000).

32 See http://beykozkonaklari.org/, accessed December 2008.

33 See http://www.acarkent.net/bogazustu.asp, accessed December 2008.

34 See http://www.habervitrini.com/haber.asp?id=251161, accessed December 2008.

35 Explicitly embracing the tenets of 'Neo-traditional New Urbanism' (represented by Leon Krier in Europe and Duany & Plater-Zyberk in Florida), Kemer Country packages its villas as remedies to the alleged destructiveness of modern urbanism and promises a much-desired return to the architectural and urban qualities of traditional environments (*Kemer Country Newsletter*, late 1990s.)

36 See http://www.istanbul-istanbul.com/, accessed 13 December 2010.

37 Göktürk Municipality publicity brochure, 2006.

38 See Şerife Geniş, 'Producing Elite Localities: The Rise of Gated Communities in Istanbul', *Urban Studies*, 44 (April 2007), pp. 771–98 about how the desired homogeneity of the property owners is ensured by careful screening of prospective buyers in Kemer Country.

39 Richard Sennett, 'Cosmopolitanism and the Social Experience of Cities', in *Conceiving Cosmopolitanism: Theory, Context and Practice*, ed. Steven Vertovec and Robin Cohen (New York, 2002), p. 47.

40 Ayfer Bartu and Biray Kolluoğlu, 'Emerging Spaces of Neoliberalism: A Gated Town and a Public Housing Project in Istanbul', *New Perspectives in Turkey*, no. 39 (2008), pp. 5–46.

41 Afife Batur, 'Akdenizli Olmak ya da Zamanlar ve Mekanlar Üzerine', Profil: Ersen Gürsel, *Arredamento Dekorasyon* (January 1994), pp. 89–97.

1 In *Arredamento Mimarlık* (December 2003), p. 38.
2 Haluk Pamir and Süha Özkan, eds, *Mimarlıkta Yeni Arayışlar. 'Genç Türk Mimarları'* (Ankara, 2000). The title may also be translated as 'Young Turkish Architects'.
3 The selected architects/firms were: Emre Arolat, Deniz Aslan/Arda Inceoğlu, Gökhan Avcıoğlu, Can Çinici, Mehmet Kütükçüoğlu/Kerem Yazgan, Nevzat Sayın/Elvan Uluutku, Murat Tabanlıoğlu/Melkan Tabanlıoğlu, Semra Teber, Han Tümertekin. The architects are not necessarily discussed here with their work submitted to the exhibition.
4 *Mimarlıkta Yeni Arayışlar. 'Genç Türk Mimarları'*, pp. 100, 104, 101.
5 Nevzat Sayın, 'Gön 2', *Arredamento Dekorasyon* (July–August 1996), pp. 104–6.
6 Nevzat Sayın and Serhan Ada, 'How to Make a Shuttle with Dust and Wind', in *Anytime*, ed. Cynthia Davidson (Cambridge, MA, 1999), pp. 34–7.
7 Tansel Korkmaz, 'Bir Mesleki Pratik Atlası', in *Nevzat Sayın. Düşler, Düşünceler, İşler*, ed. Tansel Korkmaz (Istanbul, 2004), pp. 9–34 (9).
8 Han Tümertekin, 'Sıfırda Başlamak', *Arredamento Mimarlık* (December 1999), pp. 57–8.
9 Bülent Tanju, *Mimarlıkta Sıfır Noktasını Aramak* (Istanbul, 2003); Hashim Sarkis, ed., *Han Tümertekin. Recent Work* (Cambridge, MA, 2007).
10 Gökhan Avcıoğlu in *Mimarlıkta Yeni Arayışlar.'Genç Türk Mimarları'*, p. 33.
11 Emre Arolat in *Mimarlıkta Yeni Arayışlar. 'Genç Türk Mimarları'*, p. 8. See also articles by Uğur Tanyeli, Bülent Tanju, Ihsan Bilgin, Neslihan Dostoğlu and Alpaslan Ataman in 'Emre Arolat Profile', *Arredamento Mimarlık* (September 2001), pp. 56–80.
12 Emre Arolat-Hakkı Yırtıcı interview, *Emre Arolat Yapılar. Projeler 1998–2005* (Istanbul, 2005), pp. 205–14 (205).
13 Emre Arolat Architects, 'Güncelleme', *Arredamento Mimarlık* (July–August 2006), pp. 42–63.
14 Murat Tabanlıoğlu-Emre Arolat-Haydar Karabey Interview, *Arredamento Mimarlık* (October 2002), pp. 53–74 (60).
15 Uğur Tanyeli, 'Profil. Murat Tabanlıoğlu', *Arredamento Mimarlık* (October 2002), p. 50; Uğur Tanyeli, 'Genç Türk Mimarları Seçkisi', *Mimarlıkta Yeni Arayışlar. 'Genç Türk Mimarları'*, pp. 107–8.
16 Kerem Erginoğlu and Hasan Çalışlar, interviewed by Ersin Altın and Burçak Özlüdil, *Arredamento Mimarlık* (December 2003), pp. 36–54 (37, 38).
17 Cengiz Bektaş, 'Mimarlıkta Sorumluluk Adanmışlık mı Dediniz?', *Arredamento Mimarlık* (March 2003), pp. 60–61.
18 While 831 collective housing projects have been uploaded by December 2010 in the architect-uploaded web-portal *Arkitera*, the number is much smaller for apartment buildings (276) and single-family houses (735); accessed in December 2010.
19 Manfredo Tafuri, *Architecture and Utopia* (Cambridge, MA, 1979).
20 See essays in William Saunders, ed., *The New Architectural Pragmatism* (Minneapolis, 2007).
21 Abdi Güzer, 'Fevkalade + Fevkalade = Alelade (TBMM lojmanları)', *Mimarlık*, 2 (1989), pp. 42–3.
22 Boğaçhan Dündaralp, 'Np12 Evleri İstanbul, Çamlıca', *Arredamento Mimarlık* (October 2003), pp. 113–14.
23 For the Novron housing projects, see http://arkiv.arkitera.com/m126-mehmet-kutukcuoglu.html, accessed December 2008.
24 See http://arkiv.arkitera.com/p5094-guney-tatil-sitesi.html, accessed December 2008.
25 Merih Karaaslan, *Yapıtlar, Anılar 1* (Ankara, 2001), pp. 117–27. Karaaslan repeated the stepping down terrace houses scheme in his Yamaçevler collective houses (1994), located on a steep hill in Ankara; ibid., pp. 175–91.
26 Arolat, Bilgin and Sayın also collaborated on a number of other collective housing

projects, such as Bahçekent and Ataköy houses.

27 Arolat, *Yapılar/Projeler,* pp. 155–7.

28 See http://arkiv.arkitera.com/p5264-doga-mese-park-evleri.html, accessed December 2008.

29 See http://arkiv.arkitera.com/p8332-tepe-narcity-konut-yerleskesi.html, accessed December 2008.

30 See housing projects in http://arkiv.arkitera.com/m63-emre-arolat.html, accessed December 2008.

31 See http://arkiv.arkitera.com/m470-bogachan-dundaralp.html, accessed December 2008

32 *New York Times*, 25 September 2005.

33 As theorists of modernity from Georg Simmel to Marshall Berman have pointed out eloquently, it is precisely this ambivalence of the modern metropolis (simultaneously liberating and alienating) that is its main attraction. This point is addressed in Ayfer Bartu and Biray Kolluoğlu, 'Emerging Spaces of Neoliberalism: A Gated Town and a Public Housing Project in Istanbul', *New Perspectives on Turkey*, 39 (2008), pp. 5–46.

34 Dikmen Bezmez, 'The Politics of Urban Waterfront Regeneration: The Case of Haliç (Golden Horn), Istanbul', *International Journal of Urban and Regional Research* (2009), pp. 815–40; S. F. Göncüoğlu, ed., *Dünü ve Bugünü ile Haliç Sempozyumu* (Istanbul, 2003).

35 See Sibel Bozdoğan, 'Industrial Architecture and Nation-Building in Turkey: A Historical Overview', in *Workplaces: The Transformation of Places of Production*, ed. M. Al-Asad (Istanbul, 2010), pp. 17–40.

36 See İpek Türeli, 'Modelling Citizenship in Turkey's Miniature Park', in *Orienting Istanbul*, ed. Deniz Göktürk, Levent Soysal and İpek Türeli (London and New York, 2010), pp. 104–25. See also Nick Stanley, 'Chinese Theme Parks and National Identity', in *Theme Park Landscapes*, ed. Terence Young and Robert Riley (Washington, DC, 2002), pp. 269–89 and Sherry Errington, 'Cosmic Theme Park of the Javanese', *The Death of Authentic Primitive Art and Other Tales of Progress* (Berkeley, CA, 1998), pp. 188–227 for the Chinese ('Splendid China') and Indonesian ('Taman Mini') examples, respectively.

37 İhsan Bilgin, 'SantralIstanbul: Architectural Problematics', in *Workplaces: The Transformation of Places of Production*, ed. M. Al-Asad (Istanbul, 2010), p. 182.

38 See Özlem Ünsal and Tuna Kuyucu, 'Challenging the Neoliberal Urban Regime: Regeneration and Resistance in Basbüyük and Tarlabaşı', in *Orienting Istanbul*, ed. Deniz Göktürk, Levent Soysal and Ipek Türeli (London and New York, 2010), pp. 51–70.

39 See http://www.arkitera.com/h20718-tarlabasi-ve-fener-%E2%80%93-balat-yenileme-projeleri-nde-son-durum.html, accessed 16 December 2008.

40 Esra Akcan, ed., *Küreselleşme Sürecinde 'Öteki' Coğrafyalar. Domus M* (February–March 2001). Uğur Tanyeli, editor in chief of *Arredamento Mimarlık*, has devoted issues to the varying conditions for architectural practice in the centre and on the periphery. The featured themes included avant-garde (February 2003), metropolis (December 2002, October 2002), sustainability (January 2003) and popular culture (May 2003).

41 Zaha Hadid's declaration in a daily newspaper that she did not spend much time in Kartal, since she did 'not need to give a massage to the inhabitants', did not help this perception. Pınar Öğünç, 'Kartallılara masaj yapmam gerekmiyor', *Radikal*, 17 November 2007 [interview with Zaha Hadid].

42 Ali Köksal, 'Karachi Hilton', *Arkitekt*, no. 3 (1975), pp. 108–11; Sibel Bozdoğan, 'Şevki Vanlı'nın Cezayir Projeleri. Gecikmiş bir değerlendirme yazısı', in *Küreselleşme Sürecinde 'Öteki' Coğrafyalar. Domus M*, ed. Esra Akcan (February–March 2001), pp. 47–51.

43 Hashim Sarkis, ed., *Han Tümertekin; Emre Arolat, Yapılar/Projeler 1998–2005.*

Select Bibliography

Abdurrahman Hancı: Buildings/Projects, 1945–2000 (Istanbul, 2008)

Aebli, Werner, Rolf Meyer and Ernst Winkler, eds, *Stadt und Umwelt: Festschrift zum siebzigsten Geburtstag von Ernst Egli* (Zurich, 1964)

Ahmad, Feroz, *The Making of Modern Turkey* (London, 1993)

Akcan, Esra, ed., *Küreselleşme Sürecinde 'Öteki' Coğrafyalar. Domus m* (February–March 2001)

—, ed., 'Intertwined Histories: Turkey and Central Europe', *centropa*, vii/2 (May 2007)

—, *Çeviride Modern Olan: Şehir ve Konutta Türk-Alman İlişkileri* (Istanbul, 2009)

—, 'Towards a Cosmopolitan Ethics in Architecture: Bruno Taut's Translations out of Germany', *New German Critique*, xxxiii/3 (2006), pp. 7–39; reprinted in J. F. Lejeune and M. Sabatino, ed., *Modern Architecture and the Mediterranean: Vernacular Dialogues and Contested Identities*, (London and New York, 2009), pp. 204–23

—, 'Civilizing Housewives versus Participatory Users: Margarete Schütte Lihotzky in the Employ of the Turkish Nation State', in *Cold War Kitchen: Americanization, Technology and European Users*, ed. Ruth Oldenziel and Karin Zachman (Cambridge, ma, 2009), pp. 185–207

—, *Architecture in Translation: Germany, Turkey and the Modern House* (Durham, nc, 2012)

Akpınar, İpek, 'From Secularization to Turkish Modernization: The Rebuilding of Istanbul after the Plan of Henri Prost, 1937–1960', PhD diss., Bartlett School, University of London, 2003

Akşin, Sina, ed., *Çağdaş Türkiye 1908–1980 (Türkiye Tarihi 4)* (Istanbul, 1990)

Alsaç, Üstün, *Türkiye Mimarlık Düşüncesinin Cumhuriyet Dönemindeki Evrimi* (Trabzon, 1976)

Arseven, Celal Esat, *Yeni Mimari* (Istanbul, 1931)

Aslanoğlu, Inci, *Erken Cumhuriyet Dönemi Mimarlığı, 1923-1938* (Ankara, 1980)

Atatürk için Düşünmek. Iki Eser: Katafalk ve Anıtkabir. Iki Mimar: Bruno Taut and Emin Onat (Istanbul, 1997)

Aydemir, Şevket Süreyya, *Ikinci Adam* (Istanbul, 1999)

Balamir, Aydan, ed., *Clemens Holzmeister: An Architect at the Turn of an Era* (Ankara, 2010)

Baltacıoğlu, Ismail Hakkı, *Demokrasi ve Sanat* (Istanbul, 1931)

Bartu, Ayfer, and Biray Kolluoğlu, 'Emerging Spaces of Neoliberalism: A Gated Town and a Public Housing Project in Istanbul', *New Perspectives on Turkey*, no. 39 (2008), pp. 5–46

Batur, Afife, 'Cumhuriyet Döneminde Türk Mimarlığı', *Cumhuriyet Dönemi Türkiye Ansiklopedisi* (Istanbul, 1984)

Batur, Afife, ed., *Bir Usta Bir Dünya: Mimar Vedat Tek* (Istanbul, 1999)

Baydar, Gülsüm, 'The Professionalization of the Ottoman-Turkish Architect', PhD diss., University of California, Berkeley, 1989

—, 'Between *Civilization* and *Culture*: Appropriation of Traditional Dwelling Forms in Early Republican Turkey', *Journal of Architectural Education*, xlvii/2 (November 1993), pp. 66–74

—, 'Silent Interruptions: Urban Encounters with Rural Turkey' in Sibel Bozdoğan and Reşat Kasaba, eds, *Rethinking Modernity and National Identity in Turkey* (Seattle, wa, 1997), pp. 192–210

Bayraktar, Erdoğan, *Gecekondu ve Kentsel Yenileme* (Ankara, 2006)

Behruz Çinici (Istanbul, 2001)

Berkman, Gülden, and Sevin Osmay, *1984 Sonrasında Konut Kooperatifçiliği* (Ankara, 1996)

Bilgin, İhsan, 'Anadolu'da Modernleşme Sürecinde Konut ve Yerleşme', in *Tarihten Günümüze Anadolu'da Konut ve Yerleşme*, ed. Yıldız Sey (Istanbul, 1996), pp. 472–90

—, 'Modernleşmenin ve Toplumsal Hareketliliğin Yörüngesinde Cumhuriyet'in İmarı', in *75 Yılda Değişen Kent ve Mimarlık*, ed. Yıldız Sey (Istanbul, 1998), pp. 255–72

Bilsel, Can, 'Our Anatolia: Organicism and the Making of Humanist Culture in Turkey', in Sibel Bozdoğan and Gülru Necipoğlu, eds, *Muqarnas*, 24 (Fall 2007), pp. 223–41

Bilsel, Cana, 'İzmir'de Cumhuriyet'in "Modern" Kentine Geçişte Şehircilik Deneyimi ve Model Transferi Sorunu: Danger-Prost Planı ve Le Corbusier'nin Nazım Plan Önerisi', in *Küreselleşme Sürecinde "Öteki" Coğrafyalar. Domus m*, ed. Esra Akcan (February–March 2001), pp. 42–6

Bonatz, Paul, *Leben und Bauen* (Stuttgart, 1950)

Bozay, Kemal, *Exil Türkei: Ein Forschungsbeitrag zur deutschsprachigen Emigration in die Türkei, 1933-1945* (Münster, 2001)

Bozdoğan, Sibel, Süha Özkan and Engin Yenal, *Sedad Eldem, Architect in Turkey* (Singapore, 1987)

Bozdoğan, Sibel, and Resat Kasaba, eds, *Rethinking Modernity and National Identity in Turkey* (Seattle, WA, 1997)

Bozdoğan, Sibel, *Modernism and Nation-Building: Turkish Architectural Culture in the Early Republic* (Seattle, WA, 2001)

—, 'Against Style: Bruno Taut's Pedagogical Program in Turkey, 1936-1938', in *The Education of the Architect: Historiography, Urbanism and the Growth of Architectural Knowledge*, ed. Martha Pollak (Cambridge, MA, 1997), pp. 163–92

—, 'The Legacy of an Istanbul Architect: Type, Context and Urban Identity in Sedad Eldem's Work', in *Modern Architecture and the Mediterranean: Vernacular Dialogues and Contested Identities*, ed. J. F. Lejeune and M. Sabatino (London and New York, 2009), pp. 141–55

—, 'Democracy, Development and the Americanization of Turkish Architectural Culture in the 1950s', in *Modernism and the Middle East*, ed. S. Isenstadt and K. Rizvi (Seattle, WA, 2008), pp. 116–38

—, 'Reading Ottoman Architecture through Modernist Lenses: Nationalist Historiography and the New Architecture in the Early Republic', *Muqarnas*, 24 (Fall 2007), pp. 199–221

—, 'Industrial Architecture and Nation-Building in Turkey: A Historical Overview', in *Workplaces: The Transformation of Places of Production*, ed. M. Al-Asad (Istanbul, 2010)

Buğra, Ayşe, 'The Immoral Economy of Housing in Turkey', *International Journal of Urban and Regional Research*, XXII/2 (1998), pp. 303–17

Cansever, Turgut, *Kubbeyi Yere Koymamak* (Istanbul, 2007)

—, *Islamda Şehir ve Mimari* (Istanbul, 1997)

Çeçen, Anıl, *Halkevleri* (Ankara, 1990).

Çelik, Zeynep, *The Remaking of Istanbul: The Portrait of an Ottoman City in the Nineteenth Century* (Berkeley and Los Angeles, 1986)

Çelik-Hinchliffe, Zeynep, 'Rootedness Uprooted: Paul Bonatz in Turkey, 1933-1954', in 'Intertwined Histories: Turkey and Central Europe', ed. Esra Akcan, *Centropa*, VII/2 (May 2007), pp. 180–96

Cengiz Bektaş (Istanbul, 2001)

Cengizkan, Ali, ed., *Mimar Kemalettin ve Çağı* (Ankara, 2009)

—, *Modernin Saati* (Ankara, 2002)

—, 'Discursive Formations in Turkish Residential Architecture: Ankara, 1948-1962', PhD diss., METU, Ankara, 2000

Cengizkan, M., ed., *Haluk Baysal - Melih Birsel* (Ankara, 2007)

Çınar, Alev, *Modernism, Islam and Secularism in Turkey: Bodies, Places and Time* (Minneapolis, 2005)

Danielson, Michael, and Ruşen Keleş, *The Politics of Rapid Urbanization: Government and Growth in Modern Turkey* (New York, 1985)

Derviş, Pelin, ed., *Becoming Istanbul: An Encyclopedia* (Istanbul, 2008)

Dietrich, Anne, *Deutschsein in Istanbul: Nationalisierung und Orientierung in der deutschsprachigen Community von 1843 bis 1956* (Opladen, 1998)

Doğan Tekeli: Sami Sisa (Istanbul, 2001)

Doğramacı, Burcu, *Kulturtransfer und nationale Identität: Deutschsprachige Architekten, Stadtplaner und Bildhauer in der Türkei nach 1927* (Berlin, 2008)

Doruk Pamir: Yapılar Projeler, 1963–2005 (Istanbul, 2006)

Düzenli, Halil Ibrahim, *Idrak ve İnşa: Turgut Cansever Mimarlığının İki Düzlemi* (Istanbul, 2009)

Egli, Ernst, *Climate and Town Districts: Consequences and Demands* (Erlanbach, Zurich, 1951)

Ekinci, Oktay, *Istanbul'u Sarsan On Yıl. 1983–1993* (Istanbul, 1994)

Eldem, Sedad, *50 Yıllık Meslek Jübilesi* (Istanbul, 1983)

—, *Türk Evi Plan Tipleri* (Istanbul, 1955)

—, *Türk Evi*, 3 vols (Istanbul, 1984–7)

—, *Boğaziçi Yalıları*, 2 vols (Istanbul, 1994)

Emre Arolat: Yapılar. Projeler 1998–2005 (Istanbul, 2005)

Erder, Semra, *Istanbul'a Bir Kent Kondu. Ümraniye* (Istanbul, 1996)

Ergut, Elvan Altan, and Bilge Imamoğlu, eds, *Cumhuriyet'in Mekanları, Zamanları, Insanları* (Ankara, 2010)

Eryıldız, Semih, *Batıkent* (Istanbul, 2002)

Evin, Ahmet, and Renata Holod, eds, *Modern Turkish Architecture* (Philadelphia, PA, 1984)

Franck, Oya Atalay, 'Politik und Architektur: Ernst Egli und die Suche nach einer Moderne in der Türkei', PhD diss., ETH, Zurich, 2004

Germener, Semra, 'Türk Sanatının Modernleşme Süreci', in *Modern ve Ötesi* (Istanbul, 2007)

Göçek, Fatma Müge, *The Transformation of Turkey: Redefining State and Society from the Ottoman Empire to the Modern Era* (London, 2011)

Göktürk, Deniz, Levent Soysal and Ipek Türeli, eds, *Orienting Istanbul: Cultural Capital of Europe?* (New York, 2010)

Gül, Murat, *The Emergence of Modern Istanbul* (London and New York, 2009)

Gülalp, Haldun, *Kimlikler Siyaseti: Turkiye'de Siyasal Islamin Temelleri* (Istanbul, 2003)

Insel, Ahmet, 'Cumhuriyet Döneminde Otoritarizm', *Bilanço, 1923–1998* (Istanbul, 1999), pp. 35–45

Işık, Oğuz, and Melih Pınarcıoğlu, *Nöbetleşe Yoksulluk. Sultanbeyli Örneği* (Istanbul, 2001)

Heper, Metin, Ayşe Öncü and Heinz Kramer, eds, *Turkey and the West: Changing Political and Cultural Identities* (London and New York, 1993)

Kaçel, Ela, 'Intellectualism and Consumerism: Ideologies, Practices and Criticisms of Common Sense Modernism in Postwar Turkey', PhD diss., Cornell University, 2009

Kandiyoti, Deniz, and Ayşe Saktanber, eds, *Fragments of Culture: The Everyday of Modern Turkey* (New Brunswick, NJ, 2002)

Karpat, Kemal, *The Gecekondu: Rural Migration and Urbanization* (Cambridge, 1976)

Kasaba, Resat, ed., *The Cambridge History of Turkey*, IV: *Turkey in the Modern World* (Cambridge, 2008)

Keleş, Ruşen, *Kentleşme Politikası,* 10th edn (Istanbul, 2006)

Keyder, Çağlar, *State and Class in Turkey: A Study in Capitalist Development* (London, 1987)

—, ed., *Istanbul: Between the Global and the Local* (Lanham, MD, 1999)

Kezer, Zeynep, 'The Making of a National Capital: Ideology and Socio-spatial Practices in Early Republican Ankara', PhD diss., Department of Architecture, University of California, Berkeley, 1999

Khan, Hasan-Uddin, ed., *World Architecture: A Critical Mosaic, 1900–2000*, V: *The Middle East* (New York, 2000)

Kinzer, Stephen, *Crescent and Star: Turkey between Two Worlds* (New York, 2008)

Koçak, Cemil, *Türk-Alman İlişkileri, 1923–1939* (Ankara, 1991)

Korkmaz, Tansel, *Nevzat Sayın Düşler, Düşünceler, İşler 1990–2004* (Istanbul, 2004)

Kortan, Enis, *Türkiye'de Mimarlık Haraketleri ve Eleştirisi, 1960–1970* (Ankara, 1974)

—, *1950'ler Kuşağı Mimarlık Antolojisi* (Istanbul, 1997)

Kuban, Doğan, 'Turkiye'de Cağdaş Cami Tasarımı', *Arredamento Dekorasyon* (October 1994), pp. 80–83

Kuruyazıcı Hasan, ed., *Batılılaşan İstanbul'un Ermeni Mimarları. Armenian Architects of Istanbul in the Era of Westernization* (Istanbul, 2010)

—, *Osmanlı'dan Cumhuriyete bir Mimar: Arif Hikmet Koyunoğlu* (Istanbul, 2008)

Kuyucu, Tuna, 'Bir Mülkiyet Transferi Aracı olarak TOKİ ve Kentsel Dönüşüm Projeleri', in *Osmanlı Başkentinden Küreselleşen İstanbul'a: Mimarlık ve Kent 1910-2010*, ed. İpek Akpınar (Istanbul, 2010), pp. 122–34

Lerner, David, *The Passing of Traditional Society: Modernizing the Middle East* (Glencoe, IL, 1958)

Lewis, Bernard, *The Emergence of Modern Turkey* (Oxford, 1961)

Mango, Andrew, *Atatürk: The Biography of the Founder of Modern Turkey* (London, 1999)

Mardin, Şerif, *Religion and Social Change in Modern Turkey* (Albany, NY, 1989)

Merih Karaaslan: Yapıtlar Anılar 1 (Ankara, 2001)

Mills, Amy, *Streets of Memory: Landscape, Tolerance, and National Identity in Istanbul* (Athens, 2010)

Mimaride Türk Milli Uslubu Semineri (Istanbul, 1984)

Navaro-Yaşin, Yael, *Faces of the State: Secularism and Public Life in Turkey* (Princeton, NJ, 2002)

Nicolai, Bernd, *Moderne und Exil: Deutschsprachige Architekten in der Türkei, 1925–1955* (Berlin, 1998)

—, 'Ernst Egli and the Emergence of Modern Architecture in Kemalist Turkey', in 'Intertwined Histories. Turkey and Central Europe', ed. Esra Akcan, *Centropa*, VII/2 (May 2007), pp. 153–63

Öktem, Kerem, et al., eds, *Turkey's Engagement with Modernity* (Basingstoke, 2010)

Öncü, Ayşe, 'The Politics of the Urban Land Market in Turkey, 1950–1980', *International Journal of Urban and Regional Research*, 12 (1988), pp. 38–64

Öncü, Ayşe, and Petra Weyland, eds, *Space, Culture and Power: New Identities in Globalizing Cities* (London, 1997)

Özer, Bülent, 'Rejyonalizm, Üniversalizm ve Çağdaş Mimarimiz Üzerine Bir Deneme', PhD diss., Istanbul Technical University, 1964

Özüekren, Şule, 'Konut Kooperatiflerinde Örgütsel Özellikler ve Başarı Göstergeleri Arasındaki İlişkiler', in *Konut Araştırmaları Sempozyumu* (Ankara, 1995), pp. 109–45

Özyürek, Esra, *Nostalgia for the Modern: State Secularism and Everyday Politics in Turkey* (Durham, NC, 2006)

Pamir, Haluk, and Süha Özkan, eds, *Mimarlıkta Yeni Arayışlar. 'Genç Türk Mimarları'* (Ankara, 2000)

Pamuk, Orhan, *Istanbul: Memories and the City* (New York, 2005)

Pamuk, Şevket, 'Globalization, Industrialization and Changing Politics in Turkey', *New Perspectives on Turkey*, no. 38 (2008), pp. 267–73

Pinon, Pierre, and Cana Bilsel, eds, *From the Imperial Capital to the Republican Modern City: Henri Prost's Planning of Istanbul, 1936–1951* (Istanbul, 2010)

Pope, Nicole, and Pope, Hugh, *Turkey Unveiled: A History of Modern Turkey* (Woodstock, NY, 1998)

Rigele, Georg, and Georg Loewit, *Clemens Holzmeister* (Innsbruck, 2000)

Rona, Zeynep, ed., *Bilanço, 1923–1998* (Istanbul, 1999)

Sargın, Güven A., ed., *Ankara'nın Kamusal Yüzleri* (Istanbul, 2002)

Sarkis, Hashim, ed., *Han Tümertekin: Recent Work* (Cambridge, MA, 2007)

Şevki Pekin: Mimari Calışmalar (Istanbul, 2007)

Şevki Vanlı: Düşünceler ve Tasarımlar (Ankara, 2001)

Sey, Yıldız, ed., *75 Yılda Değişen Kent ve Mimarlık* (Istanbul, 1998)

Sözen, Metin, *Cumhuriyet Dönemi Türk Mimarlığı* (Ankara, 1973)

Sözen, Metin, and Mete Tapan, *50 Yılın Türk Mimarisi* (Istanbul, 1973)

Speer, Albert, *Neue Deutsche Baukunst - Yeni Alman Mimarisi* (Berlin, 1942)

Speidel, Manfred, 'Naturlichkeit und Freiheit. Bruno Tauts Bauten in der Turkei', in *Ankara 1923–50. Bir Başkentin Oluşumu* (Ankara, 1994), pp. 52–65

Şenyapılı, Tansı, 'Cumhuriyet'in 75. Yılı, Gecekonudunun 50. Yılı', in *75 Yılda Değişen Kent ve Mimarlık*, ed. Yıldız Sey (Istanbul, 1998), pp. 301–16

—, '*Baraka'dan Gecekonduya. Ankara'da Kentsel Mekanın Dönüşümü* (Istanbul, 2004)

Tanju, Bülent, *Mimarlıkta Sıfır Noktasını Aramak* (Istanbul, 2003)

Tanju, Bülent, and Uğur Tanyeli, eds, *Sedad Eldem*, 2 vols (Istanbul, 2008–9)

Tankut, Gönül, *Bir Başkentin İmarı: Ankara, 1929-1939* (Ankara, 1990)

Tansuğ, Sezer, *Çağdaş Türk Sanatı* (Istanbul, 1986)

Tanyeli, Uğur, *Istanbul 1900-2000: Konutu ve Modernleşmeyi Metropolden Okumak* (Istanbul, 2004)

—, *Mimarlığın Aktörleri: Türkiye, 1900-2000* (Istanbul, 2007)

—, '1950'lerden Bu Yana Mimari Paradigmaların Değişimi ve "Reel" Mimarlık', in *75 Yılda Değişen Kent ve Mimarlık*, ed. Yıldız Sey (Istanbul, 1998), pp. 235–54

—, and Atilla Yücel, eds, *Turgut Cansever: Düşünce Adamı ve Mimar* (Istanbul, 2007)

Tapan, Mete, 'İstanbul'un Kentsel Planlamasının Tarihsel Gelişimi ve Planlama Eylemleri', in *75 Yılda Değişen Kent ve Mimarlık*, ed. Yıldız Sey (Istanbul, 1998), pp. 75–88

Tapper, Richard, ed., *Islam in Modern Turkey* (London, 1991)

Taut, Bruno, *Mimari Bilgisi*, trans. A. Kolatan (Istanbul, 1938)

Tekeli, İlhan, 'Türkiye'de Konut Sunumunun Davranışsal Nitelikleri ve Konut Kesiminde Bunalım', *Konut '81* (Ankara, 1982)

—, *Türkiye'de Yaşamda ve Yazında Konut Sorununun Gelişimi* (Ankara, 1996)

—, 'Türkiye'de Cumhuriyet Döneminde Kentsel Gelişme ve Kent Planlaması', in *75 Yılda Değişen Kent ve Mimarlık*, ed. Yıldız Sey (Istanbul, 1998), pp. 1–24

—, Yiğit Gülöksüz and Tarık Okyay, *Gecekondulu, Dolmuşlu, Işportalı Şehir* (Istanbul, 1976)

—, and Selim Ilkin, eds, *Mimar Kemalettin'in Yazdıkları* (Ankara, 1997)

—, *Cumhuriyetin Harcı: Modernitenin Altyapısı Oluşurken* (Istanbul, 2003)

Tezel, Y., *Cumhuriyet Döneminin Iktisadi Tarihi, 1923-1950* (Ankara, 1986)

Tümer, Gürhan, *Cumhuriyet Döneminde Yabancı Mimar Sorunu* (İzmir, 1998)

Ünalın, Çetin, *Türk Mimarlar Cemiyetinden Mimarlar Derneği 1927'ye* (Ankara, 2002)

Ünsal, Özlem, and Kuyucu, Tuna, 'Challenging the Neoliberal Urban Regime: Regeneration and Resistance in Başbüyük and Tarlabaşı', in *Orienting Istanbul*, ed. Deniz Göktürk, Levent Soysal and Ipek Türeli (London and New York, 2010), pp. 51–70

Vanlı, Şevki, *Mimarlık Sevgilim* (Istanbul, 2000)

—, *Bilinmek Istenmeyen 20. YY Türk Mimarlığı: Eleştirel Bir Bakış* (Ankara, 2006)

Yavuz, Yıldırım, *Imparatorluktan Cumhuriyete Mimar Kemalettin, 1870-1927* (Ankara, 2009)

Yeşilkaya, Neşe Gürallar, *Halkevleri, Ideoloji ve Mimarlık*, (Istanbul, 1999)

Yücel, Atilla, 'Pluralism Takes Command: The Turkish Architectural Scene Today', in *Modern Turkish Architecture*, ed. Renata Holod and Ahmet Evin (Philadelphia, PA, 1984), pp. 119–52

White, Jenny, *Islamist Mobilization in Turkey: A Study in Vernacular Politics* (Seattle, WA, 2002)

Widmann, Horst, *Exil und Bildungshilfe: Die deutschsprachige akademische Emigration in die Türkei nach 1933* (Frankfurt, 1973)

Zürcher, Erik, *Turkey: A Modern History* (London, 1993)

Acknowledgements &
Photo Acknowledgements

Our first and foremost thanks go to Vivian Constantinopoulos, not just for her support, patience and excellent editorial work with us, but also for her overall vision for the Modern Architectures in History series, the significance of which is proving to be larger than the sum of the individual volumes. Collectively, these books offer compelling evidence to the recent critical re-conceptualizations of the historiography of modern architecture and urbanism from global and trans-national perspectives, and we are very happy to be contributors to this project. Throughout the process we were inspired by the work of other authors in the series and appreciated their encouragement of ours: Jean-Louis Cohen, Diane Ghirardo and Gwendolyn Wright in particular.

In writing a synthetic book of this nature, we benefited from many existing and new studies by Turkish and international scholars and we have acknowledged them in our citations. The 'unevenness' of the existing scholarship on the historiography of modern architecture in Turkey was a concern for us. Compared to the relatively large number of new studies on the early republican period (including our own work), scholarly literature on the period from 1950 to the present is rather scarce. Consequently, our account of those more recent periods is unavoidably introductory and provisional. It is meant only as a starting point for future scholarship (many new doctoral theses are now in the works), which will undoubtedly make our story richer, more layered and more nuanced.

The writing of the book has been a prolonged but invaluable adventure spread over many years and shaped by the support of and numerous exchanges with other people too many to name individually. We will, none the less, mention some of them.

We thank all photographers who waived their fees and gave us permission to use their work, especially Ara Güler, Cemal Emden, Murat Germen, Oğuz Meriç and Pablo Martinez Muniz. We are also grateful to other scholars, and to the collectors who let us use images from their archives, especially Gökhan Akçura, Burak Asıliskender, Inci Aslanoğlu, Aydan Balamir, Cana Bilsel, Burak Boysan, Ali Cengizkan, Burhan Doğançay, Peter Dübers, Oğuz Işık, Enis Kortan, Bernd Nicolai, Uğur Tanyeli, Murat Tarman and Yıldırım Yavuz. Complete credits for the photographs are listed in the Photo Acknowledgements.

We are equally grateful to the architects who gave us material for publication and facilitated our research, in particular Zafer Akay, Emre Arolat, Kemal Ahmet Aru, Aybars Aşçı, Gökhan Avcıoğlu, Behruz Çinici, Can Çinici, Boğaçhan Dündaralp, Can Elmas, Ali Hızıroğlu, Mehmet Kütükçüoğlu, Ali Osman Öztürk, Nevzat Sayın, Murat Tabanlıoğlu, Doğan Tekeli and Han Tümertekin. We would also like to thank Edhem Eldem for being able to publish Sedad Eldem's, and Şule Karaaslan for Merih Karaaslan's works. All of these and other architects are also listed in the Photo Acknowledgements.

Along with Vivian's excellent editorship at Reaktion Books, we are also grateful to the meticulous work of the other staff members, Harry Gilonis and Robert Williams in particular. Our indexer Diana Witt did a marvellous job in a very short time.

We also have individual thanks to give. Esra Akcan expresses her gratitude to Onur Yüce Gün for his logistical support and expert 'image adjustment' help. Although not directly supporting this project, her fellowships from the Getty Research Institute, the Canadian Center for Architecture, the Clark Institute and the Transregional Studies programme hosted by the Institute for Advanced Study in Berlin gave her the release time from teaching to focus on this book alongside other commitments. In that, she owes special thanks to the University of

Illinois at Chicago for its commitment to scholarly research, and the unmatched support of her colleagues there. She would also like to express her deep appreciation for the scholars she met in these research institutes (who are too many to list but will recognize themselves in this sentence), whose work informed her on the unfolding ways of writing global, intertwined histories of modernism. Sibel Bozdoğan is particularly grateful to current and former graduate students (Ipek Akpınar, Aslıhan Demirtas, Burak Erdim, Ela Kaçel, Ömer Kanıpak, Zeynep Kezer, Burcu Kütükçüoğlu and Neyran Turan among others) whose work has enriched her own in many different ways; to Resat Kasaba who has always been there to talk about Turkish society, culture and politics; to Ihsan Bilgin for many fruitful exchanges over the years; and to her other colleagues at Istanbul Bilgi University, where thinking about modern Turkish architecture and urbanism is an ongoing and ever-provocative project.

Last but certainly not least, in the completion of this collaborative project, we owe heart-felt thanks to each other. The book has developed out of countless conversations, email exchanges and comments on the parts that we each wrote separately at first and merged into a coherent narrative afterwards. The book ultimately turned into a shared adventure in the course of which we learned from each other and got to know each other better in our similarly 'nomadic' lives between Turkey and the United States. This, in itself, was as rewarding to us as the resulting book.

Aga Khan Archives: p. 195; drawing by Zafer Akay, Erkan Gencol: p. 283 (foot); Zafer Akay: p. 283 (foot); Esra Akcan: pp. 65, 88, 97, 146 (top), 156, 162, 165, 202, 209, 214–15, 222 (foot), 224, 226, 228, 230 (top), 231, 232, 233, 239, 242, 248, 249, 279 (top), 279 (middle), 295; *Ankara Posta Kartları ve Belge Fotoğrafları Arşivi* (Ankara, 1994): pp. 52, 57, 64 (left), 74, 82; *Architectural Forum* (December 1955): p. 118; Architecture for Humanity, *Design Like You Give a Damn* (New York: Metropolis Books, 2006): p. 253; from *Arkitekt*: pp. 37 (8, no. 2 – 1938), 39 top (5, nos 11–12 – 1935), 42 foot (5, nos 11–12 – 1935), 69 top (6, no. 4 – 1936), 69 foot (8, no. 4 – 1938), 73 (8, no. 4 – 1938), 75 foot (280, no. 2 – 1955), 80 (5, no. 9 – 1935), 83 (5 – 1935), 87 top (5, no. 6 – 1935), 87 foot (no. 7 – 1936), 94 (10, nos 1–2 – 1940), 100 (no. 8 – 1938), 101 (no. 11–12 – 1950), 112 top right (nos 7–8 – 1943), 122 (no. 4 – 1959), 125 top (no. 2 – 1959), 125 middle (nos 1–4 – 1953), 135 (340, no. 4 – 1970), 143 (296, no. 3 – 1959), 144 (322, no. 2 – 1966), 151 top (nos 9–10 – 1952), 154 (305, no. 4 – 1961), 157 (374, no. 2 – 1979), 159 top (nos 9–10 – 1951), 159 foot (nos 1–2 – 1951), 160 (294, no. 1 – 1959), 184 top (308, no. 3 (1962), 185 right (296 – 1959), 190 (359, no. 5 – 1975), 193 (342, no. 2 – 1971), 194 top left and right (369, no. 1 – 1978), 194 foot (367, no. 3 – 1977); Arkitera: p. 217; courtesy of Emre Arolat Architects: pp. 269, 279, 289; *Arradamento Dekorasyon* no. 1 (1994): p. 260; Kemal Ahmet Aru: p. 151 (middle); courtesy Burak Asıliskender: p. 44; courtesy of Inci Aslanoğlu: p. 24; Aybars Aşçı for SOM: p. 297; collection of the authors: pp. 150, 200, 208, 230 (foot), 255, 257, 258, 283 (top); courtesy of Gökhan Avcıoğlu (GAD): p. 267; *Der Baumeister*: pp. 62 (2, February 1936), 78 (1, 1950); Erdoğan Bayraktar, *Gecekondu ve Kentsel Yenileme* (Ankara, 2006: pp. 243, 247; photos by Ali Bekman: pp. 269, 279 (foot); photo by Helene Binet: p. 271; Nil Birol, *Abdurrahman Hancı Yapılar Projeler 1945–2000* (Istanbul, 2008): p. 145; courtesy Sibel Bozdoğan: pp. 16 (top); Bozdoğan collection: p. 178 (foot); photos by Sibel Bozdoğan: pp. 23, 153, 212, 256; from Sibel Bozdoğan, Suha Özkan and Engin Yenal, eds. *Sedad Eldem. Architect in Turkey* (Oxford, 1991): p. 178 (top, middle), 179; *Cengiz Bektaş* (Istanbul, 2001): p. 170; courtesy of Ali Cengizkan: pp. 47 (right), 155; *Cumhuriyet Devrinde Istanbul* (Istanbul, 1949): p. 112 (foot); Behruz Çinici: pp. 127, 181, 259; courtesy of Can Çinici: pp. 219, 284, 292; photos by Veli Demur: p. 87; *Doğan Tekeli, Sami Sisa* (Istanbul, 1994): pp. 177 (top, middle), 191; courtesy of Burhan Doğançay: p. 134; Peter Dübers collection: p. 102; Boğaçhan Dündaralp: pp. 277, 286; Sedad Eldem, *Büyük Konutlar* (Ankara, 1982): pp. 146 (foot), 147 (top); Sedad Eldem, *Türk Evi Plan Tipleri* (Istanbul, 1968): p. 98; Sedad Eldem archives: p. 146 (top); courtesy of Can Elmas: pp. 250, 251; photos by Cemal Emdem: pp. 48, 77, 192 (left), 196–67, 215 (foot), 245 (top), 266, 280; *Fotoğraflarla Türkiye* (Ankara, 1938): pp. 30, 42 (top), 45; *Fotoğraflarla Yeni Ankara Garı* (Ankara, 1937): pp. 16 (foot), 72; photos by Murat Germen: pp. 262, 287, 288; Gökhan Akçura Archive: pp. 109, 117, 120; photo Ara Güler: p. 176; *Güzelleşen Istanbul*, 1943: p. 112 (top left); Henri Prost Archives (AA/Cité de l'Architecture et du Patrimoine / Centre d'Archives du xxe siècle, courtesy of Cana Bilsel): p. 111; courtesy of Ali Hızıroğlu: p. 217; photo by Markus Hilbich: p. 46 (top); Renata Holod and Ahmet Evin, eds., *Modern Turkish Architecture* (Philadelphia, 1984): pp. 126 (middle), 177 (foot), 185 (left); *Clemens Holzmeister: Bauten, Entwürfe* (Salzburg, 1937): p. 54; *II. Imar Kongresi. Sosyal Mesken Standartları*: p. 149; *InnenDekoration* 43 (1932): p. 85 (foot); photo Iskender: p. 83; *Istanbul. 1910-2010 Kent Yapılı Çevre ve Mimarlık Kültürü Sergisi* exhibition catalogue (Istanbul, 2010): p. 254; Istanbul Metropolitan and Urban Design Center: p. 293; Istanbul Vilayeti Neşriyat ve Turizm Müdürlüğü, *Istanbul'un Kitabı* (Istanbul, 1957): p. 152; Oğuz Işık and Melih Pınarcıoğlu, *Nöbetleşe Yoksulluk: gecekondulaşma ve kent yoksulları: Sultanbeyli Örneği* (Istanbul, 2001): p. 241; Kurt Junghanns, *Bruno Taut* (Milan, 1978): p. 64 (right); Merih Karaaslan, *Yapıtlar / Anılar 1* (Ankara, 2001): pp. 216, 225, 227; Kemal Karpat, *The Gecekondu: Rural Migration and Urbanization* (Cambridge, 1976): p. 163; Emine Kazmaoğlu (ed.), *Architectural Yearbook 1: Architecture in Turkey* (Ankara, 2000): p. 274; Enis Kortan (ed.), *1950ler Kuşağı Mimarlık Antalojisi* (Istanbul, 1997): pp. 138, 147 (foot), 180 (top); Enis Kortan, *Türkiye'de Mimarlık Haraketleri ve Eleştirisi (1960-70)* (Ankara, 1974): p. 182; Lilo Linke, *Allah Dethroned: a Journey Through Modern Turkey* (New York, 1937): p. 40; photo by Thomas Mayer: pp. 211, 270 (foot), 289; photo Oğuz Meriç: p. 163; *Mimar*: pp. 96 (vol. 3, no. 2, 1933); *Mimarlık*: pp. 126 middle (no. 3 - 1971), 140 (no. 1 - 1967), 174 (nos 1-2 - 1974), 184 foot (no. 7 - 1967), 198, (no. 1 - 1976); photos Pablo Martínez Muñiz: pp. 13, 244, 245 (foot); Murat Tarman Archive: p. 45; photo by Jeroen Musch: p. 270 (top); 'New German Architecture' exhibition catalogue (Ankara, 1943): p. 75 (top); courtesy of Bernd Nicolai: p. 46 (top); courtesy of NSMH (Nevzat Sayın): p. 265; *Once Upon a Time in Ankara*: p. 27; photo M. Pehlivanoğlu: p. 179; Rıfat Behar Archive, courtesy of Burak Boysan: p. 46 (middle); courtesy of Nevzat Sayın: p. 280; photos J. Scherb: p. 85; photo by Önol Soner: p. 219; *Städtebau*, 1925: p. 27; photo Ezra Stoller (courtesy Ezra Stoller/Esto): pp. 6, 121; Suzan Kapsız Archive: p. 168; Sümerbank Archives, Ankara: p. 44; courtesy of Tabanlıoğlu Architects: pp. 104, 128, 129, 211, 212, 213, 262, 270, 271, 287; photo Uğur Tangyeli: p. 220 (top); Uğur Tanyeli and Atilla Yücel, eds., *Turgut Cansever. Düşünce Adamı ve Mimar* (Istanbul, 2007): pp. 188, 220 (top); A Tasarım (Ali Osman Öztürk): p. 210; Technischen Universität Berlin (Plansammlung, Nachlass Hermann Jansen): pp. 29 (22600.1), 34 top (22878), foot (22913), 91 (23083); Teğet Architecture: pp. 273, 278, 282; *La Turquie Contemporaine*: p. 67; *La Turquie Kemaliste* (photos probably by Othmar Pflerschy): pp. 16 middle (17 – February 1937), 26 (6 – April 1935), 31 (30 – April 1939), 36 (12 – April 1936), 38 (23-24 – April 1938), 47 left (17 – February 1937), 55 (– February 1935), 56 (6 – April 1935), 60 (14 – August 1936), 63 (23-24 – April 1938), 68 (12 – April 1936), 71 (47 – December 1943), 85 (31 – June 1939), 92 (43 – June 1941), 93 (20 – August 1937); *La Turquie Moderne*, 1 (November 1935): p. 53; Han Tümertekin: p. 252; Universität für ange-wandte Kunst, Vienna (Kunstsammlung und Archiv): p. 61; *Ülkü*, 1 no. 8 (1933): p. 39 (foot); *Wasmuth* (November–December 1931): p. 85 (top); Yapı Kredi Archive: pp. 110, 113, 123 (foot); photo by Didem Yavuz: p. 133; Yıldırım Yavuz, *Kemalettin Bey*: p. 22; *Yedigün*, 12/290 (September, 1938): p. 89; published in *75 Yılda Değişen Kent ve Mimarlık* (Istanbul, 1998): p. 168.

Index

Numerals in *italics* indicate figures

334